50% OFF Online PSAT 8/9 Prep Course!

Dear Customer,

We consider it an honor and a privilege that you chose our PSAT 8/9 Study Guide. As a way of showing our appreciation and to help us better serve you, we have partnered with Mometrix Test Preparation to offer you **50% off their online PSAT 8/9 Prep Course**. Many PSAT 8/9 courses are needlessly expensive and don't deliver enough value. With their course, you get access to the best PSAT 8/9 prep material, and **you only pay half price**.

Mometrix has structured their online course to perfectly complement your printed study guide. The PSAT 8/9 Prep Course contains **in-depth lessons** that cover all the most important topics, **230+ video reviews** that explain difficult concepts, over **350 practice questions** to ensure you feel prepared, and more than **450 digital flashcards**, so you can study while you're on the go.

Online PSAT 8/9 Prep Course

Topics Included:

- Reading
  - o Command of Evidence
  - o Words in Context
- Writing
  - o Expression of Ideas
  - o Standard English Conventions
- Mathematics
  - o Foundation Math Concepts
  - o Heart of Algebra Overview

Course Features:

- PSAT 8/9 Study Guide
  - o Get content that complements our best-selling study guide.
- Full-Length Practice Tests
  - o With over 350 practice questions, you can test yourself again and again.
- Mobile Friendly
  - o If you need to study on the go, the course is easily accessible from your mobile device.
- PSAT 8/9 Flashcards
  - o Their course includes a flashcard mode with over 450 content cards to help you study.

To receive this discount, visit them at mometrix.com/university/psat89 or simply scan this QR code with your smartphone. At the checkout page, enter the discount code: **PSAT89TPB50**

If you have any questions or concerns, please contact Mometrix at support@mometrix.com.

Sincerely,

 in partnership with

FREE Test Taking Tips Video/DVD Offer

To better serve you, we created videos covering test taking tips that we want to give you for FREE. **These videos cover world-class tips that will help you succeed on your test.**

We just ask that you send us feedback about this product. Please let us know what you thought about it—whether good, bad, or indifferent.

To get your **FREE videos**, you can use the QR code below or email freevideos@studyguideteam.com with "Free Videos" in the subject line and the following information in the body of the email:

     a. The title of your product

     b. Your product rating on a scale of 1-5, with 5 being the highest

     c. Your feedback about the product

If you have any questions or concerns, please don't hesitate to contact us at info@studyguideteam.com.

Thank you!

Digital PSAT 8/9 Prep 2024-2025

6 Practice Tests and Study Guide
[5th Edition]

Lydia Morrison

Interested in buying more than 10 copies of our product? Contact us about bulk discounts:
bulkorders@studyguideteam.com

ISBN 13: 9781637756744

Table of Contents

Welcome

Dear Reader,

Welcome to your new Test Prep Books study guide! We are pleased that you chose us to help you prepare for your exam. There are many study options to choose from, and we appreciate you choosing us. Studying can be a daunting task, but we have designed a smart, effective study guide to help prepare you for what lies ahead.

Whether you're a parent helping your child learn and grow, a high school student working hard to get into your dream college, or a nursing student studying for a complex exam, we want to help give you the tools you need to succeed. We hope this study guide gives you the skills and the confidence to thrive, and we can't thank you enough for allowing us to be part of your journey.

In an effort to continue to improve our products, we welcome feedback from our customers. We look forward to hearing from you. Suggestions, success stories, and criticisms can all be communicated by emailing us at info@studyguideteam.com.

Sincerely,
Test Prep Books Team

FREE Videos/DVD OFFER

Doing well on your exam requires both knowing the test content and understanding how to use that knowledge to do well on the test. We offer completely FREE test taking tip videos. **These videos cover world-class tips that you can use to succeed on your test.**

To get your **FREE videos**, you can use the QR code below or email freevideos@studyguideteam.com with "Free Videos" in the subject line and the following information in the body of the email:

    a. The title of your product
    b. Your product rating on a scale of 1-5, with 5 being the highest
    c. Your feedback about the product

If you have any questions or concerns, please don't hesitate to contact us at info@studyguideteam.com.

1

Quick Overview

As you draw closer to taking your exam, effective preparation becomes more and more important. Thankfully, you have this study guide to help you get ready. Use this guide to help keep your studying on track and refer to it often.

This study guide contains several key sections that will help you be successful on your exam. The guide contains tips for what you should do the night before and the day of the test. Also included are test-taking tips. Knowing the right information is not always enough. Many well-prepared test takers struggle with exams. These tips will help equip you to accurately read, assess, and answer test questions.

A large part of the guide is devoted to showing you what content to expect on the exam and to helping you better understand that content. In this guide are practice test questions so that you can see how well you have grasped the content. Then, answer explanations are provided so that you can understand why you missed certain questions.

Don't try to cram the night before you take your exam. This is not a wise strategy for a few reasons. First, your retention of the information will be low. Your time would be better used by reviewing information you already know rather than trying to learn a lot of new information. Second, you will likely become stressed as you try to gain a large amount of knowledge in a short amount of time. Third, you will be depriving yourself of sleep. So be sure to go to bed at a reasonable time the night before. Being well-rested helps you focus and remain calm.

Be sure to eat a substantial breakfast the morning of the exam. If you are taking the exam in the afternoon, be sure to have a good lunch as well. Being hungry is distracting and can make it difficult to focus. You have hopefully spent lots of time preparing for the exam. Don't let an empty stomach get in the way of success!

When travelling to the testing center, leave earlier than needed. That way, you have a buffer in case you experience any delays. This will help you remain calm and will keep you from missing your appointment time at the testing center.

Be sure to pace yourself during the exam. Don't try to rush through the exam. There is no need to risk performing poorly on the exam just so you can leave the testing center early. Allow yourself to use all of the allotted time if needed.

 Remain positive while taking the exam even if you feel like you are performing poorly. Thinking about the content you should have mastered will not help you perform better on the exam.

Once the exam is complete, take some time to relax. Even if you feel that you need to take the exam again, you will be well served by some down time before you begin studying again. It's often easier to convince yourself to study if you know that it will come with a reward!

Test-Taking Strategies

1. Predicting the Answer

When you feel confident in your preparation for a multiple-choice test, try predicting the answer before reading the answer choices. This is especially useful on questions that test objective factual knowledge. By predicting the answer before reading the available choices, you eliminate the possibility that you will be distracted or led astray by an incorrect answer choice. You will feel more confident in your selection if you read the question, predict the answer, and then find your prediction among the answer choices. After using this strategy, be sure to still read all of the answer choices carefully and completely. If you feel unprepared, you should not attempt to predict the answers. This would be a waste of time and an opportunity for your mind to wander in the wrong direction.

2. Reading the Whole Question

Too often, test takers scan a multiple-choice question, recognize a few familiar words, and immediately jump to the answer choices. Test authors are aware of this common impatience, and they will sometimes prey upon it. For instance, a test author might subtly turn the question into a negative, or he or she might redirect the focus of the question right at the end. The only way to avoid falling into these traps is to read the entirety of the question carefully before reading the answer choices.

3. Looking for Wrong Answers

Long and complicated multiple-choice questions can be intimidating. One way to simplify a difficult multiple-choice question is to eliminate all of the answer choices that are clearly wrong. In most sets of answers, there will be at least one selection that can be dismissed right away. If the test is administered on paper, the test taker could draw a line through it to indicate that it may be ignored; otherwise, the test taker will have to perform this operation mentally or on scratch paper. In either case, once the obviously incorrect answers have been eliminated, the remaining choices may be considered. Sometimes identifying the clearly wrong answers will give the test taker some information about the correct answer. For instance, if one of the remaining answer choices is a direct opposite of one of the eliminated answer choices, it may well be the correct answer. The opposite of obviously wrong is obviously right! Of course, this is not always the case. Some answers are obviously incorrect simply because they are irrelevant to the question being asked. Still, identifying and eliminating some incorrect answer choices is a good way to simplify a multiple-choice question.

4. Don't Overanalyze

Anxious test takers often overanalyze questions. When you are nervous, your brain will often run wild, causing you to make associations and discover clues that don't actually exist. If you feel that this may be a problem for you, do whatever you can to slow down during the test. Try taking a deep breath or counting to ten. As you read and consider the question, restrict yourself to the particular words used by the author. Avoid thought tangents about what the author *really* meant, or what he or she was *trying* to say. The only things that matter on a multiple-choice test are the words that are actually in the question. You must avoid reading too much into a multiple-choice question, or supposing that the writer meant something other than what he or she wrote.

3

5. No Need for Panic

It is wise to learn as many strategies as possible before taking a multiple-choice test, but it is likely that you will come across a few questions for which you simply don't know the answer. In this situation, avoid panicking. Because most multiple-choice tests include dozens of questions, the relative value of a single wrong answer is small. As much as possible, you should compartmentalize each question on a multiple-choice test. In other words, you should not allow your feelings about one question to affect your success on the others. When you find a question that you either don't understand or don't know how to answer, just take a deep breath and do your best. Read the entire question slowly and carefully. Try rephrasing the question a couple of different ways. Then, read all of the answer choices carefully. After eliminating obviously wrong answers, make a selection and move on to the next question.

6. Confusing Answer Choices

When working on a difficult multiple-choice question, there may be a tendency to focus on the answer choices that are the easiest to understand. Many people, whether consciously or not, gravitate to the answer choices that require the least concentration, knowledge, and memory. This is a mistake. When you come across an answer choice that is confusing, you should give it extra attention. A question might be confusing because you do not know the subject matter to which it refers. If this is the case, don't

eliminate the answer before you have affirmatively settled on another. When you come across an answer choice of this type, set it aside as you look at the remaining choices. If you can confidently assert that one of the other choices is correct, you can leave the confusing answer aside. Otherwise, you will need to take a moment to try to better understand the confusing answer choice. Rephrasing is one way to tease out the sense of a confusing answer choice.

7. Your First Instinct

Many people struggle with multiple-choice tests because they overthink the questions. If you have studied sufficiently for the test, you should be prepared to trust your first instinct once you have carefully and completely read the question and all of the answer choices. There is a great deal of research suggesting that the mind can come to the correct conclusion very quickly once it has obtained all of the relevant information. At times, it may seem to you as if your intuition is working faster even than your reasoning mind. This may in fact be true. The knowledge you obtain while studying may be retrieved from your subconscious before you have a chance to work out the associations that support it. Verify your instinct by working out the reasons that it should be trusted.

8. Key Words

Many test takers struggle with multiple-choice questions because they have poor reading comprehension skills. Quickly reading and understanding a multiple-choice question requires a mixture of skill and experience. To help with this, try jotting down a few key words and phrases on a piece of scrap paper. Doing this concentrates the process of reading and forces the mind to weigh the relative importance of the question's parts. In selecting words and phrases to write down, the test taker thinks

about the question more deeply and carefully. This is especially true for multiple-choice questions that are preceded by a long prompt.

9. Subtle Negatives

One of the oldest tricks in the multiple-choice test writer's book is to subtly reverse the meaning of a question with a word like *not* or *except*. If you are not paying attention to each word in the question, you can easily be led astray by this trick. For instance, a common question format is, "Which of the following is…?" Obviously, if the question instead is, "Which of the following is not…?," then the answer will be quite different. Even worse, the test makers are aware of the potential for this mistake and will include one answer choice that would be correct if the question were not negated or reversed. A test taker who misses the reversal will find what he or she believes to be a correct answer and will be so confident that he or she will fail to reread the question and discover the original error. The only way to avoid this is to practice a wide variety of multiple-choice questions and to pay close attention to each and every word.

10. Reading Every Answer Choice

It may seem obvious, but you should always read every one of the answer choices! Too many test takers fall into the habit of scanning the question and assuming that they understand the question because they recognize a few key words. From there, they pick the first answer choice that answers the question they believe they have read. Test takers who read all of the answer choices might discover that one of the latter answer choices is actually *more* correct. Moreover, reading all of the answer choices can remind you of facts related to the question that can help you arrive at the correct answer. Sometimes, a misstatement or incorrect detail in one of the latter answer choices will trigger your memory of the subject and will enable you to find the right answer. Failing to read all of the answer choices is like not reading all of the items on a restaurant menu: you might miss out on the perfect choice.

11. Spot the Hedges

One of the keys to success on multiple-choice tests is paying close attention to every word. This is never truer than with words like *almost*, *most*, *some*, and *sometimes*. These words are called "hedges" because they indicate that a statement is not totally true or not true in every place and time. An absolute statement will contain no hedges, but in many subjects, the answers are not always straightforward or absolute. There are always exceptions to the rules in these subjects. For this reason,

you should favor those multiple-choice questions that contain hedging language. The presence of qualifying words indicates that the author is taking special care with his or her words, which is certainly important when composing the right answer. After all, there are many ways to be wrong, but there is only one way to be right! For this reason, it is wise to avoid answers that are absolute when taking a multiple-choice test. An absolute answer is one that says things are either all one way or all another. They often include words like *every*, *always*, *best*, and *never*. If you are taking a multiple-choice test in a subject that doesn't lend itself to absolute answers, be on your guard if you see any of these words.

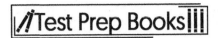
12. Long Answers

In many subject areas, the answers are not simple. As already mentioned, the right answer often requires hedges. Another common feature of the answers to a complex or subjective question are qualifying clauses, which are groups of words that subtly modify the meaning of the sentence. If the question or answer choice describes a rule to which there are exceptions or the subject matter is complicated, ambiguous, or confusing, the correct answer will require many words in order to be expressed clearly and accurately. In essence, you should not be deterred by answer choices that seem excessively long. Oftentimes, the author of the text will not be able to write the correct answer without offering some qualifications and modifications. Your job is to read the answer choices thoroughly and completely and to select the one that most accurately and precisely answers the question.

13. Restating to Understand

Sometimes, a question on a multiple-choice test is difficult not because of what it asks but because of how it is written. If this is the case, restate the question or answer choice in different words. This process serves a couple of important purposes. First, it forces you to concentrate on the core of the question. In order to rephrase the question accurately, you have to understand it well. Rephrasing the question will concentrate your mind on the key words and ideas. Second, it will present the information to your mind in a fresh way. This process may trigger your memory and render some useful scrap of information picked up while studying.

14. True Statements

Sometimes an answer choice will be true in itself, but it does not answer the question. This is one of the main reasons why it is essential to read the question carefully and completely before proceeding to the answer choices. Too often, test takers skip ahead to the answer choices and look for true statements. Having found one of these, they are content to select it without reference to the question above. The savvy test taker will always read the entire question before turning to the answer choices. Then, having settled on a correct answer choice, he or she will refer to the original question and ensure that the selected answer is relevant. The mistake of choosing a correct-but-irrelevant answer choice is especially common on questions related to specific pieces of objective knowledge.

15. No Patterns

One of the more dangerous ideas that circulates about multiple-choice tests is that the correct answers tend to fall into patterns. These erroneous ideas range from a belief that B and C are the most common right answers, to the idea that an unprepared test-taker should answer "A-B-A-C-A-D-A-B-A." It cannot be emphasized enough that pattern-seeking of this type is exactly the WRONG way to approach a multiple-choice test. To begin with, it is highly unlikely that the test maker will plot the correct answers according to some predetermined pattern. The questions are scrambled and delivered in a random order. Furthermore, even if the test maker was following a pattern in the assignation of correct answers, there is no reason why the test taker would know which pattern he or she was using. Any attempt to discern a pattern in the answer choices is a waste of time and a distraction from the real work of taking the test. A test taker would be much better served by extra preparation before the test than by reliance on a pattern in the answers.

Bonus Content

We host multiple bonus items online, including all 6 practice tests in digital format. Scan the QR code or go to this link to access this content:

testprepbooks.com/bonus/psat89

The first time you access the tests, you will need to register as a "new user" and verify your email address.

If you have any issues, please email support@testprepbooks.com.

Introduction to the PSAT 8/9

Function of the Test

The Preliminary SAT (PSAT) 8/9 is an introductory version of the PSAT/NMSQT, PSAT 10, and the SAT. Given by the College Board, the PSAT 8/9 is designed to help US eighth- and ninth-grade students determine their areas of weakness so that they can focus their preparation for future testing and optimize their success in college. Because it assesses the same knowledge and skills that the subsequent tests measure, but in an understandable form for eighth and ninth graders, the results can serve as a strong personal benchmark for test takers in terms of their areas of competency and those that need the most improvement.

The PSAT 8/9 should be used as a tool to gauge mastery of concepts learned in school and progress towards those needed to succeed in college. The College Board recommends that the best way to prepare for the exam is simply to work hard in classes, complete all assignments, study regularly, remain inquisitive and active in class, and take advantage of challenging courses that are offered. While cramming for the exam is not necessary and not likely helpful, a favorite strategy of successful test takers and students is to familiarize themselves with the types of questions asked, the format of the questions, and the content that will be measured on the exam by taking practice exams and using study guides specifically created for the PSAT and SAT suite of tests.

Test Administration

The PSAT 8/9 is offered to students in the eighth and ninth grades on various dates during the academic year at schools throughout the United States. Some schools will pay all or part of the exam registration fee for their pupils. Since the financial responsibility of the student for the exam is different for each school, it is best to consult the school's guidance department for specifics. Students can only sign up to take the PSAT 8/9 through their school, or a local school if homeschooled.

In a change from past years, the test is now entirely digital. It is administered on supported devices through the Bluebook testing application. Students with documented disabilities can contact their school counselor to make alternative arrangements to take the PSAT 8/9. Examples of accommodations that are permitted include extending testing or break time and reading and seeing aids. College Board approval is not required to grant the accommodations, although nonstandard test format requests must be received by the College Board before the ordering deadline.

Test Format

All the tests that fall under the PSAT and SAT umbrella were redesigned in 2023. The PSAT 8/9 is very similar to the new PSAT and SAT in substance, structure, and scoring methodology. The test gauges a student's proficiency in two areas: Reading and Writing are tested first, followed by Math. The PSAT 8/9 does not include an essay.

The Reading and Writing portion of the PSAT 8/9 measures comprehension, requiring candidates to read brief fiction and non-fiction passages (including informational visuals, such as charts, tables and graphs) and answer questions based on this content. It also requires students to evaluate and edit passages to produce the most effective writing.

Four critical sectors are tested for the Math section: Algebra, Advanced Math, Problem-Solving and Data Analysis, and Geometry. Unlike higher-level SAT and PSAT tests, there is no trigonometry on the PSAT 8/9.

The PSAT 8/9 contains mostly multiple-choice questions, though some of the math questions are "student response," meaning the student inputs the answer instead of selecting from several options. There are a total of 98 questions on the test. Each of the two main sections are divided into two modules. After the first module in a section is completed, the second module will be more or less difficult, based on the test taker's performance in the initial module. This helps the evaluation to determine a more precise final score. All questions in a module must be completed before moving on to the next module.

A different length of time is given for each section, for a total of 2 hours and 14 minutes. There are fewer questions than previous versions of the test, and more time is available for each question. The specific breakdown is as follows:

Section	Time (In Minutes)	Number of Questions
Reading and Writing: Module 1	32	27
Reading and Writing: Module 2	32	27
Math: Module 1	35	22
Math: Module 2	35	22
Total	**134**	**98**

Scoring

Test takers are not penalized for incorrect answers on the PSAT 8/9, so it is smart to guess, even when the test taker does not know the answer. A raw score is calculated based on the number of correct responses. This score is then equated, or scaled, to a total score that ranges from 240 to 1440. Of this, 120 to 720 is contributed from each of the two sections: Math and Reading and Writing. The score equating process allows different iterations and administrations of the PSAT 8/9 to be compared. Score reports also list sub-scores for the four subsections in Reading and Writing and the four subsections in the Math section. This is in order to give candidates an idea of their specific strengths and weaknesses.

The report ranks scores based on a User Percentile between 1 and 99 so students can see how they measured up to other test takers. The average (50th percentile) for each subtest is listed as well. Good scores are typically defined as higher than 50 percent. These percentiles are based on the actual performance of the past three "cohorts" (groups of students) that took the test. Benchmark scores are also provided. These serve to indicate whether the candidate is on track for success in college based on their relative achievement on the benchmark continuum.

Scores are not sent to colleges. The College Board only sends PSAT 8/9 scores to schools, and usually districts and states. A copy is also sent to parents by some schools directly.

Study Prep Plan for the PSAT 8/9

1   **Schedule -** Use one of our study schedules below or come up with one of your own.

2   **Relax -** Test anxiety can hurt even the best students. There are many ways to reduce stress. Find the one that works best for you.

3   **Execute -** Once you have a good plan in place, be sure to stick to it.

One Week Study Schedule

Day 1	Reading Test
Day 2	Writing and Language Test
Day 3	Math Test
Day 4	Practice Tests #1 & #2
Day 5	Practice Tests #3 & #4
Day 6	Practice Tests #5 & #6
Day 7	Take Your Exam!

Two Week Study Schedule

Day 1	Reading Test	Day 8	Problem-Solving and Data Analysis
Day 2	Rhetoric and Synthesis	Day 9	Passport to Advanced Math
Day 3	Analysis of Science Excerpts	Day 10	Interpreting Parts of Nonlinear Expressions...
Day 4	Writing and Language Test	Day 11	Practice Tests #1 & #2
Day 5	Standard English Conventions	Day 12	Practice Tests #3 & #4
Day 6	Punctuation	Day 13	Practice Tests #5 & #6
Day 7	Math Test	Day 14	Take Your Exam!

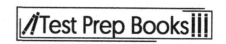

One Month Study Schedule							
Day 1	Reading Test	Day 11	Creating, Solving, and Interpreting Systems of Two...	Day 21	Answer Explanations #2
Day 2	Rhetoric and Synthesis	Day 12	Problem-Solving and Data Analysis	Day 22	Practice Test #3
Day 3	Analysis of History/ Social Studies Excerpts	Day 13	Using the Relationship Between Two...	Day 23	Answer Explanations #3
Day 4	Analysis of Science Excerpts	Day 14	Passport to Advanced Math	Day 24	Practice Test #4
Day 5	Writing and Language Test	Day 15	Solving an Equation in One Variable that...	Day 25	Answer Explanations #4
Day 6	Effective Language Use	Day 16	Interpreting Parts of Nonlinear Expressions...	Day 26	Practice Test #5
Day 7	Standard English Conventions	Day 17	Using Function Notation, and...	Day 27	Answer Explanations #5
Day 8	Usage	Day 18	Practice Test #1	Day 28	Practice Test #6
Day 9	Punctuation	Day 19	Answer Explanations #1	Day 29	Answer Explanations #6
Day 10	Math Test	Day 20	Practice Test #2	Day 30	Take Your Exam!

Build your own prep plan by visiting:
testprepbooks.com/prep

As you study for your test, we'd like to take the opportunity to remind you that you are capable of great things! With the right tools and dedication, you truly can do anything you set your mind to. The fact that you are holding this book right now shows how committed you are. In case no one has told you lately, you've got this! Our intention behind including this coloring page is to give you the chance to take some time to engage your creative side when you need a little brain-break from studying. As a company, we want to encourage people like you to achieve their dreams by providing good quality study materials for the tests and certifications that improve careers and change lives. As individuals, many of us have taken such tests in our careers, and we know how challenging this process can be. While we can't come alongside you and cheer you on personally, we can offer you the space to recall your purpose, reconnect with your passion, and refresh your brain through an artistic practice. We wish you every success, and happy studying!

Reading and Writing Test

The purpose of this guide is to help test takers understand the basic principles of reading comprehension questions contained in the PSAT 8/9. Studying this guide will help determine the types of questions that the test contains and how best to address them, provided the test's parameters. This guide is not all-inclusive, and does not contain actual test material. This guide is, and should be used, only as preparation to improve student's reading skills for the PSAT Reading and Writing section.

Each section addresses key skills test takers need to master in order to successfully complete the Reading portion of the PSAT 8/9. Each section is further broken down into sub-skills. All of the topics and related subtopics address testable material. Careful use of this guide should fully prepare test takers for a successful test experience.

The PSAT 8/9 Reading and Writing modules contain a series of brief passages that must be read along with a question pertaining to each passage. The task is not so much to recall or restate a passage's content, but to analyze how the content is presented and answer questions about how to improve it.

Craft and Structure

Words in Context

In order to successfully complete the reading comprehension section of the PSAT 8/9, the test taker should be able to identify words in context. This involves a set of skills that requires the test taker to answer questions about unfamiliar words within a brief text passage. Additionally, the test taker may be asked to answer critical thinking questions based on unfamiliar word meanings. Identifying the meaning of different words in context is very much like solving a puzzle. By using a variety of techniques, a test taker should be able to correctly identify the meaning of unfamiliar words and concepts with ease.

Using Context Clues
A context clue is a hint that an author provides to the reader in order to help define difficult or unique words. When reading a passage, a test taker should take note of any unfamiliar words, and then examine the sentence around them to look for clues to the word meanings. Let's look at an example:

> He faced a *conundrum* in making this decision. He felt as if he had come to a crossroads. This was truly a puzzle, and what he did next would determine the course of his future.

The word *conundrum* may be unfamiliar to the reader. By looking at context clues, the reader should be able to determine its meaning. In this passage, context clues include the idea of making a decision and of being unsure. Furthermore, the author restates the definition of conundrum in using the word *puzzle* as a synonym. Therefore, the reader should be able to determine that the definition of the word *conundrum* is a difficult puzzle.

Similarly, a reader can determine difficult vocabulary by identifying antonyms. Let's look at an example:

> Her *gregarious* nature was completely opposite of her twin's, who was shy, retiring, and socially nervous.

The word *gregarious* may be unfamiliar. However, by looking at the surrounding context clues, the reader can determine that *gregarious* does not mean shy. The twins' personalities are being contrasted. Therefore, *gregarious* must mean sociable, or something similar to it.

At times, an author will provide contextual clues through a cause and effect relationship. Look at the next sentence as an example:

> The athletes were excited with *elation* when they won the tournament; unfortunately, their off-court antics caused them to forfeit the win.

The word elated may be unfamiliar to the reader. However, the author defines the word by presenting a cause and effect relationship. The athletes were so elated at the win that their behavior went overboard, and they had to forfeit. In this instance, *elated* must mean something akin to overjoyed, happy, and overexcited.

Cause and effect is one technique authors use to demonstrate relationships. A cause is why something happens. The effect is what happens as a result. For example, a reader may encounter text such as *Because he was unable to sleep, he was often restless and irritable during the day*. The cause is insomnia due to lack of sleep. The effect is being restless and irritable. When reading for a cause and effect relationship, look for words such as "if", "then", "such", and "because." By using cause and effect, an author can describe direct relationships, and convey an overall theme, particularly when taking a stance on their topic.

An author can also provide contextual clues through comparison and contrast. Let's look at an example:

> Her torpid state caused her parents, and her physician, to worry about her seemingly sluggish well-being.

The word *torpid* is probably unfamiliar to the reader. However, the author has compared *torpid* to a state of being and, moreover, one that's worrisome. Therefore, the reader should be able to determine that *torpid* is not a positive, healthy state of being. In fact, through the use of comparison, it means sluggish. Similarly, an author may contrast an unfamiliar word with an idea. In the sentence *Her <u>torpid</u> state was completely opposite of her usual, bubbly self,* the meaning of *torpid*, or sluggish, is contrasted with the words *bubbly self*.

A test taker should be able to critically assess and determine unfamiliar word meanings through the use of an author's context clues in order to fully comprehend difficult text passages.

Relating Unfamiliar Words to Familiar Words

The PSAT 8/9 will test a reader's ability to use context clues, and then relate unfamiliar words to more familiar ones. Using the word *torpid* as an example, the test may ask the test taker to relate the meaning of the word to a list of vocabulary options and choose the more familiar word as closest in meaning. In this case, the test may say something like the following:

> Which of the following words means the same as the word *torpid* in the above passage?

Then they will provide the test taker with a list of familiar options such as happy, disgruntled, sluggish, and animated. By using context clues, the reader has already determined the meaning of *torpid* as slow or sluggish, so the reader should be able to correctly identify the word *sluggish* as the correct answer.

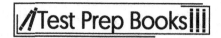

One effective way to relate unfamiliar word meanings to more familiar ones is to substitute the provided word in each answer option for the unfamiliar word in question. Although this will not always lead to a correct answer every time, this strategy will help the test taker narrow answer options. Be careful when utilizing this strategy. Pay close attention to the meaning of sentences and answer choices because it's easy to mistake answer choices as correct when they are easily substituted, especially when they are the same part of speech. Does the sentence mean the same thing with the substituted word option in place or does it change entirely? Does the substituted word make sense? Does it possibly mean the same as the unfamiliar word in question?

How an Author's Word Choice Shapes Meaning, Style, and Tone

Authors choose their words carefully in order to artfully depict meaning, style, and tone, which is most commonly inferred through the use of adjectives and verbs. The *tone* is the predominant emotion present in the text, and represents the attitude or feelings that an author has towards a character or event.

To review, an adjective is a word used to describe something, and usually precedes the noun, a person, place, or object. A verb is a word describing an action. For example, the sentence "The scary woodpecker ate the spider" includes the adjective *scary*, the noun *woodpecker*, and the verb *ate*. Reading this sentence may rouse some negative feelings, as the word *scary* carries a negative charge. The "charge" is the emotional connotation that can be derived from the adjectives and verbs and is either positive or negative. Recognizing the charge of a particular sentence or passage is an effective way to understand the meaning and tone the author is trying to convey.

Many authors have conflicting charges within the same text, but a definitive tone can be inferred by understanding the meaning of the charges relative to each other. It's important to recognize key conjunctions, or words that link sentences or clauses together. There are several types and subtypes of conjunctions. Three are most important for reading comprehension:

- *Cumulative conjunctions* add one statement to another.
- Examples: and, both, also, as well as, not only
- e.g. The juice is sweet *and* sour.
- *Adversative conjunctions* are used to contrast two clauses.
- Examples: but, while, still, yet, nevertheless
- e.g. She was tired, *but* she was happy.
- *Alternative conjunctions* express two alternatives.
- Examples: or, either, neither, nor, else, otherwise
- e.g. He must eat, *or* he will die.

Identifying the meaning and tone of a text can be accomplished with the following steps:

- Identify the adjectives and verbs.
- Recognize any important conjunctions.
- Label the adjectives and verbs as positive or negative.
- Understand what the charge means about the text.

To demonstrate these steps, examine the following passage from the classic children's poem, "The Sheep":

> Lazy sheep, pray tell me why
>
> In the pleasant fields you lie,
>
> Eating grass, and daisies white,
>
> From the morning till the night?
>
> Everything can something do,
>
> But what kind of use are you?

–Taylor, Jane and Ann. "The Sheep."

This selection is a good example of conflicting charges that work together to express an overall tone. Following the first two steps, identify the adjectives, verbs, and conjunctions within the passage. For this example, the adjectives are <u>underlined</u>, the verbs are in **bold**, and the conjunctions *italicized*:

> <u>Lazy</u> sheep, pray **tell** me why
>
> In the <u>pleasant</u> fields you **lie**,
>
> **Eating** grass, and daisies <u>white,</u>
>
> From the morning till the night?
>
> Everything can something do,
>
> *But* what kind of use are you?

For step three, read the passage and judge whether feelings of positivity or negativity arose. Then assign a charge to each of the words that were outlined. This can be done in a table format, or simply by writing a + or − next to the word.

The word <u>lazy</u> carries a negative connotation; it usually denotes somebody unwilling to work. To **tell** someone something has an exclusively neutral connotation, as it depends on what's being told, which has not yet been revealed at this point, so a charge can be assigned later. The word <u>pleasant</u> is an inherently positive word. To **lie** could be positive or negative depending on the context, but as the subject (the sheep) is lying in a pleasant field, then this is a positive experience. **Eating** is also generally positive.

After labeling the charges for each word, it might be inferred that the tone of this poem is happy and maybe even admiring or innocuously envious. However, notice the adversative conjunction, "but" and what follows. The author has listed all the pleasant things this sheep gets to do all day, but the tone changes when the author asks, "What kind of use are you?" Asking someone to prove their value is a rather hurtful thing to do, as it implies that the person asking the question doesn't believe the subject has any value, so this could be listed under negative charges. Referring back to the verb **tell**, after

17

reading the whole passage, it can be deduced that the author is asking the sheep to tell what use the sheep is, so this has a negative charge.

+	−
• Pleasant • Lie in fields • From morning to night	• Lazy • Tell me • What kind of use are you

Upon examining the charges, it might seem like there's an even amount of positive and negative emotion in this selection, and that's where the conjunction "but" becomes crucial to identifying the tone. The conjunction "but" indicates there's a contrasting view to the pleasantness of the sheep's daily life, and this view is that the sheep is lazy and useless, which is also indicated by the first line, "lazy sheep, pray tell me why."

It might be helpful to look at questions pertaining to tone. For this selection, consider the following question:

The author of the poem regards the sheep with a feeling of what?
a. Respect
b. Disgust
c. Apprehension
d. Intrigue

Considering the author views the sheep as lazy with nothing to offer, Choice *A* appears to reflect the opposite of what the author is feeling.

Choice *B* seems to mirror the author's feelings towards the sheep, as laziness is considered a disreputable trait, and people (or personified animals, in this case) with unfavorable traits might be viewed with disgust.

Choice *C* doesn't make sense within context, as laziness isn't usually feared.

Choice *D* is tricky, as it may be tempting to argue that the author is intrigued with the sheep because they ask, "pray tell me why." This is another out-of-scope answer choice as it doesn't *quite* describe the feelings the author experiences and there's also a much better fit in Choice *B*.

Focus

Good writing stays *focused* and on topic. During the test, determine the main idea for each passage and then look for times when the writer strays from the point they're trying to make. Let's go back to the seat belt example. If the writer suddenly begins talking about how well airbags, crumple zones, or other safety features work to save lives, they might be losing focus from the topic of "safety belts."

Focus can also refer to individual sentences. Sometimes the writer does address the main topic, but in a confusing way. For example:

> Thanks to seat belt usage, survival in serious car accidents has shown a consistently steady increase since the development of the retractable seat belt in the 1950s.

This statement is definitely on topic, but it's not easy to follow. A simpler, more focused version of this sentence might look like this:

> Seat belts have consistently prevented car fatalities since the 1950s.

Providing *adequate information* is another aspect of focused writing. Statements like "seat belts are important" and "many people drive cars" are true, but they're so general that they don't contribute much to the writer's case. When reading a passage, watch for these kinds of unfocused statements.

Introductions and Conclusions

Examining the writer's strategies for introductions and conclusions puts the reader in the right mindset to interpret the rest of the passage. Look for methods the writer might use for introductions such as:

- Stating the main point immediately, followed by outlining how the rest of the piece supports this claim.

- Establishing important, smaller pieces of the main idea first, and then grouping these points into a case for the main idea.

- Opening with a quotation, anecdote, question, seeming paradox, or other piece of interesting information, and then using it to lead to the main point.

Whatever method the writer chooses, the introduction should make their intention clear, establish their voice as a credible one, and encourage a person to continue reading.

Conclusions tend to follow a similar pattern. In them, the writer restates their main idea a final time, often after summarizing the smaller pieces of that idea. If the introduction uses a quote or anecdote to grab the reader's attention, the conclusion often makes reference to it again. Whatever way the writer chooses to arrange the conclusion, the final restatement of the main idea should be clear and simple for the reader to interpret. Finally, conclusions shouldn't introduce any new information.

Precision

People often think of *precision* in terms of math, but precise word choice is another key to successful writing. Since language itself is imprecise, it's important for the writer to find the exact word or words to convey the full, intended meaning of a given situation. For example:

> The number of deaths has gone down since seat belt laws started.

There are several problems with this sentence. First, the word *deaths* is too general. From the context, it's assumed that the writer is referring only to *deaths* caused by car accidents. However, without clarification, the sentence lacks impact and is probably untrue. The phrase "gone down" might be accurate, but a more precise word could provide more information and greater accuracy. Did the numbers show a slow and steady decrease of highway fatalities or a sudden drop? If the latter is true,

19

the writer is missing a chance to make their point more dramatically. Instead of "gone down" they could substitute *plummeted*, *fallen drastically*, or *rapidly diminished* to bring the information to life. Also, the phrase "seat belt laws" is unclear. Does it refer to laws requiring cars to include seat belts or to laws requiring drivers and passengers to use them? Finally, *started* is not a strong verb. Words like *enacted* or *adopted* are more direct and make the content more real. When put together, these changes create a far more powerful sentence:

> The number of highway fatalities has plummeted since laws requiring seat belt usage were enacted.

However, it's important to note that precise word choice can sometimes be taken too far. If the writer of the sentence above takes precision to an extreme, it might result in the following:

> The incidence of high-speed, automobile accident related fatalities has decreased 75% and continued to remain at historical lows since the initial set of federal legislations requiring seat belt use were enacted in 1992.

This sentence is extremely precise, but it takes so long to achieve that precision that it suffers from a lack of clarity. Precise writing is about finding the right balance between information and flow. This is also an issue of *conciseness* (discussed in the next section).

The last thing to consider with precision is a word choice that's not only unclear or uninteresting, but also confusing or misleading. For example:

> The number of highway fatalities has become hugely lower since laws requiring seat belt use were enacted.

In this case, the reader might be confused by the word *hugely*. Huge means large, but here the writer uses *hugely* to describe something small. Though most readers can decipher this, doing so disconnects them from the flow of the writing and makes the writer's point less effective.

On the test, there can be questions asking for alternatives to the writer's word choice. In answering these questions, always consider the context and look for a balance between precision and flow.

Conciseness

"Less is more" is a good rule to follow when writing a sentence. Unfortunately, writers often include extra words and phrases that seem necessary at the time, but add nothing to the main idea. This confuses the reader and creates unnecessary repetition. Writing that lacks *conciseness* is usually guilty of excessive wordiness and redundant phrases. Here's an example containing both of these issues:

> When legislators decided to begin creating legislation making it mandatory for automobile drivers and passengers to make use of seat belts while in cars, a large number of them made those laws for reasons that were political reasons.

There are several empty or "fluff" words here that take up too much space. These can be eliminated while still maintaining the writer's meaning. For example:

- "decided to begin" could be shortened to "began"
- "making it mandatory for" could be shortened to "requiring"

20

- "make use of" could be shortened to "use"
- "a large number" could be shortened to "many"

In addition, there are several examples of redundancy that can be eliminated:

- "legislators decided to begin creating legislation" and "made those laws"
- "automobile drivers and passengers" and "while in cars"
- "reasons that were political reasons"

These changes are incorporated as follows:

> When legislators began requiring drivers and passengers to use seat belts, many of them did so for political reasons.

There are many examples of redundant phrases, such as "add an additional," "complete and total," "time schedule," and "transportation vehicle." If asked to identify a redundant phrase on the test, look for words that are close together with the same (or similar) meanings.

Reading for Tone, Message, and Effect

The PSAT 8/9 does not just address a test taker's ability to find facts within a passage; it also evaluates a reader's ability to determine an author's viewpoint through the use of tone, message, and overall effect. This type of reading comprehension requires inference skills, deductive reasoning skills, the ability to draw logical conclusions, and overall critical thinking skills. Reading for factual information is straightforward. Reading for an author's tone, message, and overall effect is not. It's key to read carefully when asked test questions that address a test taker's ability to identify and analyze these writing devices. These are not questions that can be easily answered by quickly scanning for the right information.

Tone

An author's *tone* is the use of particular words, phrases, and writing style to convey an overall meaning. Tone expresses the author's attitude towards a particular topic. For example, a passage may begin like the following:

> The presidential election of 1960 ushered in a new era, a new Camelot, a new phase of forward thinking in US politics that embraced brash action and unrest and responded with admirable leadership.

From this opening statement, a reader can draw some conclusions about the author's attitude towards President John F. Kennedy. Furthermore, the reader can make additional, educated guesses about the state of the Union during the 1960 presidential election. By close reading, the test taker can determine that the repeated use of the word *new* and words such as *admirable leadership* indicate the author's tone of admiration regarding President Kennedy's boldness. In addition, the author assesses that the era during President Kennedy's administration was problematic through the use of the words *brash action* and *unrest*. Therefore, if a test taker encountered a test question asking about the author's use of tone and their assessment of the Kennedy administration, the test taker should be able to identify an answer indicating admiration. Similarly, if asked about the state of the Union during the 1960s, a test taker should be able to correctly identify an answer indicating political unrest.

When identifying an author's tone, the following list of words may be helpful. This is not an inclusive list. Generally, parts of speech that indicate attitude will also indicate tone:

- Comical
- Angry
- Ambivalent
- Scary
- Lyrical
- Matter-of-fact
- Judgmental
- Sarcastic
- Malicious
- Objective
- Pessimistic
- Patronizing
- Gloomy
- Instructional
- Satirical
- Formal
- Casual

Message

An author's *message* is the same as the overall meaning of a passage. It is the main idea, or the main concept the author wishes to convey. An author's message may be stated outright, or it may be implied. Regardless, the test taker will need to use careful reading skills to identify an author's message or purpose.

Often, the message of a particular passage can be determined by thinking about why the author wrote the information. Many historical passages are written to inform and to teach readers established, factual information. However, many historical works are also written to convey biased ideas to readers. Gleaning bias from an author's message in a historical passage can be difficult, especially if the reader is presented with a variety of established facts as well. Readers tend to accept historical writing as factual. This is not always the case. Any discerning reader who has tackled historical information on topics such as United States political party agendas can attest that two or more works on the same topic may have completely different messages supporting or refuting the value of the identical policies.

Therefore, it is important to critically assess an author's message separate from factual information. One author, for example, may point to the rise of unorthodox political candidates in an election year based on the failures of the political party in office while another may point to the rise of the same candidates in the same election year based on the current party's successes. The historical facts of what has occurred leading up to an election year are not in refute. Labeling those facts as a failure or a success is a bias within an author's overall *message*, as is excluding factual information in order to further a particular point. In a standardized testing situation, a reader must be able to critically assess what the author is trying to say separate from the historical facts that surround their message.

22

Using the example of Lincoln's Gettysburg Address, a test question may ask the following:

What message is the author trying to convey through this address?

Then they will ask the test taker to select an answer that best expresses Lincoln's *message* to his audience. Based on the options given, a test taker should be able to select the answer expressing the idea that Lincoln's audience should recognize the efforts of those who died in the war as a sacrifice to preserving human equality and self-government.

Effect

An author may want to challenge a reader's intellect, inspire imagination, or spur emotion. An author may present information to appeal to a physical, aesthetic, or transformational sense. Take the following text as an example:

In 1963, Martin Luther King stated "I have a dream." The gathering at the Lincoln Memorial was the beginning of the Civil Rights movement and, with its reference to the Emancipation Proclamation, Dr. King's words electrified those who wanted freedom and equality while rising from hatred and slavery. It was the beginning of radical change.

The test taker may be asked about the effect this statement might have on King's audience. Through careful reading of the passage, the test taker should be able to choose an answer that best identifies an effect of grabbing the audience's attention. The historical facts are in place: King made the speech in 1963 at the Lincoln Memorial, kicked off the civil rights movement, and referenced the Emancipation Proclamation. The words *electrified* and *radical change* indicate the effect the author wants the reader to understand as a result of King's speech. In this historical passage, facts are facts. However, the author's message goes beyond the facts to indicate the effect the message had on the audience and, in addition, the effect the event should have on the reader.

Information and Ideas

Command of Evidence

Command of evidence, or the ability to use contextual clues, factual statements, and corroborative phrases to support an author's message or intent, is an important part of the PSAT 8/9. A test taker's ability to parse out factual information and draw conclusions based on evidence is important to critical reading comprehension. The test will ask students to read text passages, and then answer questions based on information contained in them. These types of questions may ask test takers to identify stated facts. They may also require test takers to draw logical conclusions, identify data based on graphs, make inferences, and to generally display analytical thinking skills.

Finding Evidence in a Passage

The basic tenet of reading comprehension is the ability to read and understand a text. One way to understand a text is to look for information that supports the author's main idea, topic, or position statement. This information may be factual, or it may be based on the author's opinion. This section will focus on the test taker's ability to identify factual information, as opposed to opinionated bias. The PSAT 8/9 will ask test takers to read passages containing factual information, and then logically relate those passages by drawing conclusions based on evidence.

In order to identify factual information within one or more text passages, begin by looking for statements of fact. Factual statements can be either true or false. Identifying factual statements as opposed to opinion statements is important in demonstrating full command of evidence in reading. For example, the statement *The temperature outside was unbearably hot* may seem like a fact; however, it's not. While anyone can point to a temperature gauge as factual evidence, the statement itself reflects only an opinion. Some people may find the temperature unbearably hot. Others may find it comfortably warm. Thus, the sentence, *The temperature outside was unbearably hot,* reflects the opinion of the author who found it unbearable. If the text passage followed up the sentence with atmospheric conditions indicating heat indices above 140 degrees Fahrenheit, then the reader knows there is factual information that supports the author's assertion of *unbearably hot*.

In looking for information that can be proven or disproven, it's helpful to scan for dates, numbers, timelines, equations, statistics, and other similar data within any given text passage. These types of indicators will point to proven particulars. For example, the statement, *The temperature outside was unbearably hot on that summer day, July 10, 1913,* most likely indicates factual information, even if the reader is unaware that this is the hottest day on record in the United States. Be careful when reading biased words from an author. Biased words indicate opinion, as opposed to fact. The following list contains a sampling of common biased words:

- Good/bad
- Great/greatest
- Better/best/worst
- Amazing
- Terrible/bad/awful
- Beautiful/handsome/ugly
- More/most
- Exciting/dull/boring
- Favorite
- Very
- Probably/should/seem/possibly

Remember, most of what is written is actually opinion or carefully worded information that seems like fact when it isn't. To say, *duplicating DNA results is not cost-effective* sounds like it could be a scientific fact, but it isn't. Factual information can be verified through independent sources.

The simplest type of test question may provide a text passage, then ask the test taker to distinguish the correct factual supporting statement that best answers the corresponding question on the test. However, be aware that most questions may ask the test taker to read more than one text passage and identify which answer best supports an author's topic. While the ability to identify factual information is critical, these types of questions require the test taker to identify chunks of details, and then relate them to one another.

Displaying Analytical Thinking Skills

Analytical thinking involves being able to break down visual information into manageable portions in order to solve complex problems or process difficult concepts. This skill encompasses all aspects of command of evidence in reading comprehension.

A reader can approach analytical thinking in a series of steps. First, when approaching visual material, a reader should identify an author's thought process. Is the line of reasoning clear from the presented passage, or does it require inference and coming to a conclusion independent of the author? Next, a reader should evaluate the author's line of reasoning to determine if the logic is sound. Look for evidentiary clues and cited sources. Do these hold up under the author's argument? Third, look for bias. Bias includes generalized, emotional statements that will not hold up under scrutiny, as they are not based on fact. From there, a reader should ask if the presented evidence is trustworthy. Are the facts cited from reliable sources? Are they current? Is there any new factual information that has come to light since the passage was written that renders the argument useless? Next, a reader should carefully think about information that opposes the author's view. Do the author's arguments guide the reader to identical thoughts, or is there room for sound arguments? Finally, a reader should always be able to identify an author's conclusion and be able to weigh its effectiveness.

The ability to display analytical thinking skills while reading is key in any standardized testing situation. Test takers should be able to critically evaluate the information provided, and then answer questions related to content by using the steps above.

Making Inferences
Simply put, an inference is an educated guess drawn from evidence, logic, and reasoning. The key to making inferences is identifying clues within a passage, and then using common sense to arrive at a reasonable conclusion. Consider it "reading between the lines."

One way to make an inference is to look for main topics. When doing so, pay particular attention to any titles, headlines, or opening statements made by the author. Topic sentences or repetitive ideas can be clues in gleaning inferred ideas. For example, if a passage contains the phrase *While some consider DNA testing to be infallible, it is an inherently flawed technique,* the test taker can infer the rest of the passage will contain information that points to problems with DNA testing.

The test taker may be asked to make an inference based on prior knowledge but may also be asked to make predictions based on new ideas. For example, the test taker may have no prior knowledge of DNA other than its genetic property to replicate. However, if the reader is given passages on the flaws of DNA testing with enough factual evidence, the test taker may arrive at the inferred conclusion that the author does not support the infallibility of DNA testing in all identification cases.

When making inferences, it is important to remember that the critical thinking process involved must be fluid and open to change. While a reader may infer an idea from a main topic, general statement, or other clues, they must be open to receiving new information within a particular passage. New ideas presented by an author may require the test taker to alter an inference. Similarly, when asked questions that require making an inference, it's important to read the entire test passage and all of the answer options. Often, a test taker will need to refine a general inference based on new ideas that may be presented within the test itself.

Author's Use of Evidence to Support Claims
Authors utilize a wide range of techniques to tell a story or communicate information. Readers should be familiar with the most common of these techniques. Techniques of writing are also commonly known as rhetorical devices, and they are some of the evidence that authors use to support claims.

In nonfiction writing, authors employ argumentative techniques to present their opinion to readers in the most convincing way. Persuasive writing usually includes at least one type of appeal: an appeal to

25

logic (logos), emotion (pathos), or credibility and trustworthiness (ethos). When a writer appeals to logic, they are asking readers to agree with them based on research, evidence, and an established line of reasoning. An author's argument might also appeal to readers' emotions, perhaps by including personal stories and anecdotes (a short narrative of a specific event). A final type of appeal, appeal to authority, asks the reader to agree with the author's argument on the basis of their expertise or credentials. Consider three different approaches to arguing the same opinion:

Logic (Logos)

Below is an example of an appeal to logic. The author uses evidence to disprove the logic of the school's rule (the rule was supposed to reduce discipline problems, but the number of problems has not been reduced; therefore, the rule is not working) and call for its repeal.

> Our school should abolish its current ban on campus cell phone use. The ban was adopted last year as an attempt to reduce class disruptions and help students focus more on their lessons. However, since the rule was enacted, there has been no change in the number of disciplinary problems in class. Therefore, the rule is ineffective and should be done away with.

Emotion (Pathos)

An author's argument might also appeal to readers' emotions, perhaps by including personal stories and anecdotes.

The next example presents an appeal to emotion. By sharing the personal anecdote of one student and speaking about emotional topics like family relationships, the author invokes the reader's empathy in asking them to reconsider the school rule.

> Our school should abolish its current ban on campus cell phone use. If students aren't able to use their phones during the school day, many of them feel isolated from their loved ones. For example, last semester, one student's grandmother had a heart attack in the morning. However, because he couldn't use his cell phone, the student didn't know about his grandmother's accident until the end of the day—when she had already passed away, and it was too late to say goodbye. By preventing students from contacting their friends and family, our school is placing undue stress and anxiety on students.

Credibility (Ethos)

Finally, an appeal to authority includes a statement from a relevant expert. In this case, the author uses a doctor in the field of education to support the argument. All three examples begin from the same opinion—the school's phone ban needs to change—but rely on different argumentative styles to persuade the reader.

> Our school should abolish its current ban on campus cell phone use. According to Dr. Bartholomew Everett, a leading educational expert, "Research studies show that cell phone usage has no real impact on student attentiveness. Rather, phones provide a valuable technological resource for learning. Schools need to learn how to integrate this new technology into their curriculum." Rather than banning phones altogether, our school should follow the advice of experts and allow students to use phones as part of their learning.

Reading for Factual Information

Standardized test questions that ask for factual information are usually straightforward. These types of questions will either ask the test taker to confirm a fact by choosing a correct answer, or to select a correct answer based on a negative fact question.

For example, the test taker may encounter a passage from Lincoln's Gettysburg Address. A corresponding test question may ask the following:

> Which war is Abraham Lincoln referring to in the following passage?

> Now we are engaged in a great civil war, testing whether that nation, or any nation so conceived and so dedicated, can long endure.

This type of question is asking the test taker to confirm a simple fact. Given options such as World War I, the War of Spanish Succession, World War II, and the American Civil War, the test taker should be able to correctly identify the American Civil War based on the words "civil war" within the passage itself, and, hopefully, through general knowledge. In this case, reading the test question and scanning answer options ahead of reading the Gettysburg Address would help quickly identify the correct answer. Similarly, a test taker may be asked to confirm a historical fact based on a negative fact question. For example, a passage's corresponding test question may ask the following:

> Which option is incorrect based on the above passage?

Given a variety of choices speaking about which war Abraham Lincoln was addressing, the test taker would need to eliminate all correct answers pertaining to the American Civil War and choose the answer choice referencing a different war. In other words, the correct answer is the one that contradicts the information in the passage.

It is important to remember that reading for factual information is straightforward. The test taker must distinguish fact from bias. Factual statements can be proven or disproven independent of the author and from a variety of other sources. Remember, successfully answering questions regarding factual information may require the test taker to re-read the passage, as these types of questions test for attention to detail.

Informational Graphics

A test taker's ability to draw conclusions from an informational graphic is a sub-skill in displaying one's command of reading evidence. Drawing conclusions requires the reader to consider all information provided in the passage, then to use logic to piece it together to form a reasonably correct resolution. In this case, a test taker must look for facts as well as opinionated statements. Both should be considered in order to arrive at a conclusion. These types of questions test one's ability to conduct logical and analytical thinking.

Identifying data-driven evidence in informational graphics is very similar to analyzing factual information. However, it often involves the use of graphics in order to do so. In these types of questions, the test taker will be presented with a graph, or organizational tool, and asked questions regarding the

27

information it contains. On the following page, review the pie chart organizing percentages of primary occupations of public transportation passengers in US cities.

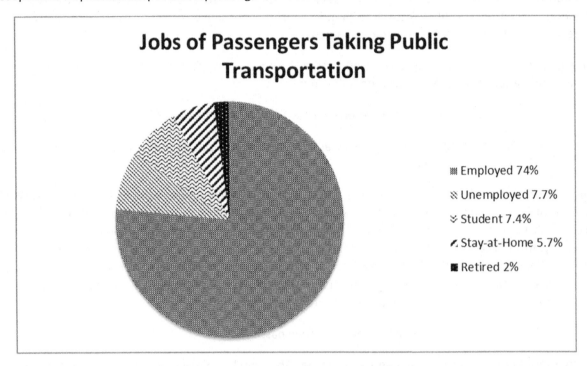

This figure depicts the jobs of passengers taking public transportation in US cities. A corresponding PSAT question may have the test taker study the chart, then answer a question regarding the values. For example, is the number of students relying on public transportation greater or less than the number of the unemployed? Similarly, the test may ask if people employed outside the home are less likely to use public transportation than homemakers. Note that the phrase *less likely* may weigh into the reader's choice of optional answers and that the test taker should look for additional passage data to arrive at a conclusion one way or another.

The PSAT 8/9 will also test the ability to draw a conclusion by presenting the test taker with more than one passage, and then ask questions that require the reader to compare the passages in order to arrive at a logical conclusion. For example, a text passage may describe the flaws in DNA testing, and then describe the near infallibility of it in the next. The test taker then may be required to glean the evidence in both passages, then answer a question such as *the central idea in the first paragraph is ...* followed by *which choice regarding the infallibility of DNA testing best refutes the previous question?* In this example, the test taker must carefully find a central concept of the flaws of DNA testing based on the two passages, and then rely on that choice to best answer the subsequent question regarding its infallibility.

Interpreting Data and Considering Implications

The PSAT 8/9 is likely to contain one or more data-driven science passages that require the test taker to examine evidence within a particular type of graphic. The test taker will then be required to interpret the data and answer questions demonstrating their ability to draw logical conclusions.

In general, there are two types of data: qualitative and quantitative. Science passages may contain both, but simply put, quantitative data is reflected numerically and qualitative is not. Qualitative data is based

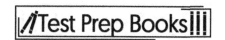

on its qualities. In other words, qualitative data tends to present information more in subjective generalities (for example, relating to size or appearance). Quantitative data is based on numerical findings such as percentages. Quantitative data will be described in numerical terms. While both types of data are valid, the test taker will more likely be faced with having to interpret quantitative data through one or more graphic(s), and then be required to answer questions regarding the numerical data.

Some writing in the test contains *infographics* such as charts, tables, or graphs. In these cases, interpret the information presented and determine how well it supports the claims made in the text. For example, if the writer makes a case that seat belts save more lives than other automobile safety measures, they might want to include a graph (like the one below) showing the number of lives saved by seat belts versus those saved by air bags.

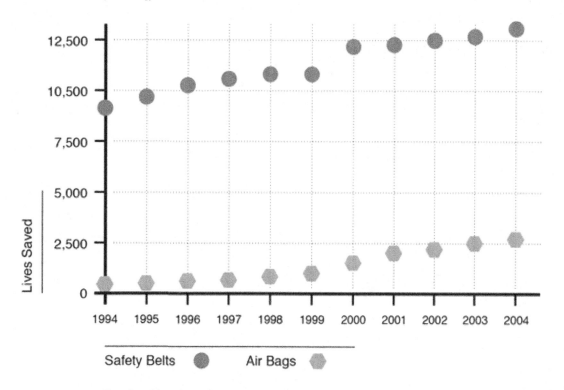

Based on data from the National Highway Traffic Safety Administration

If the graph clearly shows a higher number of lives are saved by seat belts, then it's effective. However, if the graph shows air bags save more lives than seat belts, then it doesn't support the writer's case.

Finally, graphs should be easy to understand. Their information should immediately be clear to the reader at a glance. Here are some basic things to keep in mind when interpreting infographics:

- In a *bar graph*, higher bars represent larger numbers. Lower bars represent smaller numbers.

- *Line graphs* often show trends over time. Points that are higher represent larger numbers than points that are lower. A line that consistently ascends from left to right shows a steady increase over time. A line that consistently descends from left to right shows a steady decrease over time. A line that bounces up and down represents instability or inconsistency in the trend. When

29

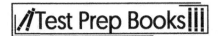
interpreting a line graph, determine the point the writer is trying to make, and then see if the graph supports that point.

- *Pie charts* are used to show proportions or percentages of a whole but are less effective in showing change over time.

- *Tables* present information in numerical form, not as graphics. When interpreting a table, make sure to look for patterns in the numbers.

More information on these infographics can be found in this section. A test taker should take the time to learn the skills it takes to interpret quantitative data.

Line Graph
An example of a line graph is as follows:

Cell Phone Use in Kiteville, 2000-2006

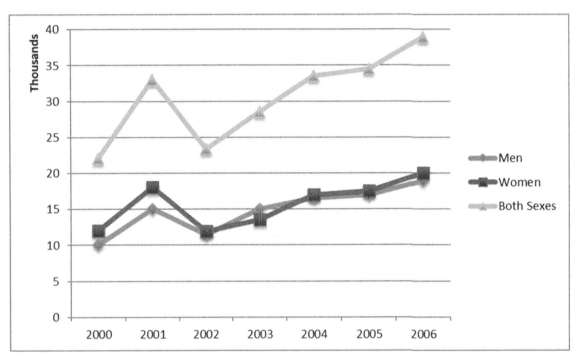

A line graph presents quantitative data on both horizontal (side to side) and vertical (up and down) axes. It requires the test taker to examine information across varying data points. When reading a line graph, a test taker should pay attention to any headings, as these indicate a title for the data it contains. In the above example, the test taker can anticipate the line graph contains numerical data regarding the use of cellphones during a certain time period. From there, a test taker should carefully read any outlying words or phrases that will help determine the meaning of data within the horizontal and vertical axes. In this example, the vertical axis displays the total number of people in increments of 5,000. Horizontally, the graph displays yearly markers, and the reader can assume the data presented accounts for a full calendar year. In addition, the line graph also uses different shapes to mark its data points. Some data points represent the number of men. Some data points represent the number of women, and a third type of data point represents the number of both sexes combined.

30

A test taker may be asked to read and interpret the graph's data, then answer questions about it. For example, the test may ask, *In which year did men seem to decrease cellphone use?* then require the test taker to select the correct answer. Similarly, the test taker may encounter a question such as *Which year yielded the highest number of cellphone users overall?* The test taker should be able to identify the correct answer as 2006.

Bar Graph

A **bar graph** presents quantitative data through the use of lines or rectangles. The height and length of these lines or rectangles corresponds to the magnitude of the numerical data for that particular category or attribute. The data presented may represent information over time, showing shaded data over time or over other defined parameters. A bar graph will also utilize horizontal and vertical axes. An example of a bar graph is as follows:

Population Growth in Major US Cities

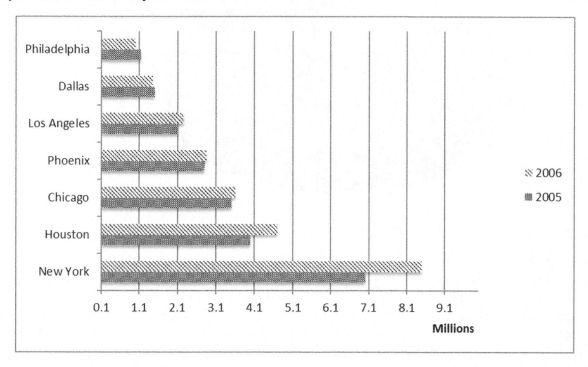

Reading the data in a bar graph is similar to the skills needed to read a line graph. The test taker should read and comprehend all heading information, as well as information provided along the horizontal and vertical axes. Note that the graph pertains to the population of some major US cities. The "values" of these cities can be found along the left side of the graph, along the vertical axis. The population values can be found along the horizontal axes. Notice how the graph uses shaded bars to depict the change in population over time, as the heading indicates. Therefore, when the test taker is asked a question such as, *Which major US city experienced the greatest amount of population growth during the depicted two year cycle,* the reader should be able to determine a correct answer of New York. It is important to pay particular attention to color, length, data points, and both axes, as well as any outlying header information in order to be able to answer graph-like test questions.

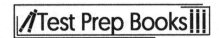
Circle Graph

A circle graph (also sometimes referred to as a pie chart) presents quantitative data in the form of a circle. The same principles apply: the test taker should look for numerical data within the confines of the circle itself but also note any outlying information that may be included in a header, footer, or to the side of the circle. A circle graph will not depict horizontal or vertical axis information, but will instead rely on the reader's ability to visually take note of segmented circle pieces and apply information accordingly. An example of a circle graph is as follows:

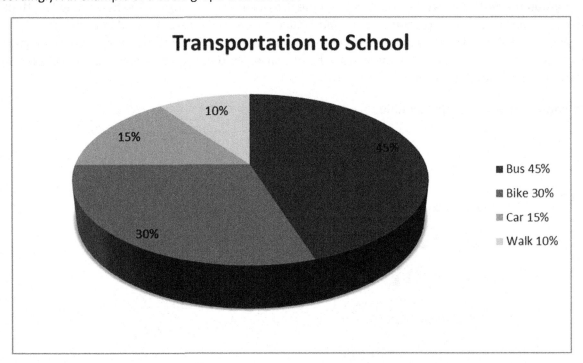

Notice the heading "Transportation to School." This should indicate to the test taker that the topic of the circle graph is how people traditionally get to school. To the right of the graph, the reader should comprehend that the data percentages contained within it directly correspond to the method of transportation. In this graph, the data is represented through the use shades and pattern. Each transportation method has its own shade. For example, if the test taker was then asked, *Which method of school transportation is most widely utilized,* the reader should be able to identify school bus as the correct answer.

Be wary of test questions that ask test takers to draw conclusions based on information that is not present. For example, it is not possible to determine, given the parameters of this circle graph, whether the population presented is of a particular gender or ethnic group. This graph does not represent data from a particular city or school district. It does not distinguish between student grade levels and, although the reader could infer that the typical student must be of driving age if cars are included, this is not necessarily the case. Elementary school students may rely on parents or others to drive them by personal methods. Therefore, do not read too much into data that is not presented. Only rely on the quantitative data that is presented in order to answer questions.

Scatter Plot

A scatter plot or scatter diagram is a graph that depicts quantitative data across plotted points. It will involve at least two sets of data. It will also involve horizontal and vertical axes.

An example of a scatter plot is as follows:

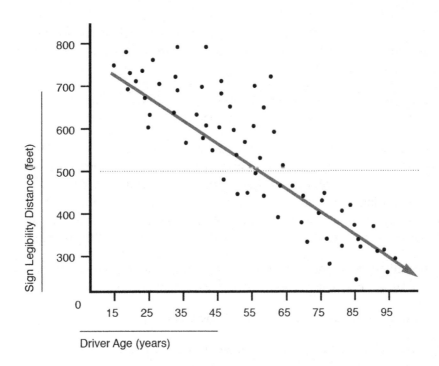

Driver Age (years)

The skills needed to address a scatter plot are essentially the same as in other graph examples. Note any topic headings, as well as horizontal or vertical axis information. In the sample above, the reader can determine the data addresses a driver's ability to correctly and legibly read road signs as related to their age. Again, note the information that is absent. The test taker is not given the data to assess a time period, location, or driver gender. It simply requires the reader to note an approximate age to the ability to correctly identify road signs from a distance measured in feet. Notice that the overall graph also displays a trend. In this case, the data indicates a negative one and possibly supports the hypothesis that as a driver ages, their ability to correctly read a road sign at over 500 feet tends to decline over time. If the test taker were to be asked, *At what approximation in feet does a sixteen-year-old driver correctly see and read a street sign,* the answer would be the option closest to 700 feet.

Reading and examining scientific data in excerpts involves all of a reader's contextual reading, data interpretation, drawing logical conclusions based only on the information presented, and their application of critical thinking skills across a set of interpretive questions. Thorough comprehension and attention to detail is necessary to achieve test success.

Standard English Conventions

Most of the topics discussed so far deal with the writer's choices and their effectiveness in a particular writing piece. In many cases, even ineffective writing can be grammatically correct. The following sections examine writing problems that actually break the rules of Standard English. These aren't questions of intent or judgment calls by the writer. These are mistakes that *must* be corrected.

Sentence Structure

Fragments and Run-Ons

A *sentence fragment* is a failed attempt to create a complete sentence because it's missing a required noun or verb. Fragments don't function properly because there isn't enough information to understand the writer's intended meaning. For example:

> Seat belt use corresponds to a lower rate of hospital visits, reducing strain on an already overburdened healthcare system. Insurance claims as well.

Look at the last sentence: *Insurance claims as well*. What does this mean? This is a fragment because it has a noun but no verb, and it leaves the reader guessing what the writer means about insurance claims. Many readers can probably infer what the writer means, but this distracts them from the flow of the writer's argument. Choosing a suitable replacement for a sentence fragment may be one of the questions on the test. The fragment is probably related to the surrounding content, so look at the overall point the writer is trying to make and choose the answer that best fits that idea.

Remember that sometimes a fragment can *look* like a complete sentence or have all the nouns and verbs it needs to make sense. Consider the following two examples:

> Seat belt use corresponds to a lower rate of hospital visits.

> Although seat belt use corresponds to a lower rate of hospital visits.

Both examples above have nouns and verbs, but only the first sentence is correct. The second sentence is a fragment, even though it's actually longer. The key is the writer's use of the word *although*. Starting a sentence with *although* turns that part into a *subordinate clause* (more on that next). Keep in mind that one doesn't have to remember that it's called a subordinate clause on the test. Just be able to recognize that the words form an incomplete thought and identify the problem as a sentence fragment.

A *run-on sentence* is, in some ways, the opposite of a fragment. It contains two or more sentences that have been improperly forced together into one. An example of a run-on sentence looks something like this:

> Seat belt use corresponds to a lower rate of hospital visits it also leads to fewer insurance claims.

Here, there are two separate ideas in one sentence. It's difficult for the reader to follow the writer's thinking because there is no transition from one idea to the next. On the test, choose the best way to correct the run-on sentence.

Here are two possibilities for the sentence above:

> Seat belt use corresponds to a lower rate of hospital visits. It also leads to fewer insurance claims.

> Seat belt use corresponds to a lower rate of hospital visits, but it also leads to fewer insurance claims.

Both solutions are grammatically correct, so which one is the best choice? That depends on the point that the writer is trying to make. Always read the surrounding text to determine what the writer wants to demonstrate, and choose the option that best supports that thought.

Subordination and Coordination

With terms like "coordinate clause" and "subordinating conjunction," grammar terminology can scare people! So, just for a minute, forget about the terms and look at how the sentences work.

Sometimes a sentence has two ideas that work together. For example, say the writer wants to make the following points:

> Seat belt laws have saved an estimated 50,000 lives.

> More lives are saved by seat belts every year.

These two ideas are directly related and appear to be of equal importance. Therefore they can be joined with a simple "and" as follows:

> Seat belt laws have saved an estimated 50,000 lives, and more lives are saved by seat belts every year.

The word *and* in the sentence helps the two ideas work together or, in other words, it "coordinates" them. It also serves as a junction where the two ideas come together, better known as a *conjunction*. Therefore the word *and* is known as a *coordinating conjunction* (a word that helps bring two equal ideas together). Now that the ideas are joined together by a conjunction, they are known as *clauses*. Other coordinating conjunctions include *or*, *but*, and *so*.

Sometimes, however, two ideas in a sentence are *not* of equal importance:

> Seat belt laws have saved an estimated 50,000 lives.

> Many more lives could be saved with stronger federal seat belt laws.

In this case, combining the two with a coordinating conjunction (*and*) creates an awkward sentence:

> Seat belt laws have saved an estimated 50,000 lives, and many more lives could be saved with stronger federal seat belt laws.

Now the writer uses a word to show the reader which clause is the most important (or the "boss") of the sentence:

> Although seat belt laws have saved an estimated 50,000 lives, many more lives could be saved with stronger federal seat belt laws.

In this example, the second clause is the key point that the writer wants to make, and the first clause works to set up that point. Since the first clause "works for" the second, it's called the *subordinate clause*. The word *although* tells the reader that this idea isn't as important as the clause that follows. This word is called the *subordinating conjunction*. Other subordinating conjunctions include *after*,

because, if, since, unless, and many more. As mentioned before, it's easy to spot subordinate clauses because they don't stand on their own (as shown in this previous example):

> Although seat belt laws have saved an estimated 50,000 lives

This is not a complete thought. It needs the other clause (called the *independent clause*) to make sense. On the test, when asked to choose the best subordinating conjunction for a sentence, look at the surrounding text. Choose the word that best allows the sentence to support the writer's argument.

Parallel Structure

Parallel structure usually has to do with lists. Look at the following sentence and spot the mistake:

> Increased seat belt legislation has been supported by the automotive industry, the insurance industry, and doctors.

Many people don't see anything wrong, but the word *doctors* breaks the sentence's parallel structure. The previous items in the list refer to an industry as a singular noun, so every item in the list must follow that same format:

> Increased seat belt legislation has been supported by the automotive industry, the insurance industry, and the healthcare industry.

Another common mistake in parallel structure might look like this:

> Before the accident, Maria enjoyed swimming, running, and played soccer.

Here, the words "played soccer" break the parallel structure. To correct it, the writer must change the final item in the list to match the format of the previous two:

> Before the accident, Maria enjoyed swimming, running, and playing soccer.

Usage

Modifier Placement

Modifiers are words or phrases (often adjectives or nouns) that add detail to, explain, or limit the meaning of other parts of a sentence. Look at the following example:

> A big pine tree is in the yard.

In the sentence, the words *big* (an adjective) and *pine* (a noun) modify *tree* (the head noun).

All related parts of a sentence must be placed together correctly. *Misplaced* and *dangling modifiers* are common writing mistakes. In fact, they're so common that many people are accustomed to seeing them and can decipher an incorrect sentence without much difficulty. On the test, expect to be asked to identify and correct this kind of error.

Misplaced Modifiers

Since *modifiers* refer to something else in the sentence (*big* and *pine* refer to *tree* in the example above), they need to be placed close to what they modify. If a modifier is so far away that the reader isn't sure what it's describing, it becomes a *misplaced modifier*. For example:

> Seat belts almost saved 5,000 lives in 2009.

It's likely that the writer means that the total number of lives saved by seat belts in 2009 is close to 5,000. However, due to the misplaced modifier (*almost*), the sentence actually says there are 5,000 instances when seat belts *almost saved lives*. In this case, the position of the modifier is actually the difference between life and death (at least in the meaning of the sentence). A clearer way to write the sentence is:

> Seat belts saved almost 5,000 lives in 2009.

Now that the modifier is close to the 5,000 lives it references, the sentence's meaning is clearer.

Another common example of a misplaced modifier occurs when the writer uses the modifier to begin a sentence. For example:

> Having saved 5,000 lives in 2009, Senator Wilson praised the seat belt legislation.

It seems unlikely that Senator Wilson saved 5,000 lives on her own, but that's what the writer is saying in this sentence. To correct this error, the writer should move the modifier closer to the intended object it modifies. Here are two possible solutions:

> Having saved 5,000 lives in 2009, the seat belt legislation was praised by Senator Wilson.

> Senator Wilson praised the seat belt legislation, which saved 5,000 lives in 2009.

When choosing a solution for a misplaced modifier, look for an option that places the modifier close to the object or idea it describes.

Dangling Modifiers

A modifier must have a target word or phrase that it's modifying. Without this, it's a *dangling modifier*. Dangling modifiers are usually found at the beginning of sentences:

> After passing the new law, there is sure to be an improvement in highway safety.

This sentence doesn't say anything about who is passing the law. Therefore, "After passing the new law" is a dangling modifier because it doesn't modify anything in the sentence. To correct this type of error, determine what the writer intended the modifier to point to:

> After passing the new law, legislators are sure to see an improvement in highway safety.

"After passing the new law" now points to *legislators*, which makes the sentence clearer and eliminates the dangling modifier.

Shifts in Construction

It's been said several times already that *good writing must be consistent*. Another common writing mistake occurs when the writer unintentionally shifts verb tense, voice, or noun-pronoun agreement.

This shift can take place within a sentence, within a paragraph, or over the course of an entire piece of writing. On the test, questions may ask that this kind of error be identified. Here are some examples.

Shift in Verb Tense

Even though test questions don't ask for verb tenses to be identified, they may cover recognizing when these tenses change unexpectedly:

> During the accident, the airbags malfunction, and the passengers were injured.

In this sentence, the writer unintentionally shifts from present tense ("airbags malfunction" is happening *now)* to past tense ("passengers were injured" has *already happened*.) This is very confusing. To correct this error, the writer must stay in the same tense throughout. Two possible solutions are:

> During the accident, the airbags malfunctioned, and the passengers were injured.

> During the accident, the airbags malfunction, and the passengers are injured.

Shift in Voice

Sometimes the writer accidentally slips from active voice to passive voice in the middle of a sentence. This is a difficult mistake to catch because it's something people often do when speaking to one another. First, it's important to understand the difference between active and passive voice. Most sentences are written in *active voice*, which means that the noun is doing what the verb in the sentence says. For example:

> Seat belts save lives.

Here, the noun (*seat belt*) is doing the saving. However, in *passive voice*, the verb is doing something to the noun:

> Lives are saved.

In this case, the noun (*lives*) is the thing *being saved*. Passive voice is difficult for many people to identify and understand, but there's a simple (and memorable) way to check: simply add "by zombies" to the end of the verb and, if it makes sense, then the verb is written in passive voice. For example: "My car was wrecked...by zombies." Also, in the above example, "Lives are saved...by zombies." If the zombie trick doesn't work, then the sentence is in active voice.

Here's what a shift in voice looks like in a sentence:

> When Amy buckled her seat belt, a satisfying click was heard.

The writer shifts from active voice in the beginning of the sentence to passive voice after the comma (remember, "a satisfying click was heard...by zombies"). To fix this mistake, the writer must remain in active voice throughout:

> When Amy buckled her seat belt, she heard a satisfying click.

This sentence is now grammatically correct, easier to read...and zombie free!

Shift in Noun-Pronoun Agreement

Pronouns are used to replace nouns so sentences don't have a lot of unnecessary repetition. This repetition can make a sentence seem awkward as in the following example:

> Seat belts are important because seat belts save lives, but seat belts can't do so unless seat belts are used.

Replacing some of the nouns (*seat belts*) with a pronoun (*they*) improves the flow of the sentence:

> Seat belts are important because they save lives, but they can't do so unless they are used.

A pronoun should agree in number (singular or plural) with the noun that precedes it. Another common writing error is the shift in *noun-pronoun agreement*. Here's an example:

> When people are getting in a car, he should always remember to buckle his seatbelt.

The first half of the sentence talks about a plural (*people*), while the second half refers to a singular person (*he* and *his*). These don't agree, so the sentence should be rewritten as:

> When people are getting in a car, they should always remember to buckle their seatbelt.

Pronouns

Pronoun Person

Pronoun person refers to the narrative voice the writer uses in a piece of writing. A great deal of nonfiction is written in third person, which uses pronouns like *he, she, it,* and *they* to convey meaning. Occasionally a writer uses first person (*I, me, we,* etc.) or second person (*you*). Any choice of pronoun person can be appropriate for a particular situation, but the writer must remain consistent and logical.

Test questions may cover examining samples that should stay in a single pronoun person, be it first, second, or third. Look out for shifts between words like *you* and *I* or *he* and *they.*

Pronoun Clarity

Pronouns always refer back to a noun. However, as the writer composes longer, more complicated sentences, the reader may be unsure which noun the pronoun should replace. For example:

> An amendment was made to the bill, but now it has been voted down.

Was the amendment voted down or the entire bill? It's impossible to tell from this sentence. To correct this error, the writer needs to restate the appropriate noun rather than using a pronoun:

> An amendment was made to the bill, but now the bill has been voted down.

Pronouns in Combination

Writers often make mistakes when choosing pronouns to use in combination with other nouns. The most common mistakes are found in sentences like this:

> Please join Senator Wilson and I at the event tomorrow.

Notice anything wrong? Though many people think the sentence sounds perfectly fine, the use of the pronoun *I* is actually incorrect. To double-check this, take the other person out of the sentence:

Please join I at the event tomorrow.

Now the sentence is obviously incorrect, as it should read, "Please join *me* at the event tomorrow." Thus, the first sentence should replace *I* with *me*:

Please join Senator Wilson and me at the event tomorrow.

For many people, this sounds wrong because they're used to hearing and saying it incorrectly. Take extra care when answering this kind of question and follow the double-checking procedure.

Agreement

In English writing, certain words connect to other words. People often learn these connections (or *agreements*) as young children and use the correct combinations without a second thought. However, the questions on the test dealing with agreement probably aren't simple ones.

Subject-Verb Agreement

Which of the following sentences is correct?

A large crowd of protesters was on hand.

A large crowd of protesters were on hand.

Many people would say the second sentence is correct, but they'd be wrong. However, they probably wouldn't be alone. Most people just look at two words: *protesters were*. Together they make sense. They sound right. The problem is that the verb *were* doesn't refer to the word *protesters*. Here, the word *protesters* is part of a prepositional phrase that clarifies the actual subject of the sentence (*crowd*). Take the phrase "of protesters" away and re-examine the sentences:

A large crowd was on hand.

A large crowd were on hand.

Without the prepositional phrase to separate the subject and verb, the answer is obvious. The first sentence is correct. On the test, look for confusing prepositional phrases when answering questions about subject-verb agreement. Take the phrase away, and then recheck the sentence.

Noun Agreement

Nouns that refer to other nouns must also match in number. Take the following example:

John and Emily both served as an intern for Senator Wilson.

Two people are involved in this sentence: John and Emily. Therefore, the word *intern* should be plural to match. Here is how the sentence should read:

John and Emily both served as interns for Senator Wilson.

40

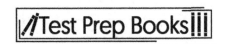

Frequently Confused Words

The English language is interesting because many of its words sound so similar or identical that they confuse readers and writers alike. Errors involving these words are hard to spot because they *sound* right even when they're wrong. Also, because these mistakes are so pervasive, many people think they're correct. Here are a few examples that may be encountered on the test:

They're vs. Their vs. There

This set of words is probably the all-time winner of misuse. The word *they're* is a contraction of "they are." Remember that contractions combine two words, using an apostrophe to replace any eliminated letters. If a question asks whether the writer is using the word *they're* correctly, change the word to "they are" and reread the sentence. Look at the following example:

> Legislators can be proud of they're work on this issue.

This sentence *sounds* correct, but replace the contraction *they're* with "they are" to see what happens:

> Legislators can be proud of they are work on this issue.

The result doesn't make sense, which shows that it's an incorrect use of the word *they're*. Did the writer mean to use the word *their* instead? The word *their* indicates possession because it shows that something *belongs* to something else. Now put the word *their* into the sentence:

> Legislators can be proud of their work on this issue.

To check the answer, find the word that comes right after the word *their* (which in this case is *work*). Pose this question: whose *work* is it? If the question can be answered in the sentence, then the word signifies possession. In the sentence above, it's the legislators' work. Therefore, the writer is using the word *their* correctly.

If the words *they're* and *their* don't make sense in the sentence, then the correct word is almost always *there*. The word *there* can be used in many different ways, so it's easy to remember to use it when *they're* and *their* don't work. Now test these methods with the following sentences:

> Their going to have a hard time passing these laws.

> Enforcement officials will have there hands full.

> They're are many issues to consider when discussing car safety.

In the first sentence, asking the question "Whose going is it?" doesn't make sense. Thus the word *their* is wrong. However, when replaced with the conjunction *they're* (or *they are*), the sentence works. Thus the correct word for the first sentence should be *they're*.

In the second sentence, ask this question: "Whose hands are full?" The answer (*enforcement officials*) is correct in the sentence. Therefore, the word *their* should replace *there* in this sentence.

In the third sentence, changing the word *they're* to "they are" ("They are are many issues") doesn't make sense. Ask this question: "Whose are is it?" This makes even less sense, since neither of the words *they're* or *their* makes sense. Therefore, the correct word must be *there*.

41

Who's vs. Whose

Who's is a contraction of "who is" while the word *whose* indicates possession. Look at the following sentence:

> Who's job is it to protect America's drivers?

The easiest way to check for correct usage is to replace the word *who's* with "who is" and see if the sentence makes sense:

> Who is job is it to protect America's drivers?

By changing the contraction to "Who is" the sentence no longer makes sense. Therefore, the correct word must be *whose*.

Your vs. You're

The word *your* indicates possession, while *you're* is a contraction for "you are." Look at the following example:

> Your going to have to write your congressman if you want to see action.

Again, the easiest way to check correct usage is to replace the word *Your* with "You are" and see if the sentence still makes sense.

> You are going to have to write your congressman if you want to see action.

By replacing Your with "You are," the sentence still makes sense. Thus, in this case, the writer should have used "You're."

Its vs. It's

Its is a word that indicates possession, while the word *it's* is a contraction of "it is." Once again, the easiest way to check for correct usage is to replace the word with "it is" and see if the sentence makes sense. Look at the following sentence:

> It's going to take a lot of work to pass this law.

Replacing *it's* with "it is" results in this: "It is going to take a lot of work to pass this law." This makes sense, so the contraction (*it's*) is correct. Now look at another example:

> The car company will have to redesign it's vehicles.

Replacing *it's* with "it is" results in this: "The car company will have to redesign it is vehicles." This sentence doesn't make sense, so the contraction (*it's*) is incorrect.

Than vs. Then

Than is used in sentences that involve comparisons, while *then* is used to indicate an order of events. Consider the following sentence:

> Japan has more traffic fatalities than the US.

The use of the word *than* is correct because it compares Japan to the US. Now look at another example:

> Laws must be passed, and then we'll see a change in behavior.

Here the use of the word *then* is correct because one thing happens after the other.

Affect vs. Effect

Affect is a verb that means to change something, while *effect* is a noun that indicates such a change. Look at the following sentence:

> There are thousands of people affected by the new law.

This sentence is correct because *affected* is a verb that tells what's happening. Now look at this sentence:

> The law will have a dramatic effect.

This sentence is also correct because *effect* is a noun and the thing that happens.

Note that a noun version of *affect* is occasionally used. It means "emotion" or "desire," usually in a psychological sense.

Two vs. Too vs. To

Two is the number (2). *Too* refers to an amount of something, or it can mean *also*. *To* is used for everything else. Look at the following sentence:

> Two senators still haven't signed the bill.

This is correct because there are *two* (2) senators. Here's another example:

> There are too many questions about this issue.

In this sentence, the word *too* refers to an amount ("too many questions"). Now here's another example:

> Senator Wilson is supporting this legislation, too.

In this sentence, the word *also* can be substituted for the word *too*, so it's also correct. Finally, one last example:

> I look forward to signing this bill into law.

In this sentence, the tests for *two* and *too* don't work. Thus the word *to* fits the bill!

Other Common Writing Confusions

In addition to all of the above, there are other words that writers often misuse. This doesn't happen because the words sound alike, but because the writer is not aware of the proper way to use them.

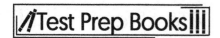
Logical Comparison

Writers often make comparisons in their writing. However, it's easy to make mistakes in sentences that involve comparisons, and those mistakes are difficult to spot. Try to find the error in the following sentence:

Senator Wilson's proposed seat belt legislation was similar to Senator Abernathy.

Can't find it? First, ask what two things are actually being compared. It seems like the writer *wants* to compare two different types of legislation, but the sentence actually compares legislation ("Senator Wilson's proposed seat belt legislation") to a person ("Senator Abernathy"). This is a strange and illogical comparison to make.

So how can the writer correct this mistake? The answer is to make sure that the second half of the sentence logically refers back to the first half. The most obvious way to do this is to repeat words:

Senator Wilson's proposed seat belt legislation was similar to Senator Abernathy's seat belt legislation.

Now the sentence is logically correct, but it's a little wordy and awkward. A better solution is to eliminate the word-for-word repetition by using suitable replacement words:

Senator Wilson's proposed seat belt legislation was similar to that of Senator Abernathy.

Senator Wilson's proposed seat belt legislation was similar to the bill offered by Senator Abernathy.

Here's another similar example:

More lives in the US are saved by seat belts than Japan.

The writer probably means to compare lives saved by seat belts in the US to lives saved by seat belts in Japan. Unfortunately, the sentence's meaning is garbled by an illogical comparison, and instead refers to US lives saved *by Japan* rather than *in Japan.* To resolve this issue, first repeat the words and phrases needed to make an identical comparison:

More lives in the US are saved by seat belts than lives in Japan are saved by seat belts.

Then, use a replacement word to clean up the repetitive text:

More lives in the US are saved by seat belts than in Japan.

Punctuation

On the test there may be a sentence where all the words are correct, but the writer uses *punctuation* incorrectly. It probably won't be something as simple as a missing period or question mark. Instead it could be one of the commonly misunderstood punctuation marks.

Colons

Colons can be used in the following situations and examples:

- To introduce lists
- Carmakers have three choices: improve seat belt design, pay financial penalties, or go out of business.
- To introduce new ideas
- There is only one person who can champion this legislation: Senator Wilson.
- To separate titles and subtitles
- Show Some Restraint: The History of Seat Belts

Semicolons

Semicolons can be used in the following situations:

- To separate two related independent clauses
- The proposed bill was voted down; opponents were concerned about the tax implications.

    Note: These are known as *independent clauses* because each one stands on its own as a complete sentence. Semicolons *cannot* be used to separate an independent clause from a dependent clause, nor to separate two dependent clauses.

- To separate complex items in a list
- Joining Senator Wilson onstage were Jim Robinson, head of the NHTSA; Kristin Gabber, a consumer advocate; and Milton Webster, an accident survivor.

    Note: While items in a list are usually separated by commas, readers can easily get confused if the list items themselves contain internal commas.

Hyphens vs. Dashes

Hyphens (-) and *dashes* (–) are not the same. *Hyphens* are shorter, and they help combine or clarify words in certain situations like:

- Creating an adjective: *safety-conscious*
- Creating compound numbers: *fifty-nine*
- Avoiding confusion with another word: *re-sent* vs. *resent*
- Avoiding awkward letter combinations: *semi-intellectual* vs. *semiintellectual*

Dashes are longer and show an interruption in the flow of the sentence. In this context, they can be used much the same way as commas or parentheses:

- The legislation—which was supported by 80 percent of Americans—did not pass.

Commas

Commas are used in many different situations. Here are some of the most misunderstood examples:

- Separating simple items in a list
- The legislation had the support of Republicans, Democrats, and Independents.
- Separating adjectives that modify the same noun
- The weak, meaningless platitudes had no effect on the listeners.

45

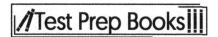
- Separating independent and dependent clauses
- After passing the bill, the lawmakers celebrated.
- Note: "After passing the bill" is a *dependent clause* because it's not a complete sentence on its own.
- Separating quotations from introductory text
- Senator Wilson asked, "How can we get this bill passed?"
- Showing interruption in the flow of a sentence. In this context, commas can be used in the same way as semicolons or parentheses.
- The legislation, which was supported by 80 percent of Americans, did not pass.
- Note: Commas cannot be used if the clause or phrase in question is essential to the meaning of the sentence.

During the test, it may be hard to remember all the rules for comma usage. Read the sentence and listen to its ebb and flow. If a particular answer looks, sounds, or feels wrong for some reason, there's probably a good reason for it. Look at another option instead.

Apostrophes

Apostrophes are often misused. For the purpose of the test, there are three things to know about using apostrophes:

- Use apostrophes to show possession
- Senator Wilson's bill just passed committee.
- Use apostrophes in contractions to replace eliminated letters
- Does not → Doesn't

Note: It's common to see acronyms made plural using apostrophes (RV's, DVD's, TV's), but these are incorrect. Acronyms function as words, so they are pluralized the same way (RVs, DVDs, TVs).

On the test, when an apostrophe-related question is asked, determine if it shows possession or is part of a contraction. If neither answer fits, then the apostrophe probably doesn't belong there.

Final Tips

Usage Conventions

On the test, don't overlook simple, obvious writing errors such as these:

- Is the first word in a sentence capitalized?
- Are countries, geographical features, and proper nouns capitalized?
- Conversely, are words capitalized that should *not* be?
- Do sentences end with proper punctuation marks?
- Are commas and quotation marks used appropriately?
- Do contractions include apostrophes?
- Are apostrophes used for plurals? (Almost never!)

Look for Context

Keep in mind that the test may give several choices to replace a writing selection, and all of them may be grammatically correct. In such cases, choose the answer that makes the most sense in the context of

the piece. What's the writer trying to say? What's their main idea? Look for the answer that best supports this theme.

Use Your Instincts

With the few notable exceptions above, instinct is often the best guide to spotting writing problems. If something sounds wrong, then it may very well be wrong. The good thing about a test like this is that the problem doesn't have to be labeled as an example of "faulty parallelism" or "improper noun-pronoun agreement." It's enough just to recognize that a problem exists and choose the best solution.

Take a Break

After reading and thinking about all of these aspects of grammar so intensely, the brain may start shutting down. If the words aren't making sense, or reading the same sentence several times still has no meaning, it's time to stop. Take a thirty-second vacation. Forget about grammar, syntax, and writing for half a minute to clear the mind. Take a few deep breaths and think about something to do after the test is over. It's surprising how quickly the brain refreshes itself!

Expression of Ideas

Organization

Good writing is not merely a random collection of sentences. No matter how well written, sentences must relate and coordinate appropriately to one another. If not, the writing seems random, haphazard, and disorganized. Therefore, good writing must be *organized* (where each sentence fits a larger context and relates to the sentences around it).

Transition Words

The writer should act as a guide, showing the reader how all the sentences fit together. Consider this example:

> Seat belts save more lives than any other automobile safety feature. Many studies show that airbags save lives as well. Not all cars have airbags. Many older cars don't. Air bags aren't entirely reliable. Studies show that in 15% of accidents, airbags don't deploy as designed. Seat belt malfunctions are extremely rare.

There's nothing wrong with any of these sentences individually, but together they're disjointed and difficult to follow. The best way for the writer to communicate information is through the use of *transition words*. Here are examples of transition words and phrases that tie sentences together, enabling a more natural flow:

- To show causality: as a result, therefore, and consequently
- To compare and contrast: *however, but*, and *on the other hand*
- To introduce examples: *for instance, namely*, and *including*
- To show order of importance: *foremost, primarily, secondly*, and *lastly*

The above is not a complete list of transitions. There are many more that can be used; however, most fit into these or similar categories. The important point is that the words should clearly show the relationship between sentences, supporting information, and the main idea.

Here is an update to the previous example using transition words. These changes make it easier to read and bring clarity to the writer's points:

> Seat belts save more lives than any other automobile safety feature. Many studies show that airbags save lives as well. However, not all cars have airbags. For instance, some older cars don't. Furthermore, air bags aren't entirely reliable. For example, studies show that in 15% of accidents, airbags don't deploy as designed. But, on the other hand, seat belt malfunctions are extremely rare.

Also be prepared to analyze whether the writer is using the best transition word or phrase for the situation. Take this sentence for example: "As a result, seat belt malfunctions are extremely rare." This sentence doesn't make sense in the context above because the writer is trying to show the *contrast* between seat belts and airbags, not the causality.

Logical Sequence

Even if the writer includes plenty of information to support their point, the writing is only effective when the information is in a logical order. *Logical sequencing* is really just common sense, but it's also an important writing technique. First, the writer should introduce the main idea, whether for a paragraph, a section, or the entire piece. Second, they should present evidence to support the main idea by using transitional language. This shows the reader how the information relates to the main idea and to the sentences around it. The writer should then take time to interpret the information, making sure necessary connections are obvious to the reader. Finally, the writer can summarize the information in a closing section.

Although most writing follows this pattern, it isn't a set rule. Sometimes writers change the order for effect. For example, the writer can begin with a surprising piece of supporting information to grab the reader's attention, and then transition to the main idea. Thus, if a passage doesn't follow the logical order, don't immediately assume it's wrong. However, most writing usually settles into a logical sequence after a nontraditional beginning.

Rhetoric and Synthesis

Rhetoric

The PSAT 8/9 will test a reader's ability to identify an author's use of rhetoric within text passages. Rhetoric is the use of positional or persuasive language to convey one or more central ideas. The idea behind the use of rhetoric is to convince the reader of something. Its use is meant to persuade or motivate the reader. An author may choose to appeal to their audience through logic, emotion, the use of ideology, or by conveying that the central idea is timely, and thus, important to the reader. There are a variety of rhetorical techniques an author can use to achieve this goal.

An author may choose to use traditional elements of style to persuade the reader. They may also use a story's setting, mood, characters, or a central conflict to build emotion in the reader. Similarly, an author may choose to use specific techniques such as alliteration, irony, metaphor, simile, hyperbole, allegory, imagery, onomatopoeia, and personification to persuasively illustrate one or more central ideas they wish the reader to adopt. In order to be successful in a standardized reading comprehension test situation, a reader needs to be well acquainted in recognizing rhetoric and rhetorical devices.

Identifying Elements of Style

A writer's style is unique. The combinations of elements are carefully designed to create an effect on the reader. For example, the novels of J.R.R Tolkien are very different in style than the novels of Stephen King, yet both are designed to tell a compelling tale and to entertain readers. Furthermore, the articles found in *National Geographic* are vastly different from those a reader may encounter in *People* magazine, yet both have the same objective: to inform the reader. The difference is in the elements of style.

While there are many elements of style an author can employ, it's important to look at three things: the words they choose to use, the voice an author selects, and the fluency of sentence structure. Word choice is critical in persuasive or pictorial writing. While effective authors will choose words that are succinct, different authors will choose various words based on what they are trying to accomplish. For example, a reader would not expect to encounter the same words in a gothic novel that they would read in a scholastic article on gene therapy. An author whose intent is to paint a picture of a foreboding scene, will choose different words than an author who wants to persuade the reader that a particular political party has the most sound, ideological platform. A romance novelist will sound very different than a true crime writer.

The voice an author selects is also important to note. An author's voice is that element of style that indicates their personality. It's important that authors move us as readers; therefore, they will choose a voice that helps them do that. An author's voice may be satirical or authoritative. It may be light-hearted or serious in tone. It may be silly or humorous as well. Voice, as an element of style, can be vague in nature and difficult to identify, since it's also referred to as an author's tone, but it is that element unique to the author. It is the author's "self." A reader can expect an author's voice to vary across literary genres. A non-fiction author will generally employ a more neutral voice than an author of fiction, but use caution when trying to identify voice. Do not confuse an author's voice with a particular character's voice.

Another critical element of style involves how an author structures their sentences. An effective writer—one who wants to paint a vivid picture or strongly illustrate a central idea—will use a variety of sentence structures and sentence lengths. A reader is more likely to be confused if an author uses choppy, unrelated sentences. Similarly, a reader will become bored and lose interest if an author repeatedly uses the same sentence structure. Good writing is fluent. It flows. Varying sentence structure keeps a reader engaged and helps reading comprehension. Consider the following example:

> The morning started off early. It was bright out. It was just daylight. The Moon was still in the sky. He was tired from his sleepless night.

Then consider this text:

> Morning hit hard. He didn't remember the last time light hurt this bad. Sleep had been absent, and the very thought of moving towards the new day seemed like a hurdle he couldn't overcome.

Note the variety in sentence structure. The second passage is more interesting to read because the sentence fluency is more effective. Both passages paint the picture of a central character's reaction to dawn, but the second passage is more effective because it uses a variety of sentences and is more fluent than the first.

Elements of style can also include more recognizable components such as a story's setting, the type of narrative an author chooses, the mood they set, and the character conflicts employed. The ability to effectively understand the use of rhetoric demands the reader take note of an author's word choices, writing voice, and the ease of fluency employed to persuade, entertain, illustrate, or otherwise captivate a reader.

Identifying Rhetorical Devices

If a writer feels strongly about a subject, or has a passion for it, strong words and phrases can be chosen. Think of the types of rhetoric (or language) our politicians use. Each word, phrase, and idea is carefully crafted to elicit a response. Hopefully, that response is one of agreement to a certain point of view, especially among voters. Authors use the same types of language to achieve the same results. For example, the word "bad" has a certain connotation, but the words "horrid," "repugnant," and "abhorrent" paint a far better picture for the reader. They're more precise. They're interesting to read and they should all illicit stronger feelings in the reader than the word "bad." An author generally uses other devices beyond mere word choice to persuade, convince, entertain, or otherwise engage a reader.

Rhetorical devices are those elements an author utilizes in painting sensory, and hopefully persuasive ideas to which a reader can relate. They are numerable. Test takers will likely encounter one or more standardized test questions addressing various rhetorical devices. This study guide will address the more common types: alliteration, irony, metaphor, simile, hyperbole, allegory, imagery, onomatopoeia, and personification, providing examples of each.

Alliteration is a device that uses repetitive beginning sounds in words to appeal to the reader. Classic tongue twisters are a great example of alliteration. *She sells sea shells down by the sea shore* is an extreme example of alliteration. Authors will use alliterative devices to capture a reader's attention. It's interesting to note that marketing also utilizes alliteration in the same way. A reader will likely remember products that have the brand name and item starting with the same letter. Similarly, many songs, poems, and catchy phrases use this device. It's memorable. Use of alliteration draws a reader's attention to ideas that an author wants to highlight.

Irony is a device that authors use when pitting two contrasting items or ideas against each other in order to create an effect. It's frequently used when an author wants to employ humor or convey a sarcastic tone. Additionally, it's often used in fictional works to build tension between characters, or between a particular character and the reader. An author may use *verbal irony* (sarcasm), *situational irony* (where actions or events have the opposite effect than what's expected), and *dramatic irony* (where the reader knows something a character does not). Examples of irony include:

- Dramatic Irony: An author describing the presence of a hidden killer in a murder mystery, unbeknownst to the characters but known to the reader.

- Situational Irony: An author relating the tale of a fire captain who loses her home in a five-alarm conflagration.

- Verbal Irony: This is where an author or character says one thing but means another. For example, telling a police officer "Thanks a lot" after receiving a ticket.

Metaphor is a device that uses a figure of speech to paint a visual picture of something that is not literally applicable. Authors relate strong images to readers, and evoke similar strong feelings using metaphors. Most often, authors will mention one thing in comparison to another more familiar to the

50

reader. It's important to note that metaphors do not use the comparative words "like" or "as." At times, metaphors encompass common phrases such as clichés. At other times, authors may use mixed metaphors in making identification between two dissimilar things. Examples of metaphors include:

- An author describing a character's anger as *a flaming sheet of fire.*
- An author relating a politician as having been a folding chair under close questioning.
- A novel's character telling another character to *take a flying hike.*
- Shakespeare's assertion that *all the world's a stage.*

Simile is a device that compares two dissimilar things using the words "like" and "as." When using similes, an author tries to catch a reader's attention and use comparison of unlike items to make a point. Similes are commonly used and often develop into figures of speech and catch phrases.

Examples of similes include:

- An author describing a character as having a complexion like a faded lily.

- An investigative journalist describing his interview subject as being like cold steel and with a demeanor hard as ice.

- An author asserting the current political arena is just like a three-ring circus and as dry as day old bread.

When utilizing simile, an author will state one thing is like another. A metaphor states one thing is another. An example of the difference would be if an author states a character is *just like a fierce tiger and twice as angry,* as opposed to stating the character *is a fierce tiger and twice as angry.*

Hyperbole is an exaggeration that is not taken literally. A potential test taker will have heard or employed hyperbole in daily speech, as it is a common device we all use. Authors will use hyperbole to draw a reader's eye toward important points and to illicit strong emotional and relatable responses. Examples of hyperbole include:

- An author describing a character and how they weigh a "ton."

- An author stating the city's water problem as being "a million times worse" than it was last year.

- A journalist stating the mayoral candidate "died of embarrassment" when her tax records were made public.

Allegories are stories or poems with hidden meanings that make political or moral observations. Authors will frequently use allegory when leading the reader to a conclusion, usually about a corruption overlooked in society. As an example, Jonathan Swift's work *Gulliver's Travels into Several Remote Nations of the World* is a political allegory of England during Jonathan Swift's lifetime. Set in a travel-journal style of a giant amongst smaller people, and a smaller Gulliver amongst the larger, the novel is a political commentary on England and certain areas of governmental corruption during the 18th century. George Orwell's *Animal Farm* is also an allegorical story of animals that conquer men and form their own society with swine at the top. However, it is not a literal story in any sense. It's Orwell's political

51

commentary of Russian society during and after the Communist revolution of 1917. Other examples of allegory in popular culture include:

- Aesop's fable "The Tortoise and the Hare," which teaches readers that being steady is more important than being fast and impulsive.

- The popular *Hunger Games* by Suzanne Collins that teaches readers that media can numb society to what is truly real and important.

- Dr. Seuss's *Yertle the Turtle* which is a warning against totalitarianism and, at the time it was written, against the despotic rule of Adolf Hitler.

Imagery is a rhetorical device that an author employs when they use visual or descriptive language to evoke a reader's emotion. Use of imagery as a rhetorical device is broader in scope than this study guide addresses, but in general, the function of imagery is to create a vibrant scene in the reader's imagination and, in turn, tease the reader's ability to identify through strong emotion and sensory experience. In the simplest of terms, imagery, as a rhetoric device, beautifies literature.

An example of poetic imagery is below:

Pain has an element of blank

It cannot recollect

When it began, or if there were

A day when it was not.

It has no future but itself,

Its infinite realms contain

Its past, enlightened to perceive

New periods of pain.

In the above poem, Emily Dickenson uses strong imagery. Pain is equivalent to an "element of blank" or of nothingness. Pain cannot recollect a beginning or end, as if it was a person (see *personification* below). Dickenson appeals to the reader's sense of a painful experience by discussing the unlikelihood that discomfort sees a future, but does visualize a past and present. She simply indicates that pain, through the use of imagery, is cyclical and never ending. Dickenson's theme is one of painful depression, and it is through the use of imagery that she conveys this to her readers.

Onomatopoeia is the author's use of words that create sound. Words like *pop* and *sizzle* are examples of onomatopoeia. When an author wants to draw a reader's attention in an auditory sense, they will use onomatopoeia. An author may also use onomatopoeia to create sounds as interjection or commentary. Examples include:

- An author describing a cat's vocalization as the kitten's chirrup echoed throughout the empty cabin.
- A description of a campfire as crackling and whining against its burning green wood.

52

- An author relating the sound of a car accident as *metallic screeching against crunching asphalt*.
- A description of an animal roadblock as being *a symphonic melody of groans, baas, and moans*.

Personification is a rhetorical device that an author uses to attribute human qualities to inanimate objects or animals. Once again, this device is useful when an author wants the reader to strongly relate to an idea. As in the example of George Orwell's *Animal Farm*, many of the animals are given the human abilities to speak, reason, apply logic, and otherwise interact as humans do. This helps the reader see how easily it is for any society to segregate into the haves and the have-nots through the manipulation of power. Personification is a device that enables the reader to empathize through human experience.

Examples of personification include:

- An author describing the wind as *whispering through the trees*.

- A description of a stone wall as being a hardened, unmovable creature made of cement and brick.

- An author attributing a city building as having slit eyes and an unapproachable, foreboding façade.

- An author describing spring as a beautiful bride, blooming in white, ready for summer's matrimony.

When identifying rhetorical devices, look for words and phrases that capture one's attention. Make note of the author's use of comparison between the inanimate and the animate. Consider words that make the reader feel sounds and envision imagery. Pay attention to the rhythm of fluid sentences and to the use of words that evoke emotion. The ability to identify rhetorical devices is another step in achieving successful reading comprehension and in being able to correctly answer standardized questions related to those devices.

Synthesis

Synthesis in reading involves the ability to fully comprehend text passages, and then going further by making new connections to see things in a new or different way. It involves a full thought process and requires readers to change the way they think about what they read. The PSAT 8/9 will require a test taker to integrate new information that he or she already knows, and demonstrate an ability to express new thoughts.

Synthesis goes further than summary. When summarizing, a reader collects all of the information an author presents in a text passage, and restates it in an effective manner. Synthesis requires that the test taker not only summarize reading material, but be able to express new ideas based on the author's message. It is a full culmination of all reading comprehension strategies. It will require the test taker to order, recount, summarize, and recreate information into a whole new idea.

In utilizing synthesis, a reader must be able to form mental images about what they read, recall any background information they have about the topic, ask critical questions about the material, determine the importance of points an author makes, make inferences based on the reading, and finally be able to form new ideas based on all of the above skills. Synthesis requires the reader to make connections, visualize concepts, determine their importance, ask questions, make inferences, then fully synthesize all of this information into new thought.

Making Connections in Reading

There are three helpful thinking strategies to keep in mind when attempting to synthesize text passages:

- Think about how the content of a passage relates to life experience.
- Think about how the content of a passage relates to other text.
- Think about how the content of a passage relates to the world in general.

When reading a given passage, the test taker should actively think about how the content relates to their life experience. While the author's message may express an opinion different from what the reader believes, or express ideas with which the reader is unfamiliar, a good reader will try to relate any of the author's details to their own familiar ground. A reader should use context clues to understand unfamiliar terminology, and recognize familiar information they have encountered in prior experience. Bringing prior life experience and knowledge to the test-taking situation is helpful in making connections. The ability to relate an unfamiliar idea to something the reader already knows is critical in understanding unique and new ideas.

When trying to make connections while reading, keep the following questions in mind:

- How does this feel familiar in personal experience?
- How is this similar to or different from other reading?
- How is this familiar in the real world?
- How does this relate to the world in general?

A reader should ask themself these questions during the act of reading in order to actively make connections to past and present experiences. Utilizing the ability to make connections is an important step in achieving synthesis.

Determining Importance in Reading

Being able to determine what is most important while reading is critical to synthesis. It is the difference between being able to tell what is necessary to full comprehension and that which is interesting but not necessary.

When determining the importance of an author's ideas, consider the following:

- Ask how critical an author's particular idea, assertion, or concept is to the overall message.

- Ask "is this an interesting fact or is this information essential to understanding the author's main idea?"

- Make a simple chart. On one side, list all of the important, essential points an author makes and on the other, list all of the interesting yet non-critical ideas.

- Highlight, circle, or underline any dates or data in non-fiction passages. Pay attention to headings, captions, and any graphs or diagrams.

- When reading a fictional passage, delineate important information such as theme, character, setting, conflict (what the problem is), and resolution (how the problem is fixed). Most often, these are the most important aspects contained in fictional text.

- If a non-fiction passage is instructional in nature, take physical note of any steps in the order of their importance as presented by the author. Look for words such as *first*, *next*, *then*, and *last*.

Determining the importance of an author's ideas is critical to synthesis in that it requires the test taker to parse out any unnecessary information and demonstrate they have the ability to make sound determination on what is important to the author, and what is merely a supporting or less critical detail.

Asking Questions While Reading

A reader must ask questions while reading. This demonstrates their ability to critically approach information and apply higher thinking skills to an author's content. Some of these questions have been addressed earlier in this section. A reader must ask what is or isn't important, what relates to their experience, and what relates to the world in general. However, it's important to ask other questions as well in order to make connections and synthesize reading material. Consider the following partial list of possibilities:

- What type of passage is this? Is it fiction? Non-fiction? Does it include data?

- Based on the type of passage, what information should be noted in order to make connections, visualize details, and determine importance?

- What is the author's message or theme? What is it they want the reader to understand?

- Is this passage trying to convince readers of something? What is it? If so, is the argument logical, convincing, and effective? How so? If not, how not?

- What do readers already know about this topic? Are there other viewpoints that support or contradict it?

- Is the information in this passage current and up to date?

- Is the author trying to teach readers a lesson? If so, what is it? Is there a moral to this story?

- How does this passage relate to experience?

- What is not as understandable in this passage? What context clues can help with understanding?

- What conclusions can be drawn? What predictions can be made?

Again, the above should be considered only a small example of the possibilities. Any question the reader asks while reading will help achieve synthesis and full reading comprehension.

This test is about *how* the information is communicated rather than the subject matter itself. The good news is there isn't any writing! Instead, it's like being an editor helping the writer find the best ways to express their ideas. Things to consider include: how well a topic is developed, how accurately facts are presented, whether the writing flows logically and cohesively, and how effectively the writer uses

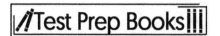

language. This can seem like a lot to remember, but these concepts are the same ones taught way back in elementary school.

One last thing to remember while going through this guide is not to be intimidated by the terminology. Phrases like "pronoun-antecedent agreement" and "possessive determiners" can sound confusing and complicated, but the ideas are often quite simple and easy to understand.

Proposition

The *proposition* (also called the *claim* since it can be true or false) is a clear statement of the point or idea the writer is trying to make. The length or format of a proposition can vary, but it often takes the form of a *topic sentence*. A good topic sentence is:

- Clear: does not weave a complicated web of words for the reader to decode or unwrap

- Concise: presents only the information needed to make the claim and doesn't clutter up the statement with unnecessary details

- Precise: clarifies the exact point the writer wants to make and doesn't use broad, overreaching statements

Look at the following example:

> The civil rights movement, from its genesis in the Emancipation Proclamation to its current struggles with de facto discrimination, has changed the face of the United States more than any other factor in its history.

Is the statement clear? Yes, the statement is fairly clear, although other words can be substituted for "genesis" and "de facto" to make it easier to understand.

Is the statement concise? No, the statement is not concise. Details about the Emancipation Proclamation and the current state of the movement are unnecessary for a topic sentence. Those details should be saved for the body of the text.

Is the statement precise? No, the statement is not precise. What exactly does the writer mean by "changed the face of the United States"? The writer should be more specific about the effects of the movement. Also, suggesting that something has a greater impact than anything else in US history is far too ambitious a statement to make.

A better version might look like this:

> The civil rights movement has greatly increased the career opportunities available for Black Americans.

The unnecessary language and details are removed, and the claim can now be measured and supported.

Support

Once the main idea or proposition is stated, the writer attempts to prove or *support* the claim with text evidence and supporting details.

Take for example the sentence, "Seat belts save lives." Though most people can't argue with this statement, its impact on the reader is much greater when supported by additional content. The writer can support this idea by:

- Providing statistics on the rate of highway fatalities alongside statistics for estimated seat belt usage.

- Explaining the science behind a car accident and what happens to a passenger who doesn't use a seat belt.

- Offering anecdotal evidence or true stories from reliable sources on how seat belts prevent fatal injuries in car crashes.

However, using only one form of supporting evidence is not nearly as effective as using a variety to support a claim. Presenting only a list of statistics can be boring to the reader, but providing a true story that's both interesting and humanizing helps. In addition, one example isn't always enough to prove the writer's larger point, so combining it with other examples is extremely effective for the writing. Thus, when reading a passage, don't just look for a single form of supporting evidence.

Another key aspect of supporting evidence is a *reliable source*. Does the writer include the source of the information? If so, is the source well known and trustworthy? Is there a potential for bias? For example, a seat belt study done by a seat belt manufacturer may have its own agenda to promote.

Effective Language Use

Language can be analyzed in a variety of ways. But one of the primary ways is its effectiveness in communicating and especially convincing others.

Rhetoric is a literary technique used to make the writing (or speaking) more effective or persuasive. Rhetoric makes use of other effective language devices such as irony, metaphors, allusion, and repetition. An example of the rhetorical use of repetition would be: "Let go, I say, let go!!!".

Figures of Speech

A *figure of speech* (sometimes called an *idiom*) is a rhetorical device. It's a phrase that's not intended to be taken literally.

When the writer uses a figure of speech, their intention must be clear if it's to be used effectively. Some phrases can be interpreted in a number of ways, causing confusion for the reader. In the PSAT Writing and Language Test, questions may ask for an alternative to a problematic word or phrase. Look for clues to the writer's true intention to determine the best replacement. Likewise, some figures of speech may seem out of place in a more formal piece of writing. To show this, here is the previous seat belt example but with one slight change:

Seat belts save more lives than any other automobile safety feature. Many studies show that airbags save lives as well. However, not all cars have airbags. For instance, some older cars don't. In addition, air bags aren't entirely reliable. For example, studies show that in 15% of

accidents, airbags don't deploy as designed. But, on the other hand, seat belt malfunctions happen once in a blue moon.

Most people know that "once in a blue moon" refers to something that rarely happens. However, because the rest of the paragraph is straightforward and direct, using this figurative phrase distracts the reader. In this example, the earlier version is much more effective.

Now it's important to take a moment and review the meaning of the word *literally*. This is because it's one of the most misunderstood and misused words in the English language. *Literally* means that something is exactly what it says it is, and there can be no interpretation or exaggeration. Unfortunately, *literally* is often used for emphasis as in the following example:

This morning, I literally couldn't get out of bed.

This sentence meant to say that the person was extremely tired and wasn't able to get up. However, the sentence can't *literally* be true unless that person was tied down to the bed, paralyzed, or affected by a strange situation that the writer (most likely) didn't intend. Here's another example:

I literally died laughing.

The writer tried to say that something was very funny. However, unless they're writing this from beyond the grave, it can't *literally* be true.

Rhetorical Fallacies

A *rhetorical fallacy* is an argument that doesn't make sense. It usually involves distracting the reader from the issue at hand in some way. There are many kinds of rhetorical fallacies. Here are just a few, along with examples of each:

- *Ad Hominem*: Makes an irrelevant attack against the person making the claim, rather than addressing the claim itself.

- Senator Wilson opposed the new seat belt legislation, but should we really listen to someone who's been divorced four times?

- *Exaggeration*: Represents an idea or person in an obviously excessive manner.

- Senator Wilson opposed the new seat belt legislation. Maybe she thinks if more people die in car accidents, it will help with overpopulation.

- *Stereotyping (or Categorical Claim)*: Claims that all people of a certain group are the same in some way.

- Senator Wilson still opposes the new seat belt legislation. You know women can never admit when they're wrong.

When examining a possible rhetorical fallacy, carefully consider the point the writer is trying to make and if the argument directly relates to that point. If something feels wrong, there's a good chance that a fallacy is at play. The PSAT Writing and Language Test doesn't expect the fallacy to be named using specific terms like those above. However, questions can include identifying why something is a fallacy or suggesting a sounder argument.

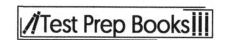

Style, Tone, and Mood

Style, *tone*, and *mood* are often thought to be the same thing. Though they're closely related, there are important differences to keep in mind. The easiest way to do this is to remember that style "creates and affects" tone and mood. More specifically, style is *how the writer uses words* to create the desired tone and mood for their writing.

Style

Style can include any number of technical writing choices, and some may have to be analyzed on the test. A few examples of style choices include:

- Sentence Construction: When presenting facts, does the writer use shorter sentences to create a quicker sense of the supporting evidence, or do they use longer sentences to elaborate and explain the information?

- Technical Language: Does the writer use jargon to demonstrate their expertise in the subject, or do they use ordinary language to help the reader understand things in simple terms?

- Formal Language: Does the writer refrain from using contractions such as *won't* or *can't* to create a more formal tone, or do they use a colloquial, conversational style to connect to the reader?

- Formatting: Does the writer use a series of shorter paragraphs to help the reader follow a line of argument, or do they use longer paragraphs to examine an issue in great detail and demonstrate their knowledge of the topic?

On the test, examine the writer's style and how their writing choices affect the way the passage comes across.

Tone

Tone refers to the writer's attitude toward the subject matter. Tone is usually explained in terms of a work of fiction. For example, the tone conveys how the writer feels about their characters and the situations in which they're involved. Nonfiction writing is sometimes thought to have no tone at all, but this is incorrect.

A lot of nonfiction writing has a neutral tone, which is an extremely important tone for the writer to take. A neutral tone demonstrates that the writer is presenting a topic impartially and letting the information speak for itself. On the other hand, nonfiction writing can be just as effective and appropriate if the tone isn't neutral. For instance, take the previous examples involving seat belt use. In them, the writer mostly chooses to retain a neutral tone when presenting information. If the writer would instead include their own personal experience of losing a friend or family member in a car accident, the tone would change dramatically. The tone would no longer be neutral. Now it would show that the writer has a personal stake in the content, allowing them to interpret the information in a different way. When analyzing tone, consider what the writer is trying to achieve in the passage, and how they *create* the tone using style.

Mood

Mood refers to the feelings and atmosphere that the writer's words create for the reader. Like tone, many nonfiction pieces can have a neutral mood. To return to the previous example, if the writer would

59

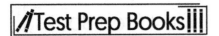

choose to include information about a person they know being killed in a car accident, the passage would suddenly carry an emotional component that is absent in the previous examples. Depending on how they present the information, the writer can create a sad, angry, or even hopeful mood. When analyzing the mood, consider what the writer wants to accomplish and whether the best choice was made to achieve that end.

Consistency

Whatever style, tone, and mood the writer uses, good writing should remain *consistent* throughout. If the writer chooses to include the tragic, personal experience above, it would affect the style, tone, and mood of the entire piece. It would seem out of place for such an example to be used in the middle of a neutral, measured, and analytical piece. To adjust the rest of the piece, the writer needs to make additional choices to remain consistent. For example, the writer might decide to use the word *tragedy* in place of the more neutral *fatality*, or they could describe a series of car-related deaths as an *epidemic*. Adverbs and adjectives such as *devastating* or *horribly* could be included to maintain this consistent attitude toward the content. When analyzing writing, look for sudden shifts in style, tone, and mood, and consider whether the writer would be wiser to maintain the prevailing strategy.

Syntax

Syntax is the order of words in a sentence. While most of the writing on the test has proper syntax, there may be questions on ways to vary the syntax for effectiveness. One of the easiest writing mistakes to spot is *repetitive sentence structure*. For example:

> Seat belts are important. They save lives. People don't like to use them. We have to pass seat belt laws. Then more people will wear seat belts. More lives will be saved.

What's the first thing that comes to mind when reading this example? The short, choppy, and repetitive sentences! In fact, most people notice this syntax issue more than the content itself. By combining some sentences and changing the syntax of others, the writer can create a more effective writing passage:

> Seat belts are important because they save lives. Since people don't like to use seat belts, though, more laws requiring their usage need to be passed. Only then will more people wear them and only then will more lives be saved.

Many rhetorical devices can be used to vary syntax (more than can possibly be named here). These often have intimidating names like *anadiplosis*, *metastasis*, and *paremptosis*. The test questions don't ask for definitions of these tricky techniques, but they can ask how the writer plays with the words and what effect that has on the writing. For example, *anadiplosis* is when the last word (or phrase) from a sentence is used to begin the next sentence:

> Cars are driven by people. People cause accidents. Accidents cost taxpayers money.

The test doesn't ask for this technique by name, but be prepared to recognize what the writer is doing and why they're using the technique in this situation. In this example, the writer is probably using *anadiplosis* to demonstrate causation.

Practice Quiz

The next question is based on the following passage:

> The research team evaluated various options but found that the proposed solution was not _____. Factors such as the high cost and limited potential for success informed their conclusion.

1. Which choice completes the text with the most logical and precise word or phrase?
   a. squalid
   b. inscrutable
   c. reflective
   d. viable

The next question is based on the following passage:

> Christopher Columbus is often credited for discovering America. This is incorrect. First, it is impossible to "discover" somewhere where people already live. However, another correction must be made, as well: Christopher Columbus was not the first European explorer to reach the present-day Americas! Rather, it was Leif Erikson who first came to the New World nearly five hundred years before Christopher Columbus.
>
> Leif Erikson, the son of Erik the Red (a famous Viking outlaw and explorer in his own right), was born in either 970 or 980, depending on which historian you read. When he was still young, he killed a man during a dispute, and the ruling council banished the Erikson clan to Greenland.
>
> Years later, in 999, on a voyage from Norway to his adopted homeland in Greenland, Leif's ship was blown off course and he arrived in a strange new land: present-day Newfoundland, Canada. When he finally returned Greenland, Leif consulted with a merchant who had also seen the shores of this previously unknown land we now know as Canada. The son of the legendary Viking explorer then gathered a crew of 35 men and set sail. Leif became the first European to set foot in the New World as he explored present-day Baffin Island and Labrador, Canada. His crew called the land "Vinland," since it was plentiful with grapes.
>
> Eventually, in 1003, Leif set sail for home and arrived at Greenland with a ship full of timber. In 1020, seventeen years later, the legendary Viking died. Many believe that Leif Erikson should receive more credit for his contributions in exploring the New World.

2. Which of the following is an opinion, rather than a historical fact, expressed by the author?
   a. Leif Erikson was definitely the son of Erik the Red; however, historians debate the year of his birth.
   b. Leif Erikson's crew called the land "Vinland," since it was plentiful with grapes.
   c. Leif Erikson deserves more credit for his contributions in exploring the New World.
   d. Leif Erikson explored the Americas nearly five hundred years before Christopher Columbus.

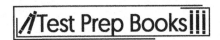

The next question is based on the following passage:

Flooding can result in severe devastation of nearby areas. Flash floods and tsunamis can result in sweeping waters that travel at destructive speeds. Fast-moving water has the power to demolish all obstacles in its path such as homes, trees, bridges, and buildings. Animals, plants, and humans may all lose their lives during a flood.

_____ in adverse circumstances. For thousands of years, peoples have inhabited floodplains of rivers. Examples include the Mississippi Valley of the United States, the Nile River in Egypt, and the Tigris River of the Middle East. The flooding of such rivers causes nutrient-rich silts to be deposited on the floodplains. Thus, after the floods recede, an extremely fertile soil is left behind. This soil is conducive to the agriculture of bountiful crops and has sustained the diets of humans for millennium.

3. Which choice most logically completes the text?
   a. Although often associated with devastation, not all flooding results
   b. Although often associated with devastation not all flooding results
   c. Although often associated with devastation. Not all flooding results
   d. While often associated with devastation, not all flooding results

The next question is based on the following passage:

Technologies now allow scientists to predict where and when flooding is likely to occur. Such technologies can also be used _____ the severity of an anticipated flood. In this way, local inhabitants can be warned and take preventative measures such as boarding up their homes, gathering necessary provisions, and moving themselves and their possessions to higher grounds.

The picturesque views of coastal regions and rivers have long enticed people to build near such locations. Due to the costs associated with the repairs needed after the flooding of such residencies, many governments now require inhabitants of flood-prone areas to purchase flood insurance and build flood-resistant structures. Pictures of all items within a building or home should be taken so that proper reimbursement for losses can be made in the event that a flood does occur.

4. Which choice completes the text so that it conforms to the conventions of Standard English?
   a. projected
   b. projecting
   c. project
   d. to project

The next question is based on the following passage:

A turbocharger is a forced induction device that compresses and pressurizes intake air in order to increase engine power without increasing fuel consumption. _____ the turbocharger being invented in 1905, "turbo lag" prevented turbochargers from being used on most passenger cars until the 1980s.

5. Which choice completes the text with the most logical transition?
   a. On account of
   b. Despite
   c. Following
   d. Opposite to

See answers on the next page.

Answer Explanations

1. D: Choice *D* is the best answer, as *viable* means feasible or capable of working successfully. The research team concluded the proposed solution was too expensive and held no guarantee of success; therefore, it was not guaranteed to be successful, or viable. *Squalid* means dirty or impure, so Choice *A* does not make sense in context. Choice *B* is inappropriate because *inscrutable* means impossible to understand; the proposed solution was undesirable but not difficult to comprehend. Finally, Choice *C* does not work because *reflective* means thoughtful or meditative and does not make sense here.

2. C: Choice *A* is incorrect because it describes facts: Leif Erikson was the son of Erik the Red and historians debate Leif's date of birth. These are not opinions. Choices *B* and *D* are incorrect; that Erikson called the land "Vinland" is a verifiable fact, as is the statement that he came to the New World almost 500 years before Columbus. Choice *C* is the correct answer because it is the author's opinion that Erikson deserves more credit. That, in fact, is the author's conclusion in the piece, but another person could argue that Columbus or another explorer deserves more credit for opening up the New World to exploration. Rather than being an indisputable fact, it is a subjective value claim.

3. A: Choice *C* can be eliminated because creating a new sentence with *not* is grammatically incorrect and throws off the rest of the sentence. Choice *B* is wrong because a comma is definitely needed after *devastation* in the sentence. Choice *D* is also incorrect because *while* is a poor substitute for *although*. *Although* in this context is meant to show contradiction with the idea that floods are associated with devastation. Therefore, Choice *A* is the correct answer.

4. D: To *project* means to anticipate or forecast. This goes very well with the sentence because it describes how new technology is trying to estimate flood activity in order to prevent damage and save lives. *Project* in this case needs to be assisted by *to* in order to function in the sentence. Therefore, Choice *D* is correct. Choices *A* and *B* are the incorrect tenses. Choice *C* is wrong because it lacks *to*.

5. B: Choice *B* is best as it properly sets up the discussion as to why the turbocharger, a century-old invention, was not able to be used for the first eighty years of its life. Choice *A* is incorrect as it implies that the turbocharger was not able to be used on engines immediately because of when it was invented. Choice *C* is somewhat correct but places focus on the chronology of the turbocharger's history rather than the reasoning for its significant lag in popularity among engineers. Choice *D* is incorrect as it places the lack of turbocharger use in direct contrast with the timing of its invention rather than its technological limits at the time.

Math Test

Algebra

Creating, Solving, or Interpreting a Linear Expression or Equation in One Variable

Linear expressions and equations are concise mathematical statements that can be written to model a variety of scenarios. Questions found pertaining to this topic will contain one variable only. A variable is an unknown quantity, usually denoted by a letter (x, n, p, etc.). In the case of linear expressions and equations, the power of the variable (its exponent) is 1. A variable without a visible exponent is raised to the first power.

Writing Linear Expressions and Equations

A linear expression is a statement about an unknown quantity expressed in mathematical symbols. The statement "five times a number added to forty" can be expressed as $5x + 40$. A linear equation is a statement in which two expressions (at least one containing a variable) are equal to each other. The statement "five times a number added to forty is equal to ten" can be expressed as $5x + 40 = 10$. Real-world scenarios can also be expressed mathematically. Consider the following:

> Bob had \$20 and Tom had \$4. After selling 4 ice cream cones to Bob, Tom has as much money as Bob.

The cost of an ice cream cone is an unknown quantity and can be represented by a variable. The amount of money Bob has after his purchase is four times the cost of an ice cream cone subtracted from his original \$20. The amount of money Tom has after his sale is four times the cost of an ice cream cone added to his original \$4. This can be expressed as: $20 - 4x = 4x + 4$, where x represents the cost of an ice cream cone.

When expressing a verbal or written statement mathematically, it is key to understand words or phrases that can be represented with symbols. The following are examples:

Symbol	Phrase
$+$	added to, increased by, sum of, more than
$-$	decreased by, difference between, less than, take away
x	multiplied by, 3 (4, 5 ...) times as large, product of
$\div$	divided by, quotient of, half (third, etc.) of
$=$	is, the same as, results in, as much as
$x, t, n, etc.$	a number, unknown quantity, value of

Evaluating and Simplifying Algebraic Expressions

Given an algebraic expression, students may be asked to evaluate for given values of variable(s). In doing so, students will arrive at a numerical value as an answer. For example:

$$\text{Evaluate } a - 2b + ab \text{ for } a = 3 \text{ and } b = -1$$

65

To evaluate an expression, the given values should be substituted for the variables and simplified using the order of operations. In this case:

$$(3) - 2(-1) + (3)(-1)$$

Parentheses are used when substituting.

Given an algebraic expression, students may be asked to simplify the expression. For example:

$$\text{Simplify } 5x^2 - 10x + 2 - 8x^2 + x - 1.$$

Simplifying algebraic expressions requires combining like terms. A term is a number, variable, or product of a number and variables separated by addition and subtraction. The terms in the above expression are: $5x^2, -10x, 2, -8x^2, x$, and -1. Like terms have the same variables raised to the same powers (exponents). To combine like terms, the coefficients (numerical factor of the term including sign) are added, while the variables and their powers are kept the same. The example above simplifies to $-3x^2 - 9x + 1$.

Solving Linear Equations

When asked to solve a linear equation, it requires determining a numerical value for the unknown variable. Given a linear equation involving addition, subtraction, multiplication, and division, isolation of the variable is done by working backward. Addition and subtraction are inverse operations, as are multiplication and division; therefore, they can be used to cancel each other out.

The first steps to solving linear equations are to distribute if necessary and combine any like terms that are on the same side of the equation. Sides of an equation are separated by an $=$ sign. Next, the equation should be manipulated to get the variable on one side. Whatever is done to one side of an equation, must be done to the other side to remain equal. Then, the variable should be isolated by using inverse operations to undo the order of operations backward. Undo addition and subtraction, then undo multiplication and division.

Creating, Solving, or Interpreting Linear Inequalities in One Variable

Linear inequalities and linear equations are both comparisons of two algebraic expressions. However, unlike equations in which the expressions are equal to each other, linear inequalities compare expressions that are unequal. Linear equations typically have one value for the variable that makes the statement true. Linear inequalities generally have an infinite number of values that make the statement true.

Writing Linear Inequalities

Linear inequalities are a concise mathematical way to express the relationship between unequal values. More specifically, they describe in what way the values are unequal. A value could be greater than ($>$); less than ($<$); greater than or equal to ($\geq$); or less than or equal to ($\leq$) another value. The statement "five times a number added to forty is more than sixty-five" can be expressed as $5x + 40 > 65$. Common words and phrases that express inequalities are:

Symbol	Phrase
$<$	is under, is below, smaller than, beneath
$>$	is above, is over, bigger than, exceeds
$\leq$	no more than, at most, maximum
$\geq$	no less than, at least, minimum

Solving Linear Inequalities

When solving a linear inequality, the solution is the set of all numbers that makes the statement true. The inequality $x + 2 \geq 6$ has a solution set of 4 and every number greater than 4 (4.0001, 5, 12, 107, etc.). Adding 2 to 4 or any number greater than 4 would result in a value that is greater than or equal to 6. Therefore, $x \geq 4$ would be the solution set.

Solution sets for linear inequalities often will be displayed using a number line. If a value is included in the set ($\geq$ or $\leq$), there is a shaded dot placed on that value and an arrow extending in the direction of the solutions. For a variable $>$ or $\geq$ a number, the arrow would point right on the number line (the direction where the numbers increase); and if a variable is $<$ or $\leq$ a number, the arrow would point left (where the numbers decrease). If the value is not included in the set ($>$ or $<$), an open circle on that value would be used with an arrow in the appropriate direction.

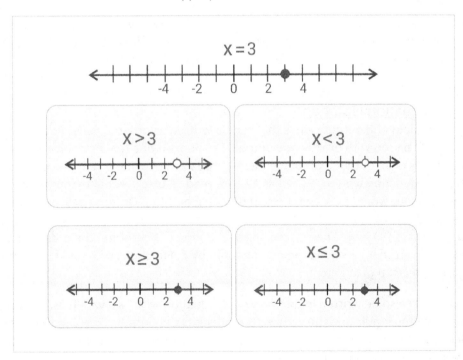

Students may be asked to write a linear inequality given a graph of its solution set. To do so, they should identify whether the value is included (shaded dot or open circle) and the direction in which the arrow is pointing.

In order to algebraically solve a linear inequality, the same steps should be followed as in solving a linear equation. The inequality symbol stays the same for all operations EXCEPT when multiplying or dividing by a negative number. If multiplying or dividing by a negative number while solving an inequality, the relationship reverses (the sign flips). Multiplying or dividing by a positive does not change the relationship, so the sign stays the same. In other words, $>$ switches to $<$ and vice versa. An example is shown below.

Solve $-2(x + 4) \leq 22$ for the value of x.

First, distribute -2 to the binomial by multiplying:

$$-2x - 8 \leq 22$$

Next, add 8 to both sides to isolate the variable:

$$-2x \leq 30$$

Divide both sides by -2 to solve for x:

$$x \geq -15$$

Building a Linear Function that Models a Linear Relationship Between Two Quantities

Linear relationships between two quantities can be expressed in two ways: function notation or as a linear equation with two variables. The relationship is referred to as linear because its graph is represented by a line. For a relationship to be linear, both variables must be raised to the first power only.

Function/Linear Equation Notation

A relation is a set of input and output values that can be written as ordered pairs. A function is a relation in which each input is paired with exactly one output. The domain of a function consists of all inputs, and the range consists of all outputs. Graphing the ordered pairs of a linear function produces a straight line. An example of a function would be $f(x) = 4x + 4$, read "f of x is equal to four times x plus four." In this example, the input would be x and the output would be $f(x)$. Ordered pairs would be represented as $(x, f(x))$. To find the output for an input value of 3, 3 would be substituted for x into the function as follows: $f(3) = 4(3) + 4$, resulting in $f(3) = 16$. Therefore, the ordered pair $(3, f(3)) = (3, 16)$. Note $f(x)$ is a function of x denoted by f. Functions of x could be named $g(x)$, read "g of x"; $p(x)$, read "p of x"; etc.

A linear function could also be written in the form of an equation with two variables. Typically, the variable x represents the inputs and the variable y represents the outputs. The variable x is considered the independent variable and y the dependent variable. The above function would be written as $y = 4x + 4$. Ordered pairs are written in the form (x, y).

Writing Linear Equations in Two Variables

When writing linear equations in two variables, the process depends on the information given. Questions will typically provide the slope of the line and its y-intercept, an ordered pair and the slope, or two ordered pairs.

Given the Slope and Y-Intercept

Linear equations are commonly written in slope-intercept form, $y = mx + b$, where m represents the slope of the line and b represents the y-intercept. The slope is the rate of change between the variables, usually expressed as a whole number or fraction. The y-intercept is the value of y when $x = 0$ (the point where the line intercepts the y-axis on a graph). Given the slope and y-intercept of a line, the values are substituted for m and b into the equation. A line with a slope of $\frac{1}{2}$ and y intercept of -2 would have an equation $y = \frac{1}{2}x - 2$.

Given an Ordered Pair and the Slope

The point-slope form of a line, $y - y_1 = m(x - x_1)$, is used to write an equation when given an ordered pair (point on the equation's graph) for the function and its rate of change (slope of the line). The values for the slope, m, and the point (x_1, y_1) are substituted into the point-slope form to obtain the equation of the line. A line with a slope of 3 and an ordered pair $(4, -2)$ would have an equation $y - (-2) = 3(x - 4)$. If a question specifies that the equation be written in slope-intercept form, the equation should be manipulated to isolate y:

Solve: $y - (-2) = 3(x - 4)$

Distribute: $y + 2 = 3x - 12$

Subtract 2 from both sides: $y = 3x - 14$

Given Two Ordered Pairs

Given two ordered pairs for a function, (x_1, y_1) and (x_2, y_2), it is possible to determine the rate of change between the variables (slope of the line). To calculate the slope of the line, m, the values for the ordered pairs should be substituted into the formula:

$$m = \frac{y_2 - y_1}{x_2 - x_1}$$

The expression is substituted to obtain a whole number or fraction for the slope. Once the slope is calculated, the slope and either of the ordered pairs should be substituted into the point-slope form to obtain the equation of the line.

Creating, Solving, and Interpreting Systems of Linear Inequalities in Two Variables

Expressing Linear Inequalities in Two Variables

A linear inequality in two variables is a statement expressing an unequal relationship between those two variables. Typically written in slope-intercept form, the variable y can be greater than; less than; greater

69

than or equal to; or less than or equal to a linear expression including the variable x. Examples include $y > 3x$ and $y \leq \frac{1}{2}x - 3$. Questions may instruct students to model real world scenarios such as:

> You work part-time cutting lawns for $15 each and cleaning houses for $25 each. Your goal is to make more than $90 this week. Write an inequality to represent the possible pairs of lawns and houses needed to reach your goal.

This scenario can be expressed as $15x + 25y > 90$ where x is the number of lawns cut and y is the number of houses cleaned.

Graphing Solution Sets for Linear Inequalities in Two Variables

A graph of the solution set for a linear inequality shows the ordered pairs that make the statement true. The graph consists of a boundary line dividing the coordinate plane and shading on one side of the boundary. The boundary line should be graphed just as a linear equation would be graphed. If the inequality symbol is > or <, a dashed line can be used to indicate that the line is not part of the solution set. If the inequality symbol is ≥ or ≤, a solid line can be used to indicate that the boundary line is included in the solution set. An ordered pair (x, y) on either side of the line should be chosen to test in the inequality statement. If substituting the values for x and y results in a true statement $(15(3) + 25(2) > 90)$, that ordered pair and all others on that side of the boundary line are part of the solution set. To indicate this, that region of the graph should be shaded. If substituting the ordered pair results in a false statement, the ordered pair and all others on that side are not part of the solution set.

Therefore, the other region of the graph contains the solutions and should be shaded.

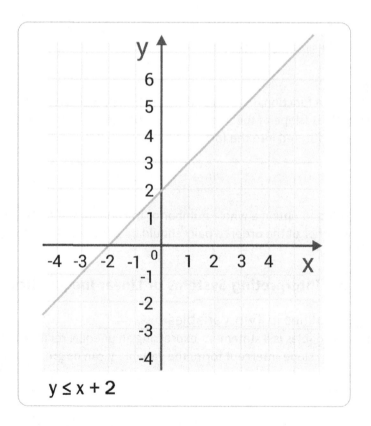

$y \leq x + 2$

70

A question may simply ask whether a given ordered pair is a solution to a given inequality. To determine this, the values should be substituted for the ordered pair into the inequality. If the result is a true statement, the ordered pair is a solution; if the result is a false statement, the ordered pair is not a solution.

Expressing Systems of Linear Inequalities in Two Variables

A system of linear inequalities consists of two linear inequalities making comparisons between two variables. Students may be given a scenario and asked to express it as a system of inequalities:

> A consumer study calls for at least 60 adult participants. It cannot use more than 25 men. Express these constraints as a system of inequalities.

This can be modeled by the system: $x + y \geq 60$; $x \leq 25$, where x represents the number of men and y represents the number of women. A solution to the system is an ordered pair that makes both inequalities true when substituting the values for x and y.

Graphing Solution Sets for Systems of Linear Inequalities in Two Variables

The solution set for a system of inequalities is the region of a graph consisting of ordered pairs that make both inequalities true. To graph the solution set, each linear inequality should first be graphed with appropriate shading. The region of the graph should be identified where the shading for the two inequalities overlaps. This region contains the solution set for the system.

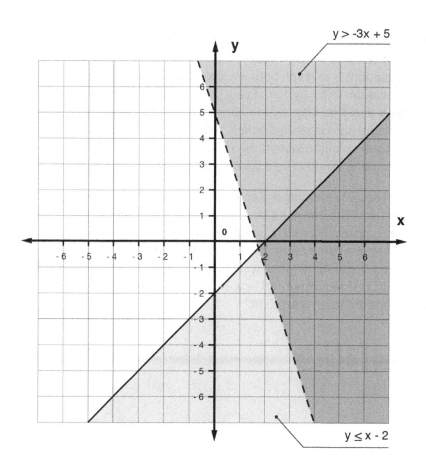

71

An ordered pair from the region of solutions can be selected to test in the system of inequalities.

Just as with manipulating linear inequalities in one variable, if dividing by a negative number in working with a linear inequality in two variables, the relationship reverses and the inequality sign should be flipped.

Creating, Solving, and Interpreting Systems of Two Linear Equations in Two Variables

Expressing Systems of Two Linear Equations in Two Variables

A system of two linear equations in two variables is a set of equations that use the same variables, usually x and y. Here's a sample problem:

> An Internet provider charges an installation fee and a monthly charge. It advertises that two months of its offering costs $100 and six months costs $200. Find the monthly charge and the installation fee.

The two unknown quantities (variables) are the monthly charge and the installation fee. There are two different statements given relating the variables: two months added to the installation fee is $100; and six months added to the installation fee is $200. Using the variable x as the monthly charge and y as the installation fee, the statements can be written as the following: $2x + y = 100$; $6x + y = 200$. These two equations taken together form a system modeling the given scenario.

Solutions of a System of Two Linear Equations in Two Variables

A solution for a system of equations is an ordered pair that makes both equations true. One method for solving a system of equations is to graph both lines on a coordinate plane. If the lines intersect, the point of intersection is the solution to the system. Every point on a line represents an ordered pair that makes its equation true. The ordered pair represented by this point of intersection lies on both lines and therefore makes both equations true. This ordered pair should be checked by substituting its values into both of the original equations of the system. Note that given a system of equations and an ordered pair, the ordered pair can be determined to be a solution or not by checking it in both equations.

If, when graphed, the lines representing the equations of a system do not intersect, then the two lines are parallel to each other or they are the same exact line. Parallel lines extend in the same direction without ever meeting. A system consisting of parallel lines has no solution. If the equations for a system represent the same exact line, then every point on the line is a solution to the system. In this case, there would be an infinite number of solutions. A system consisting of intersecting lines is referred to as independent; a system consisting of parallel lines is referred to as inconsistent; and a system consisting of coinciding lines is referred to as dependent.

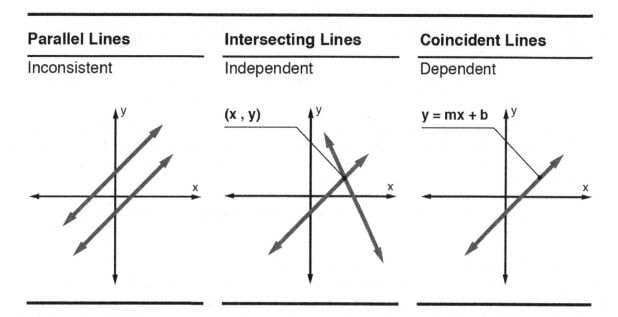

Parallel Lines	**Intersecting Lines**	**Coincident Lines**
Inconsistent	Independent	Dependent

Algebraically Solving Linear Equations (or Inequalities) in One Variable

Linear equations in one variable and linear inequalities in one variable can be solved following similar processes. Although they typically have one solution, a linear equation can have no solution or can have a solution set of all real numbers. Solution sets for linear inequalities typically consist of an infinite number of values either greater or less than a given value (where the given value may or may not be included in the set). However, a linear inequality can have no solution or can have a solution set consisting of all real numbers.

<u>Linear Equations in One Variable – Special Cases</u>
Solving a linear equation produces a value for the variable that makes the algebraic statement true. If there is no value for the variable that would make the statement true, there is no solution to the equation. Here's a sample equation:

$$x + 3 = x - 1$$

There is no value for *x* in which adding 3 to the value would produce the same result as subtracting 1 from that value. Conversely, if any value for the variable would make a true statement, the equation has an infinite number of solutions. Here's another sample equation

$$3x + 6 = 3(x + 2)$$

Any real number substituted for *x* would result in a true statement (both sides of the equation are equal).

By manipulating equations similar to the two above, the variable of the equation will cancel out completely. If the constants that are left express a true statement (ex., $6 = 6$), then all real numbers are solutions to the equation. If the constants left express a false statement (ex., $3 = -1$), then there is no solution to the equation.

A question on this material may present a linear equation with an unknown value for either a constant or a coefficient of the variable and ask to determine the value that produces an equation with no solution or infinite solutions. For example:

$3x + 7 = 3x + 10 + n$; Find the value of n that would create an equation with an infinite number of solutions for the variable x.

To solve this problem, the equation should be manipulated so the variable x will cancel. To do this, $3x$ should be subtracted from both sides, which would leave $7 = 10 + n$. By subtracting 10 on both sides, it is determined that $n = -3$. Therefore, a value of -3 for n would result in an equation with a solution set of all real numbers.

If the same problem asked for the equation to have no solution, the value of n would be all real numbers except -3.

Linear Inequalities in One Variable – Special Cases

A linear inequality can have a solution set consisting of all real numbers or can contain no solution. When solved algebraically, a linear inequality in which the variable cancels out and results in a true statement (ex., $7 \geq 2$) has a solution set of all real numbers. A linear inequality in which the variable cancels out and results in a false statement (ex., $7 \leq 2$) has no solution.

Compound Inequalities

A compound inequality is a pair of inequalities joined by *and* or *or*. Given a compound inequality, to determine its solution set, both inequalities should be solved for the given variable. The solution set for a compound inequality containing *and* consists of all the values for the variable that make both inequalities true. If solving the compound inequality results in $x > -9$ and $x \leq 6$, the solution set would consist of all values between -2 and 3, including 3. This may also be written as follows: $-9 < x \leq 6$. Due to the graphs of their solution sets (shown below), compound inequalities such as these are referred to as conjunctions.

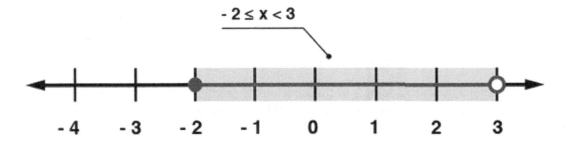

If there are no values that would make both inequalities of a compound inequality containing *and* true, then there is no solution. An example would be $x > 2$ and $x \leq 0$.

The solution set for a compound inequality containing *or* consists of all the values for the variable that make at least one of the inequalities true. The solution set for the compound inequality $x < 3$ or $x \geq 6$

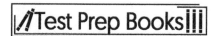

consists of all values less than 3, 6, and all values greater than 6. Due to the graphs of their solution sets (shown below), compound inequalities such as these are referred to as disjunctions.

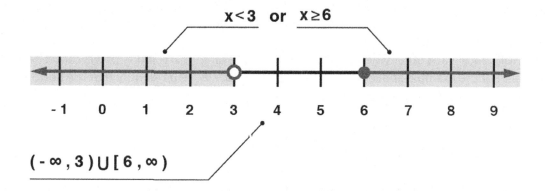

If the two inequalities for a compound inequality containing *or* "overlap," then the solution set contains all real numbers. An example would be $x > 2$ or $x < 7$. Any number would make at least one of these true.

Algebraically Solving Systems of Two Linear Equations in Two Variables

A system of two linear equations in two variables is a set of equations that use the same variables (typically x and y). A solution to the system is an ordered pair that makes both equations true. One method for solving a system is by graphing. This method, however, is not always practical. Students may not have graph paper; or the solution may not consist of integers, making it difficult to identify the exact point of intersection on a graph. There are two methods for solving systems of equations algebraically: substitution and elimination. The method used will depend on the characteristics of the equations in the system.

Solving Systems of Equations with the Substitution Method

If one of the equations in a system has an isolated variable ($x =$ or $y =$) or a variable that can be easily isolated, the substitution method can be used. Here's a sample system: $x + 3y = 7; 2x - 4y = 24$. The first equation can easily be solved for x. By subtracting $3y$ on both sides, the resulting equation is $x = 7 - 3y$. When one equation is solved for a variable, the expression that it is equal can be substituted into the other equation. For this example, $(7 - 3y)$ would be substituted for x into the second equation as follows:

$$2(7 - 3y) + 4y = 24$$

Solving this equation results in $y = -5$. Once the value for one variable is known, this value should be substituted into either of the original equations to determine the value of the other variable. For the example, -5 would be substituted for y in either of the original equations. Substituting into the first equation results in $x + 3(-5) = 7$, and solving this equation yields $x = 22$. The solution to a system is an ordered pair, so the solution to the example is written as $(22, 7)$. The solution can be checked by substituting it into both equations of the system to ensure it results in two true statements.

75

Solving Systems of Equations with the Elimination Method

The elimination method for solving a system of equations involves canceling out (or eliminating) one of the variables. This method is typically used when both equations of a system are written in standard form ($Ax + By = C$). An example is $2x + 3y = 12; 5x - y = 13$. To perform the elimination method, the equations in the system should be arranged vertically to be added together and then one or both of the equations should be multiplied so that one variable will be eliminated when the two are added. Opposites will cancel each other when added together. For example, $8x$ and $-8x$ will cancel each other when added. For the example above, writing the system vertically helps identify that the bottom equation should be multiplied by 3 to eliminate the variable y.

$$2x + 3y = 12 \quad \rightarrow \quad 2x + 3y = 12$$

$$3(5x - y = 13) \quad \rightarrow \quad 15x - 3y = 39$$

Adding the two equations together vertically results in $17x = 51$. Solving yields $x = 3$. Once the value for one variable is known, it can be substituted into either of the original equations to determine the value of the other variable. Once this is obtained, the solution can be written as an ordered pair (x, y) and checked in both equations of the system. In this example, the solution is $(3, 2)$.

Systems of Equations with No Solution or an Infinite Number of Solutions

A system of equations can have one solution, no solution, or an infinite number of solutions. If, while solving a system algebraically, both variables cancel out, then the system has either no solution or has an infinite number of solutions. If the remaining constants result in a true statement (ex., $7 = 7$), then there is an infinite number of solutions. This would indicate coinciding lines. If the remaining constants result in a false statement, then there is no solution to the system. This would indicate parallel lines.

Interpreting Variables and Constants in Expressions for Linear Functions

Linear functions, also written as linear equations in two variables, can be written to model real-world scenarios. Questions on this material will provide information about a scenario and then request a linear equation to represent the scenario. The algebraic process for writing the equation will depend on the given information. The key to writing linear models is to decipher the information given to determine what it represents in the context of a linear equation (variables, slope, ordered pairs, etc.).

Identifying Variables for Linear Models

The first step to writing a linear model is to identify what the variables represent. A variable represents an unknown quantity, and in the case of a linear equation, a specific relationship exists between the two variables (usually x and y). Within a given scenario, the variables are the two quantities that are changing. The variable x is considered the independent variable and represents the inputs of a function. The variable y is considered the dependent variable and represents the outputs of a function. For example, if a scenario describes distance traveled and time traveled, distance would be represented by y and time represented by x. The distance traveled depends on the time spent traveling (time is independent). If a scenario describes the cost of a cab ride and the distance traveled, the cost would be represented by y and the distance represented by x. The cost of a cab ride depends on the distance traveled.

Identifying the Slope and Y-Intercept for Linear Models

The slope of the graph of a line represents the rate of change between the variables of an equation. In the context of a real-world scenario, the slope will tell the way in which the unknown quantities

(variables) change with respect to each other. A scenario involving distance and time might state that someone is traveling at a rate of 45 miles per hour. The slope of the linear model would be 45. A scenario involving the cost of a cab ride and distance traveled might state that the person is charged $3 for each mile. The slope of the linear model would be 3.

The y-intercept of a linear function is the value of y when $x = 0$ (the point where the line intercepts the y-axis on the graph of the equation). It is sometimes helpful to think of this as a "starting point" for a linear function. Suppose for the scenario about the cab ride that the person is told that the cab company charges a flat fee of $5 plus $3 for each mile. Before traveling any distance ($x = 0$), the cost is $5. The y-intercept for the linear model would be 5.

Identifying Ordered Pairs for Linear Models

A linear equation with two variables can be written given a point (ordered pair) and the slope or given two points on a line. An ordered pair gives a set of corresponding values for the two variables (x and y). As an example, for a scenario involving distance and time, it is given that the person traveled 112.5 miles in 2 ½ hours. Knowing that x represents time and y represents distance, this information can be written as the ordered pair (2.5, 112.5).

Understanding Connections Between Algebraic and Graphical Representations

The solution set to a linear equation in two variables can be represented visually by a line graphed on the coordinate plane. Every point on this line represents an ordered pair (x, y), which makes the equation true. The process for graphing a line depends on the form in which its equation is written: slope-intercept form or standard form.

Graphing a Line in Slope-Intercept Form

When an equation is written in slope-intercept form, $y = mx + b$, m represents the slope of the line and b represents the y-intercept. The y-intercept is the value of y when $x = 0$ and the point at which the graph of the line crosses the y-axis. The slope is the rate of change between the variables, expressed as a fraction. The fraction expresses the change in y compared to the change in x. If the slope is an integer, it should be written as a fraction with a denominator of 1. For example, 5 would be written as 5/1.

To graph a line given an equation in slope-intercept form, the y-intercept should first be plotted. For example, to graph $y = -\frac{2}{3}x + 7$, the y-intercept of 7 would be plotted on the y-axis (vertical axis) at the point $(0, 7)$. Next, the slope would be used to determine a second point for the line. Note that all that is necessary to graph a line is two points on that line. The slope will indicate how to get from one point on the line to another. The slope expresses vertical change (y) compared to horizontal change (x) and therefore is sometimes referred to as $\frac{rise}{run}$. The numerator indicates the change in the y-value (move up for positive integers and move down for negative integers), and the denominator indicates the change in the x-value. For the previous example, using the slope of $-\frac{2}{3}$, from the first point at the y-intercept, the second point should be found by counting down 2 and to the right 3. This point would be located at (3, 5).

Graphing a Line in Standard Form

When an equation is written in standard form, $Ax + By = C$, it is easy to identify the x- and y-intercepts for the graph of the line. Just as the y-intercept is the point at which the line intercepts the y-

77

axis, the x-intercept is the point at which the line intercepts the x-axis. At the y-intercept, $x = 0$; and at the x-intercept, $y = 0$. Given an equation in standard form, $x = 0$ should be used to find the y-intercept. Likewise, $y = 0$ should be used to find the x-intercept. For example, to graph $3x + 2y = 6$, 0 for y results in:

$$3x + 2(0) = 6$$

Solving for y yields $x = 2$; therefore, an ordered pair for the line is $(2, 0)$. Substituting 0 for x results in:

$$3(0) + 2y = 6$$

Solving for y yields $y = 3$; therefore, an ordered pair for the line is $(0, 3)$. The two ordered pairs (the x- and y-intercepts) can be plotted, and a straight line through them can be constructed.

T - chart		Intercepts
x	**y**	**x** - intercept : (2,0)
0	3	**y** - intercept : (0,3)
2	0	

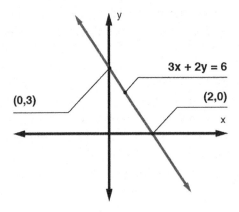

Writing the Equation of a Line Given its Graph

Given the graph of a line, its equation can be written in two ways. If the y-intercept is easily identified (is an integer), it and another point can be used to determine the slope. When determining $\frac{\text{change in } y}{\text{change in } x}$ from one point to another on the graph, the distance for $\frac{rise}{run}$ is being figured. The equation should be written in slope-intercept form, $y = mx + b$, with m representing the slope and b representing the y-intercept.

The equation of a line can also be written by identifying two points on the graph of the line. To do so, the slope is calculated and then the values are substituted for the slope and either of the ordered pairs into the point-slope form of an equation.

Vertical, Horizontal, Parallel, and Perpendicular Lines

For a vertical line, the value of x remains constant (for all ordered pairs (x, y) on the line, the value of x is the same); therefore, the equations for all vertical lines are written in the form $x = number$. For

example, a vertical line that crosses the x-axis at -2 would have an equation of $x = -2$. For a horizontal line, the value of y remains constant; therefore, the equations for all horizontal lines are written in the form $y = number$.

Parallel lines extend in the same exact direction without ever meeting. Their equations have the same slopes and different y-intercepts. For example, given a line with an equation of $y = -3x + 2$, a parallel line would have a slope of -3 and a y-intercept of any value other than 2. Perpendicular lines intersect to form a right angle. Their equations have slopes that are opposite reciprocal (the sign is changed and the fraction is flipped; for example, $-\frac{2}{3}$ and $\frac{3}{2}$) and y-intercepts that may or may not be the same. For example, given a line with an equation of $y = \frac{1}{2}x + 7$, a perpendicular line would have a slope of $-\frac{2}{1}$ and any value for its y-intercept.

Advanced Math

Creating a Quadratic or Exponential Function

Quadratic Models

A quadratic function can be written in the standard form: $y = ax^2 + bx + c$. It can be represented by a u-shaped graph called a parabola. For a quadratic function where the value of a is positive, as the inputs increase, the outputs increase until a certain value (maximum of the function) is reached. As inputs increase past the value that corresponds with the maximum output, the relationship reverses, and the outputs decrease. For a quadratic function where a is negative, as the inputs increase, the outputs (1) decrease, (2) reach a maximum, and (3) then increase.

Consider a ball thrown straight up into the air. As time passes, the height of the ball increases until it reaches its maximum height. After reaching the maximum height, as time increases, the height of the ball decreases (it is falling toward the ground). This relationship can be expressed as a quadratic function where time is the input (x), and the height of the ball is the output (y).

Given a scenario that can be modeled by a quadratic function, to write its equation, the following is needed: its vertex and any other ordered pair; or any three ordered pairs for the function. Given three ordered pairs, they should be substituted into the general form ($y = ax^2 + bx + c$) to create a system of three equations. For example, given the ordered pairs $(2, 3)$, $(3, 13)$, and $(4, 29)$, it yields:

$$3 = a(2)2 + b(2) + c \rightarrow 4a + 2b + c = 3$$

$$13 = a(3)2 + b(3) + c \rightarrow 9a + 3b + c = 13$$

$$29 = a(4)2 + b(4) + c \rightarrow 16a + 24b + c = 29$$

The values for a, b, and c in the system can be found and substituted into the general form to write the equation of the function. In this case, the equation is:

$$y = 3x^2 - 5x + 1$$

Exponential Models

Exponential functions can be written in the form:

$$y = a \times b^x$$

79

Scenarios involving growth and decay can be modeled by exponential functions.

The equation for an exponential function can be written given the y-intercept (a) and the growth rate (b). The y-intercept is the output (y) when the input (x) equals zero. It can be thought of as an "original value" or starting point. The value of b is the rate at which the original value increases ($b > 1$) or decreases ($b < 1$). Suppose someone deposits \$1,200 into a bank account that accrues 1% interest per month. The y-intercept, a, would be \$1,200, while the growth rate, b, would be 1.01 (100% of the original value + 1% interest). This scenario could be written as the exponential function $y = 1200 \times 1.01^x$, where x represents the number of months since the deposit and y represents money in the account.

Given a scenario that models an exponential function, the equation can also be written when provided two ordered pairs.

Determining the Most Suitable Form of an Expression

It is possible for algebraic expressions and equations to be written that look completely different, yet are still equivalent. For instance, the expression $4(2x - 3) - 3x + 5$ is equivalent to the expression $5x - 7$. Given two algebraic expressions, it can be determined if they are equivalent by writing them in simplest form. Distribution should be used, if applicable, and like terms should be combined. Given two algebraic equations, it can be determined if they are equivalent by solving each for the same variable. Here are two sample equations to consider: $3x - 4y = 7$ and $x + 2 = \frac{4}{3}y + 4\frac{1}{3}$. To determine if they are equivalent, solving for x is required.

$$3x - 4y = 7 \qquad\qquad x + 2 = \frac{4}{3}y + 4\frac{1}{3}$$

$$3x = 4y + 7 \qquad\qquad x = \frac{4}{3}y + 2\frac{1}{3}$$

$$x = \frac{4}{3}y + \frac{7}{3} \qquad\qquad x = \frac{4}{3}y + 2\frac{1}{3}$$

The equations are equivalent.

Equivalent Forms of Functions

Equations in two variables can often be written in different forms to easily recognize a given trait of the function or its graph. Linear equations written in slope-intercept form allow for recognition of the slope and y-intercept; linear equations written in standard form allow for identification of the x and y-intercepts. Quadratic functions written in standard form allow for identification of the y-intercept and for easy calculation of outputs; quadratic functions written in vertex form allow for identification of the function's minimum or maximum output and its graph's vertex. Polynomial functions written in factored form allow for identification of the zeros of the function.

The method of substituting the same inputs (x-values) into functions to determine if they produce the same outputs can reveal if functions are not equivalent (different outputs). However, corresponding inputs and outputs do not necessarily indicate equivalent functions.

Create Equivalent Expressions Involving Rational Exponents

Converting To and From Radical Form

Algebraic expressions involving radicals ($\sqrt{}$, $\sqrt[3]{}$, etc.) can be written without the radical by using rational (fraction) exponents. For radical expressions, the value under the root symbol is called the radicand, and the type of root determines the index. For example, the expression $\sqrt{6x}$ has a radicand of $6x$ and an index of 2 (it is a square root). If the exponent of the radicand is 1, then $\sqrt[n]{a} = a^{\frac{1}{n}}$ where n is the index. A number or variable without a power has an implied exponent of 1. For example, $\sqrt{6} = 6^{\frac{1}{2}}$ and $125^{\frac{1}{3}} = \sqrt[3]{125}$. For any exponent of the radicand:

$$\sqrt[n]{a^m} = \left(\sqrt[n]{a}\right)^m = a^{\frac{m}{n}}$$

For example, $64^{\frac{5}{3}} = \sqrt[3]{64^5}$ or $\left(\sqrt[3]{64}\right)^5$; and $(xy)^{\frac{2}{3}} = \sqrt[3]{(xy)^2}$ or $\left(\sqrt[3]{xy}\right)^2$.

Simplifying Expressions with Rational Exponents

When simplifying expressions with rational exponents, all basic properties for exponents hold true. When multiplying powers of the same base (same value with or without the same exponent), the exponents are added.

For example:

$$x^{\frac{2}{7}} \times x^{\frac{3}{14}} = x^{\frac{1}{2}} \left(\frac{2}{7} + \frac{3}{14} = \frac{1}{2}\right)$$

When dividing powers of the same base, the exponents are subtracted. For example:

$$\frac{5^{\frac{2}{3}}}{5^{\frac{1}{2}}} = 5^{\frac{1}{6}} \left(\frac{2}{3} - \frac{1}{2} = \frac{1}{6}\right)$$

When raising a power to a power, the exponents are multiplied. For example:

$$\left(5^{\frac{1}{2}}\right)^4 = 5^2 \left(\frac{1}{2} \times 4 = 2\right)$$

When simplifying expressions with exponents, a number should never be raised to a power or a negative exponent. If a number has an integer exponent, its value should be determined. If the number has a rational exponent, it should be rewritten as a radical and the value determined if possible. A base with a negative exponent moves from the numerator to the denominator of a fraction (or vice versa) and is written with a positive exponent. For example, $x^{-3} = \frac{1}{x^3}$ and $\frac{2}{5x^{-2}} = \frac{2x^2}{5}$. The exponent of 5 is 1, and therefore the 5 does not move.

Here's a sample expression: $(27x^{-9})^{\frac{1}{3}}$. After the implied exponents are noted, a power should be raised to a power by multiplying exponents, which yields $27^{\frac{1}{3}}x^{-3}$. Next, the negative exponent is eliminated by

81

moving the base and power: $\frac{27^{\frac{1}{3}}}{x^3}$. Then the value of the number is determined to a power by writing it in radical form: $\frac{\sqrt[3]{27}}{x^3}$. Simplifying yields $\frac{3}{x^3}$.

Creating an Equivalent Form of an Algebraic Expression

There are many different ways to write algebraic expressions and equations that are equivalent to each other. Converting expressions from standard form to factored form and vice versa are skills commonly used in advanced mathematics. Standard form of an expression arranges terms with variables powers in descending order (highest exponent to lowest and then constants). Factored form displays an expression as the product of its factors (what can be multiplied to produce the expression).

Converting Standard Form to Factored Form

To factor an expression, a greatest common factor needs to be factored out first. Then, if possible, the remaining expression needs to be factored into the product of binomials. A binomial is an expression with two terms.

Greatest Common Factor

The **greatest common factor (GCF)** of a monomial (one term) consists of the largest number that divides evenly into all coefficients (number part of a term), and if all terms contain the same variable, the variable with the lowest exponent. The GCF of $3x^4 - 9x^3 + 12x^2$ would be $3x^2$. To write the factored expression, every term needs to be divided by the GCF, then the product of the resulting quotient and the GCF (using parentheses to show multiplication) should be written. For the previous example, the factored expression would be:

$$3x^2(x^2 - 3x + 4)$$

Factoring Ax² + Bx + C When A = 1

To factor a quadratic expression in standard form when the value of a is equal to 1, the factors that multiply to equal the value of c should be found and then added to equal the value of b (the signs of b and c should be included). The factored form for the expression will be the product of binomials: $(x + factor1)(x + factor2)$. Here's a sample expression: $x^2 - 4x - 5$. The two factors that multiply to equal $c(-5)$ and add together to equal $b(-4)$ are -5 and 1. Therefore, the factored expression would be $(x - 5)(x + 1)$. Note $(x + 1)(x - 5)$ is equivalent.

Factoring a Difference of Squares

A difference of squares is a binomial expression where both terms are perfect squares (perfect square-perfect square). Perfect squares include 1, 4, 9, 16 … and x^2, x^4, x^6 … The factored form of a difference of squares will be:

$$(\sqrt{term1} + \sqrt{term2})(\sqrt{term1} - \sqrt{term2})$$

For example:

$$x2 - 4 = (x + 2)(x - 2)$$

and

$$25x6 - 81 = (5x3 + 9)(5x3 - 9)$$

82

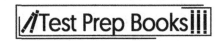

Factoring $Ax^2 + Bx + C$ when $A \neq 1$

To factor a quadratic expression in standard form when the value of a is not equal to 1, the factors that multiply to equal the value of $a \times c$ should be found and then added to equal the value of b. Next, the expression splitting the bx term should be rewritten using those factors. Instead of three terms, there will now be four. Then the first two terms should be factored using GCF, and a common binomial should be factored from the last two terms. The factored form will be: (common binomial) (2 terms out of binomials). In the sample expression $2x^2 + 11x + 12$, the value of $a \times c$ (or 2×12) equals 24.

Two factors that multiply to 24 and added together to yield b (11) are 8 and 3. The bx term ($11x$) can be rewritten by splitting it into the factors:

$$2x^2 + 8x + 3x + 12$$

A GCF from the first two terms can be factored as:

$$2x(x + 4) + 3x + 12$$

A common binomial from the last two terms can then be factored as:

$$2(x + 4) + 3(x + 4)$$

The factored form can be written as a product of binomials:

$$(x + 4)(2x + 3)$$

Converting Factored Form to Standard Form

To convert an expression from factored form to standard form, the factors are multiplied.

Solving a Quadratic Equation

A quadratic equation is one in which the highest exponent of the variable is 2. A quadratic equation can have two, one, or zero real solutions. Depending on its structure, a quadratic equation can be solved by (1) factoring, (2) taking square roots, or (3) using the quadratic formula.

Solving Quadratic Equations by Factoring

To solve a quadratic equation by factoring, the equation should first be manipulated to set the quadratic expression equal to zero. Next, the quadratic expression should be factored using the appropriate method(s). Then each factor should be set equal to zero. If two factors multiply to equal zero, then one or both factors must equal zero. Finally, each equation should be solved. Here's a sample:

$$x^2 - 10 = 3x - 6$$

The expression should be set equal to zero:

$$x^2 - 3x - 4 = 0$$

The expression should be factored:

$$(x - 4)(x + 1) = 0$$

83

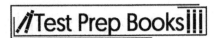

Each factor should be set equal to zero:

$$x - 4 = 0; x + 1 = 0$$

Solving yields $x = 4$ or $x = -1$.

Solving Quadratic Equations by Taking Square Roots

If a quadratic equation does not have a linear term (variable to the first power), it can be solved by taking square roots. This means x^2 needs to be isolated and then the square root of both sides of the equation should be isolated. There will be two solutions because square roots can be positive or negative. ($\sqrt{4} = \pm 2$ (2 or -2) because $2 \times 2 = 4$ and $-2 \times -2 = 4$.) Here's a sample equation:

$$3x^2 - 12 = 0$$

Isolating x^2 yields $x^2 = 4$. The square root of both sides is then solved: $x = 2$ or -2.

The Quadratic Formula

When a quadratic expression cannot be factored or is difficult to factor, the quadratic formula can be used to solve the equation. To do so, the equation must be in the form:

$$ax^2 + bx + c = 0$$

The quadratic formula is:

$$x = \frac{-b \pm \sqrt{b^2 - 4ac}}{2a}$$

(The $\pm$ symbol indicates that two calculations are necessary, one using $+$ and one using $-$.) Here's a sample equation:

$$3x^2 - 2x = 3x + 2$$

First, the quadratic expression should be set equal to zero:

$$3x^2 - 5x - 2 = 0$$

Then the values are substituted for a (3), b (-5), and c (-2) into the formula:

$$x = \frac{-(-5) \pm \sqrt{(-5)^2 - 4(3)(-2)}}{2(3)}$$

Simplification yields:

$$x = \frac{5 \pm \sqrt{49}}{6} \rightarrow x = \frac{5 \pm 7}{6}$$

Calculating two values for x using $+$ and $-$ yields:

$$x = \frac{5 + 7}{6}; x = \frac{5 - 7}{6}$$

84

Simplification yields:

$$x = 2 \text{ or } -\frac{1}{3}.$$

Just as with any equation, solutions should be checked by substituting the value into the original equation.

Adding, Subtracting, and Multiplying Polynomial Expressions

A polynomial expression is a monomial (one term) or the sum of monomials (more than one term separated by addition or subtraction). A polynomial in standard form consists of terms with variables written in descending exponential order and with any like terms combined.

Adding/Subtracting Polynomials
When adding or subtracting polynomials, each polynomial should be written in parenthesis; the negative sign should be distributed when necessary, and like terms need to be combined. Here's a sample equation: add $3x^3 + 4x - 3$ to $x^3 - 3x^2 + 2x - 2$. The sum is set as follows:

$$(x^3 - 3x^3 + 2x - 2) + (3x^3 + 4x - 3)$$

In front of each set of parentheses is an implied positive 1, which, when distributed, does not change any of the terms.

Therefore, the parentheses should be dropped and like terms should be combined:

$$x^3 - 3x^2 + 2x - 2 + 3x^3 + 4x - 3$$

$$4x^3 - 3x^2 + 6x - 5$$

Here's another sample equation: subtract $3x^3 + 4x - 3$ from $x^3 - 3x^2 + 2x - 2$. The difference should be set as follows:

$$(x^3 - 3x^2 + 2x - 2) - (3x^3 + 4x - 3)$$

The implied $+1$ in front of the first set of parentheses will not change those four terms; however, distributing the implied -1 in front of the second set of parentheses will change the sign of each of those three terms:

$$x^3 - 3x^2 + 2x - 2 - 3x^3 - 4x + 3$$

Combining like terms yields:

$$-2x^3 - 3x^2 - 2x + 1$$

Multiplying Polynomials
When multiplying monomials, the coefficients are multiplied, and exponents of the same variable are added. For example:

$$-5x^3y^2z \times 2x^2y^5z^3 = -10x^5y^7z^4$$

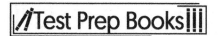

When multiplying polynomials, the monomials should be distributed and multiplied, then any like terms should be combined and written in standard form. Here's a sample equation:

$$2x^3(3x^2 + 2x - 4)$$

First, $2x^3$ should be multiplied by each of the three terms in parentheses:

$$2x^3 \times 3x^2 + 2x^3 \times 2x + 2x^3 \times -4$$

$$6x^5 + 4x^4 - 8x^3$$

Multiplying binomials will sometimes be taught using the FOIL method (where the products of the first, outside, inside, and last terms are added together). However, it may be easier and more consistent to think of it in terms of distributing. Both terms of the first binomial should be distributed to both terms of the second binomial. For example, the product of binomials $(2x + 3)(x - 4)$ can be calculated by distributing $2x$ and distributing 3:

$$2x \times x + 2x \times -4 + 3 \times x + 3 \times -4$$

$$2x^2 - 8x + 3x - 12$$

Combining like terms yields:

$$2x^2 - 5x - 12$$

The general principle of distributing each term can be applied when multiplying polynomials of any size. To multiply $(x^2 + 3x - 1)(5x^3 - 2x^2 + 2x + 3)$, all three terms should be distributed from the first polynomial to each of the four terms in the second polynomial and then any like terms should be combined. If a problem requires multiplying more than two polynomials, two at a time can be multiplied and combined until all have been multiplied. To multiply $(x + 3)(2x - 1)(x + 5)$, two polynomials should be chosen to multiply together first. Multiplying the last two results in:

$$(2x - 1)(x + 5) = 2x^2 + 9x - 5$$

That product should then be multiplied by the third polynomial:

$$(x + 3)(2x^2 + 9x - 5)$$

The final answer should equal:

$$2x^3 + 15x^2 + 36x - 15$$

Solving an Equation in One Variable that Contains Radicals or Contains the Variable in the Denominator of a Fraction

Equations with radicals containing numbers only as the radicand are solved the same way that an equation without a radical would be. For example, $3x + \sqrt{81} = 45$ would be solved using the same steps as if solving:

$$2x + 4 = 12$$

Radical equations are those in which the variable is part of the radicand. For example, $\sqrt{5x+1} - 6 = 0$ and $\sqrt{x-3} + 5 = x$ would be considered radical equations.

Radical Equations

To solve a radical equation, the radical should be isolated and both sides of the equation should be raised to the same power to cancel the radical. Raising both sides to the second power will cancel a square root, raising to the third power will cancel a cube root, etc. To solve $\sqrt{5x+1} - 6 = 0$, the radical should be isolated first:

$$\sqrt{5x+1} = 6$$

Then both sides should be raised to the second power:

$$(\sqrt{5x+1})^2 = (6)^2 \rightarrow 5x + 1 = 36$$

Lastly, the linear equation should be solved: $x = 7$.

Radical Equations with Extraneous Solutions

If a radical equation contains a variable in the radicand and a variable outside of the radicand, it must be checked for extraneous solutions. An extraneous solution is one obtained by following the proper process for solving an equation but does not "check out" when substituted into the original equation. Here's a sample equation:

$$\sqrt{x-3} + 5 = x$$

Isolating the radical yields:

$$\sqrt{x-3} = x - 5$$

Next, both sides should be squared to cancel the radical:

$$\left(\sqrt{x-3}\right)^2 = (x-5)^2 \rightarrow x - 3$$

$$(x-5)(x-5)$$

The binomials should be multiplied:

$$x - 3 = x^2 - 10x + 25$$

The quadratic equation is then solved:

$$0 = x^2 - 11x + 28$$

$$0 = (x-7)(x-4)$$

$$x - 7 = 0; x - 4 = 0$$

$$x = 7 \text{ or } x = 4$$

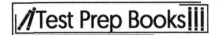

To check for extraneous solutions, each answer can be substituted, one at a time, into the original equation. Substituting 7 for x, results in $7 = 7$. Therefore, 7 is a solution. Substituting 4 for x results in $6 = 4$. This is false; therefore, 4 is an extraneous solution.

Equations with a Variable in the Denominator of a Fraction

For equations with variables in the denominator, if the equation contains two rational expressions (on opposite sides of the equation, or on the same side and equal to zero), it can be solved like a proportion. Here's an equation to consider:

$$\frac{5}{2x - 2} = \frac{15}{x^2 - 1}$$

First, cross-multiplying yields:

$$5(x^2 - 1) = 15(2x - 2)$$

Distributing yields:

$$5x^2 - 5 = 30x - 30$$

In solving the quadratic equation, it is determined that $x = 1$ or $x = 5$. Solutions must be checked to see if they are extraneous. Extraneous solutions either produce a false statement when substituted into the original equation or create a rational expression with a denominator of zero (dividing by zero is undefined). Substituting 5 into the original equation produces $\frac{5}{8} = \frac{5}{8}$; therefore, 5 is a solution. Substituting 1 into the original equation results in both denominators equal to zero; therefore, 1 is an extraneous solution.

If an equation contains three or more rational expressions: the least common denominator (LCD) needs to be found for all the expressions, then both sides of the equation should be multiplied by the LCD. The LCD consists of the lowest number that all coefficients divide evenly into and for every variable, the highest power of that variable. Here's a sample equation:

$$\frac{3}{5x} - \frac{4}{3x} = \frac{1}{3}$$

The LCD would be $15x$. Both sides of the equation should be multiplied by $15x$:

$$15x \left(\frac{3}{5x} - \frac{4}{3x}\right) = 15x \left(\frac{1}{3}\right)$$

$$\frac{45x}{5x} - \frac{60x}{3x} = \frac{15x}{3}$$

$$9 - 20 = 5x$$

$$x = -2\frac{1}{2}$$

Any extraneous solutions should be identified.

88

Solving a System of One Linear Equation and One Quadratic Equation

A system of equations consists of two variables in two equations. A solution to the system is an ordered pair (x, y) that makes both equations true. When displayed graphically, a solution to a system is a point of intersection between the graphs of the equations. When a system consists of one linear equation and one quadratic equation, there may be one, two, or no solutions. If the line and parabola intersect at two points, there are two solutions to the system; if they intersect at one point, there is one solution; if they do not intersect, there is no solution.

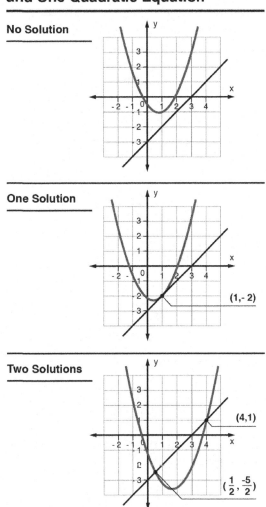

One method for solving a system of one linear equation and one quadratic equation is to graph both functions and identify point(s) of intersection. This, however, is not always practical. Graph paper may not be available, or the intersection points may not be easily identified. Solving the system algebraically involves using the substitution method. Consider the following system: $y = x^2 + 9x + 11$; $y = 2x - 1$. The equivalent value of y should be substituted from the linear equation ($2x - 1$) into the quadratic equation. The resulting equation is $2x - 1 = x^2 + 9x + 11$. Next, this quadratic equation should be

solved using the appropriate method: factoring, taking square roots, or using the quadratic formula. Solving this quadratic equation by factoring results in $x = -4$ or $x = -3$. Next, the corresponding y-values should be found by substituting the x-values into the original linear equation: $y = 2(-4) - 1; y = 2(-3) - 1$. The solutions should be written as ordered pairs: $(-4, -9)$ and $(-3, -7)$. Finally, the possible solutions should be checked by substituting each into both of the original equations. In this case, both solutions "check out."

Rewriting Simple Rational Expressions

A rational expression is an algebraic expression including variables that look like a fraction. In simplest form, the numerator and denominator of a rational expression do not have common divisors (factors). To simplify a rational expression, the numerator and denominator should be factored; then any common factors in the numerator and denominator should be canceled. To simplify, the numerator and denominator should be written as a product of its factors:

$$\frac{3x^2y}{12xy^3}$$

$$\frac{3 \times x \times x \times y}{2 \times 2 \times 3 \times x \times x \times y \times y \times y}$$

Canceling common factors leaves:

$$\frac{x}{2 \times 2 \times y \times y}$$

Multiplying the remaining factors results in $\frac{x}{4y^2}$.

Here's a rational expression:

$$\frac{x^2 - 1}{x^2 - x - 2}$$

Factoring the numerator and denominator produces:

$$\frac{(x + 1)(x - 1)}{(X - 2)(x + 1)}$$

Each binomial in parentheses is a factor and only the exact same binomial would cancel that factor. By canceling factors, the expression is simplified to:

$$\frac{x - 1}{x - 2}$$

The variable x itself is not a factor. Therefore, they do not cancel each other out.

Multiplying/Dividing Rational Expressions

When multiplying or dividing rational expressions, the basic concepts of operations with fractions are used. To multiply, (1) all numerators and denominators need to be factored, (2) common factors should be canceled between any numerator and any denominator, (3) the remaining factors of the numerator

and the remaining factors of the denominator should be multiplied, and (4) the expression should be checked to see whether it can be simplified further.

To multiply the following, each numerator and denominator should be written as a product of its factors:

$$\frac{4a^4}{3} \times \frac{6}{5a^2}$$

$$\frac{2 \times 2 \times a \times a \times a \times a}{3} \times \frac{3 \times 2}{5 \times a \times a}$$

After canceling common factors, the remaining expression is:

$$\frac{2 \times 2 \times a \times a}{1} \times \frac{2}{5}$$

A factor of 1 remains if all others are canceled. Multiplying remaining factors produces:

$$\frac{8a^2}{5}$$

To divide rational expressions, the expression should be changed to multiplying by the reciprocal of the divisor (just as with fractions: $\frac{1}{2} \div \frac{3}{4} = \frac{1}{2} \times \frac{4}{3}$); then follow the process for multiplying rational expressions.

Here's a sample expression:

$$\frac{2x}{x^2 - 16} \div \frac{4x^2 + 6x}{x^2 + 6x + 8}$$

First, the division problem should be changed to a multiplication problem:

$$\frac{2x}{x^2 - 16} \times \frac{x^2 + 6x + 8}{4x^2 + 6x}$$

Then, the equation should be factored:

$$\frac{2x}{(x + 4)(x - 4)} \times \frac{(x + 4)(x + 2)}{2x(2x + 3)}$$

Canceling yields:

$$\frac{1}{(x - 4)} \times \frac{(x + 2)}{(2x + 3)}$$

Multiplying the remaining factors produces:

$$\frac{x + 2}{2x^2 - 5x - 12}$$

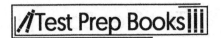
Adding/Subtracting Rational Expressions

Just as with adding and subtracting fractions, to add or subtract rational expressions, a common denominator is needed. (The numerator is added or subtracted, and the denominator stays the same.) If the expressions have like denominators, subtraction should be changed to add the opposite (a -1 is distributed to each term in the numerator of the expression being subtracted); the denominators should be factored and the expressions added; the numerator should then be factored; and the equation should be simplified if possible. Here's a sample expression:

$$\frac{2x^2 + 4x - 3}{x + 3} - \frac{x^2 - 2x - 12}{x + 3}$$

Changing subtraction to add the opposite yields:

$$\frac{2x^2 + 4x - 3}{x + 3} + \frac{-x^2 + 2x + 12}{x + 3}$$

The denominator cannot be factored, so the expression should be added, resulting in:

$$\frac{x^2 + 6x + 9}{x + 3}$$

Simplification is performed by factoring the numerator:

$$\frac{(x + 3)(x + 3)}{(x + 3)}$$

Canceling yields: $\frac{x + 3}{1}$, or simply $x + 3$.

To add or subtract rational expressions with unlike denominators, the denominators must be changed by finding the least common multiple (LCM) of the expressions. To find the LCM, each expression should be factored, and the product should be formed using each factor the greatest number of times it occurs. The LCM of $12xy^2$ and $15x^3y$ would be $60x^3y^2$. The LCM of $x^2 + 5x + 4$ (which factors to $(x + 4)(x + 1)$) and $x^2 + 2x + 1$ (which factors to $(x + 1)(x + 1)$) would be $(x + 4)(x + 1)(x + 1)$.

To add or subtract expressions with unlike denominators: (1) subtraction should be changed to add the opposite; (2) the denominators are factored; (3) an LCM should be determined for the denominators; (4) the numerator and denominator of each expression should be multiplied by the missing factor(s); (5) the expressions that now have like denominators should be added; (6) the numerator should be factored; and (7) simplification should be performed if possible. Here's a sample expression:

$$\frac{x^2 + 6x + 11}{x^2 + 7x + 12} - \frac{2}{x + 3}$$

First, subtraction should be changed to addition:

$$\frac{x^2 + 6x + 11}{x^2 + 7x + 12} + \frac{-2}{x + 3}$$

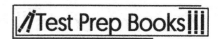

Then, the denominators are factored:

$$\frac{x^2 + 6x + 11}{(x + 4)(x + 3)} + \frac{-2}{x + 3}$$

The LCM of $(x + 4)(x + 3)$ and $(x + 3)$ should be determined, which is $(x + 4)(x + 3)$.

The numerator and denominator should be multiplied by the missing factor:

$$\frac{x^2 + 6x + 11}{(x + 4)(x + 3)} + \frac{-2}{x + 3} \times \frac{(x + 4)}{(x + 4)}$$

$$\frac{x^2 + 6x + 11}{(x + 4)(x + 3)} + \frac{-2x - 8}{(x + 4)(x + 3)}$$

The expressions should be added, resulting in:

$$\frac{x^2 + 4x + 3}{(x + 4)(x + 3)}$$

The numerator should be factored:

$$\frac{(x + 3)(x + 1)}{(x + 4)(x + 3)}$$

Simplifying yields:

$$\frac{x + 1}{x + 4}$$

Interpreting Parts of Nonlinear Expressions in Terms of Their Context

When a nonlinear function is used to model a real-life scenario, some aspects of the function may be relevant while others may not. The context of each scenario will dictate what should be used. In general, x- and y-intercepts will be points of interest. A y-intercept is the value of y when x equals zero; and an x-intercept is the value of x when y equals zero. Suppose a nonlinear function models the value of an investment (y) over the course of time (x). It would be relevant to determine the initial value (the y-intercept where time equals zero), as well as any point in time in which the value would be zero (the x-intercept).

Another aspect of a function that is typically desired is the rate of change. This tells how fast the outputs are growing or decaying with respect to given inputs. For polynomial functions, the rate of change can be estimated by the highest power of the function. Polynomial functions also include absolute and/or relative minimums and maximums. Functions modeling production or expenses should be considered. Maximum and minimum values would be relevant aspects of these models.

Finally, the domain and range for a function should be considered for relevance. The domain consists of all input values, and the range consists of all output values. For instance, a function could model the volume of a container to be produced in relation to its height. Although the function that models the scenario may include negative values for inputs and outputs, these parts of the function would obviously not be relevant.

93

Understanding the Relationship Between Zeros and Factors of Polynomials

The zeros of a function are the x-intercepts of its graph. They are called zeros because they are the x-values for which $y = 0$.

Finding Zeros

To find the zeros of a polynomial function, it should be written in factored form, then each factor should be set equal to zero and solved. To find the zeros of the function $y = 3x^3 - 3x^2 - 36x$, the polynomial should be factored first. Factoring out a GCF results in:

$$y = 3x(x^2 - x - 12)$$

Then factoring the quadratic function yields:

$$y = 3x(x - 4)(x + 3)$$

Next, each factor should be set equal to zero: $3x = 0$; $x - 4 = 0$; $x + 3 = 0$. By solving each equation, it is determined that the function has zeros, or x-intercepts, at 0, 4, and -3.

Writing a Polynomial with Given Zeros

Given zeros for a polynomial function, to write the function, a linear factor corresponding to each zero should be written. The linear factor will be the opposite value of the zero added to x. Then the factors should be multiplied, and the function written in standard form. To write a polynomial with zeros at -2, 3, and 3, three linear factors should be written:

$$y = (x + 2)(x - 3)(x - 3)$$

Then, multiplication is used to convert the equation to standard form, producing:

$$y = x^3 - 4x^2 - 3x + 18$$

Dividing Polynomials by Linear Factors

To determine if a linear binomial is a factor of a polynomial, the polynomial should be divided by the binomial. If there is no remainder (it divides evenly), then the binomial is a factor of the polynomial. To determine if a value is a zero of a function, a binomial can be written from that zero and tested by division. To divide a polynomial by a linear factor, the terms of the dividend should be divided by the linear term of the divisor; the same process as long division of numbers (divide, multiply, subtract, drop down, and repeat) should be followed.

$$\frac{divisor\sqrt{quotient}}{dividend}$$

Remember that when subtracting a binomial, the signs of both terms should be changed. Here's a sample equation: divide $9x^3 - 18x^2 - x + 2$ by $3x + 1$. First, the problem should be set up as long division:

$$3x + 1 \overline{)\ 9x^3 - 18x^2 - x + 2}$$

94

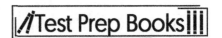

Then the first term of the dividend $(9x^3)$ should be divided by the linear term of the divisor $(3x)$:

$$\frac{3x^2}{3x+1\overline{)\ 9x^3-18x^2-\ x+2}}$$

Next, the divisor should be multiplied by that term of the quotient:

$$
\begin{array}{r}
3x^2-7x+2 \\
3x+1\overline{)\ 9x^3-18x^2-\ x+2} \\
-9x^3-\ 3x^2 \\
\end{array}
$$

Subtraction should come next:

$$
\begin{array}{r}
3x^2-7x+2 \\
3x+1\overline{)\ 9x^3-18x^2-\ x+2} \\
-9x^3-\ 3x^2 \\
\hline
-21x^2 \\
\end{array}
$$

Now, the next term $(-x)$ should be dropped down:

$$
\begin{array}{r}
3x^2-7x+2 \\
3x+1\overline{)\ 9x^3-18x^2-\ x+2} \\
-9x^3-\ 3x^2 \\
\hline
-21x^2-\ x \\
\end{array}
$$

Then, the process should be repeated, dividing $-21x^2$ by $3x$:

$$
\begin{array}{r}
3x^2-7x+2 \\
3x+1\overline{)\ 9x^3-18x^2-\ x+2} \\
-9x^3-\ 3x^2 \\
\hline
-21x^2-\ x \\
+21x^2+7x \\
\hline
6x \\
\end{array}
$$

The next term (2) should be dropped and repeated by dividing $6x$ by $3x$:

$$
\begin{array}{r}
3x^2 - 7x + 2 \\
3x + 1 \overline{\smash{\big)}\ 9x^3 - 18x^2 - x + 2} \\
\underline{-9x^3 - 3x^2} \\
-21x^2 - x \\
\underline{+21x^2 + 7x} \\
6x + 2 \\
\underline{-6x - 2} \\
0
\end{array}
$$

There is no remainder; therefore, $3x + 1$ is a factor of:

$$9x^3 - 18x^2 - x + 2$$

By the definition of factors:

$$(3x + 1)(3x^2 - 7x + 2) = 9x^3 - 18x^2 - x + 2$$

The quadratic expression can further be factored to produce:

$$(3x + 1)(3x - 1)(x - 2)$$

Understanding a Nonlinear Relationship Between Two Variables

Questions on this material will assess the ability of test takers to make connections between linear or nonlinear equations and their graphical representations. It will also require interpreting graphs in relation to systems of equations.

Graphs of Polynomial Functions

A polynomial function consists of a monomial or sum of monomials arranged in descending exponential order. The graph of a polynomial function is a smooth continuous curve that extends infinitely on both ends. From the equation of a polynomial function, the following can be determined: (1) the end behavior of the graph—does it rise or fall to the left and to the right; (2) the y-intercept and x-intercept(s) and whether the graph simply touches or passes through each x-intercept; and (3) the largest possible number of turning points, where the curve changes from rising to falling or vice versa. To graph the function, these three aspects of the graph should be determined and extra points between the intercepts should be found if necessary.

End Behavior

The end behavior of the graph of a polynomial function can be determined by the degree of the function (largest exponent) and the leading coefficient (coefficient of the term with the largest exponent). There are four possible scenarios for the end behavior: (1) if the degree is odd and the coefficient is positive, the graph falls to the left and rises to the right; (2) if the degree is odd and the coefficient is negative, the graph rises to the left and falls to the right; (3) if the degree is even and the coefficient is positive, the graph rises to the left and rises to the right, or (4) if the degree is even and the coefficient is negative, the graph falls to the left and falls to the right.

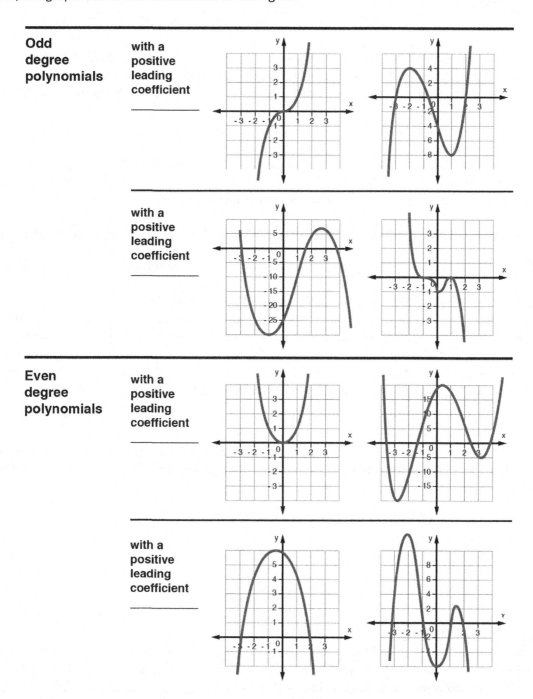

X and Y-Intercepts

The y-intercept for any function is the point at which the graph crosses the y-axis. At this point $x = 0$; therefore, to determine the y-intercept, $x = 0$ should be substituted into the function and solved for y. For a given zero of a function, the graph can either pass through that point or simply touch that point (the graph turns at that zero). This is determined by the multiplicity of that zero. The multiplicity of a

97

zero is the number of times its corresponding factor is multiplied to obtain the function in standard form. For example, $y = x^3 - 4x^2 - 3x + 18$ can be written in factored form as:

$$y = (x + 2)(x - 3)(x - 3) \text{ or } y = (x + 2)(x - 3)^2$$

The zeros of the function would be -2 and 3. The zero at -2 would have a multiplicity of 1, and the zero at 3 would have a multiplicity of 2. If a zero has an even multiplicity, then the graph touches the x-axis at that zero and turns around. If a zero has an odd multiplicity, then the graph crosses the x-axis at that zero.

Turning Points

The graph of a polynomial function can have, at most, a number of turning points equal to one less than the degree of the function. It is possible to have fewer turning points than this value. For example, the function $y = 3x^5 + 2x^2 - 3x$ could have no more than four turning points.

Using Function Notation, and Interpreting Statements Using Function Notation.

Function notation is covered in the *Function/Linear Equation Notation* section under *Heart of Algebra*.

Addition, Subtraction, Multiplication and Division of Functions

Functions denoted by $f(x)$, $g(x)$, etc., can be added, subtracted, multiplied, or divided. For example, the function $f(x) = 15x + 100$ represents the cost to have a catered party at a banquet hall (where x represents the number of guests); and the function $g(x) = 10x$ represents the cost for unlimited drinks at the party. The total cost of a catered party with unlimited drinks can be represented by adding the functions $f(x)$ and $g(x)$. In this case $f(x) + g(x) = (15x + 100) + (10x)$; therefore:

$$f(x) + g(x) = 25x + 100$$

$(f(x) + g(x)$ can also be written $(f + g)(x))$. To add, subtract, multiply, or divide functions, the values of the functions should be substituted and the rules for operations with polynomials should be followed. It should be noted:

$$(f - g)(x) = f(x) - g(x); \ (f \times g)(x) = f(x) \times g(x)$$

and

$$\left(\frac{f}{g}\right)(x) = \frac{f(x)}{g(x)}$$

Composition of Functions

A composite function is one in which two functions are combined such that the output from the first function becomes the input for the second function (one function should be applied after another function). The composition of a function written as $(g \circ f)(x)$ or $g(f(x))$ is read "g of f of x." The inner function, $f(x)$, would be evaluated first and the answer would be used as the input of the outer function, $g(x)$. To determine the value of a composite function, the value of the inner function should be substituted for the variable of the outer function.

98

Here's a sample problem:

> A store is offering a 20% discount on all of its merchandise. You have a coupon worth $5 off any item.

The cost of an item with the 20% discount can be modeled by the function: $d(x) = 0.8x$. The cost of an item with the coupon can be modeled by the function $c(x) = x - 5$. A composition of functions to model the cost of an item applying the discount first and then the coupon would be $c(d(x))$. Replacing $d(x)$ with its value $(0.8x)$ results in $c(0.8x)$. By evaluating the function $c(x)$ with an input of $0.8x$, it is determined that:

$$c(d(x)) = 0.8x - 5$$

To model the cost of an item if the coupon is applied first and then the discount, $d(c(x))$ should be determined. The result would be:

$$d(c(x) = 0.8x - 4$$

Evaluating Functions

If a problem asks to evaluate with operations between functions, the new function should be determined and then the given value should be substituted as the input of the new function. To find $(f \times g)(3)$ given $f(x) = x + 1$ and $g(x) = 2x - 3$, the following should be determined:

$$(f \times g)(x) = f(x) \times g(x)$$

$$(x + 1)(2x - 3) = 2x^2 - x - 3$$

Therefore:

$$(f \times g)(x) = 2x^2 - x - 3$$

To find $(f \times g)(3)$, the function $(f \times g)(x)$ needs to be evaluated for an input of 3:

$$(f \times g)(3) = 2(3)^2 - (3) - 3 = 12$$

Therefore:

$$(f \times g)(3) = 12$$

Using Structure to Isolate or Identify a Quantity of Interest

Formulas are mathematical expressions that define the value of one quantity given the value of one or more different quantities. A formula or equation expressed in terms of one variable can be manipulated to express the relationship in terms of any other variable. The equation $y = 3x + 2$ is expressed in terms of the variable y. By manipulating the equation, it can be written as $x = \frac{y - 2}{3}$, which is expressed in terms of the variable x. To manipulate an equation or formula to solve for a variable of interest, how the equation would be solved if all other variables were numbers should be considered. The same steps for solving should be followed, leaving operations in terms of the variables, instead of calculating numerical values.

The formula $P = 2l + 2w$ expresses how to calculate the perimeter of a rectangle given its length and width. To write a formula to calculate the width of a rectangle given its length and perimeter, the previous formula relating the three variables should be used and the variable w should be solved. If P and l were numerical values, this would be a two-step linear equation solved by subtraction and division. To solve the equation $P = 2l + 2w$ for w, $2l$ should be subtracted from both sides: $P - 2l = 2w$. Then both sides should be divided by 2: $\frac{P - 2l}{2} = w$ or $\frac{P}{2} - l = w$.

The distance formula between two points on a coordinate plane can be found using the formula:

$$d = \sqrt{(x_2 - x_1)^2 + (y_2 - y_1)^2}$$

A problem might require determining the x-coordinate of one point (x_2), given its y-coordinate (y_2) and the distance (d) between that point and another given point (x_1, y_1). To do so, the above formula for x_1 should be solved just as a radical equation containing numerical values in place of the other variables. Both sides should be squared; the quantity should be subtracted $(y_2 - y_1)^2$; the square root of both sides should be taken; x_1 should be subtracted to produce:

$$\sqrt{d^2 - (y_2 - y_1)^2} + x_1 = x_2$$

Problem-Solving and Data Analysis

Using Ratios, Rates, Proportions, and Scale Drawings to Solve Single- and Multistep Problems

Ratios, rates, proportions, and scale drawings are used when comparing two quantities. Questions on this material will include expressing relationships in simplest terms and solving for missing quantities.

Ratios

A ratio is a comparison of two quantities that represent separate groups. For example, if a recipe calls for 2 eggs for every 3 cups of milk, it can be expressed as a ratio. Ratios can be written three ways: (1) with the word "to"; (2) using a colon; or (3) as a fraction. For the previous example, the ratio of eggs to cups of milk can be written as: 2 to 3, 2:3, or $\frac{2}{3}$. When writing ratios, the order is important. The ratio of eggs to cups of milk is not the same as the ratio of cups of milk to eggs, 3:2.

In simplest form, both quantities of a ratio should be written as integers. These should also be reduced just as a fraction would be. For example, 5:10 would reduce to 1:2. Given a ratio where one or both quantities are expressed as a decimal or fraction, both should be multiplied by the same number to produce integers. To write the ratio $\frac{1}{3}$ to 2 in simplest form, both quantities should be multiplied by 3. The resulting ratio is 1 to 6.

When a problem involving ratios gives a comparison between two groups, then: (1) a total should be provided and a part should be requested; or (2) a part should be provided and a total should be requested. Consider the following:

> The ratio of boys to girls in the 11th grade is 5:4. If there is a total of 270 11th grade students, how many are girls?

To solve this, the total number of "ratio pieces" first needs to be determined. The total number of 11th grade students is divided into 9 pieces. The ratio of boys to total students is 5:9; and the ratio of girls to total students is 4:9. Knowing the total number of students, the number of girls can be determined by setting up a proportion: $\frac{4}{9} = \frac{x}{270}$. Solving the proportion, it shows that there are 120 11th grade girls.

Rates
A rate is a ratio comparing two quantities expressed in different units. A unit rate is one in which the second is one unit. Rates often include the word *per*. Examples include miles per hour, beats per minute, and price per pound. The word *per* can be represented with a / symbol or abbreviated with the letter "p" and the units abbreviated. For example, miles per hour would be written mi/h. Given a rate that is not in simplest form (second quantity is not one unit), both quantities should be divided by the value of the second quantity. Suppose a patient had 99 heartbeats in 1½ minutes. To determine the heart rate, 1½ should divide both quantities. The result is 66 bpm.

Scale Drawings
Scale drawings are used in designs to model the actual measurements of a real-world object. For example, the blueprint of a house might indicate that it is drawn at a scale of 3 inches to 8 feet. Given one value and asked to determine the width of the house, a proportion should be set up to solve the problem. Given the scale of 3in:8ft and a blueprint width of 1 ft (12 in.), to find the actual width of the building, the proportion $\frac{3}{8} = \frac{12}{x}$ should be used. This results in an actual width of 32 ft.

Proportions
A proportion is a statement consisting of two equal ratios. Proportions will typically give three of four quantities and require solving for the missing value. The key to solving proportions is to set them up properly. Here's a sample problem:

If 7 gallons of gas costs $14.70, how many gallons can you get for $20?

The information should be written as equal ratios with a variable representing the missing quantity

$$\left(\frac{\text{gallons}}{\text{cost}} = \frac{\text{gallons}}{\text{cost}}\right) : \frac{7 \text{ gallons}}{\$14.70} = \frac{x}{\$20}$$

To solve, cross multiply (multiply the numerator of the first ratio by the denominator of the second and vice versa) is used, and the products are set equal to each other. Cross-multiplying results in:

$$(7)(20) = (14.7)(x)$$

Solving the equation for x, it can be determined that 9.5 gallons of gas can be purchased for $20.

Indirect Proportions
The proportions described above are referred to as direct proportions or direct variation. For direct proportions, as one quantity increases, the other quantity also increases. For indirect proportions (also referred to as indirect variations, inverse proportions, or inverse variations), as one quantity increases,

the other decreases. Direct proportions can be written: $\frac{y_1}{x_1} = \frac{y_2}{x_2}$. Conversely, indirect proportions are written: $y_1x_1 = y_2x_2$. Here's a sample problem:

> It takes 3 carpenters 10 days to build the frame of a house. How long should it take 5 carpenters to build the same frame?

In this scenario, as one quantity increases (number of carpenters), the other decreases (number of days building); therefore, this is an inverse proportion. To solve, the products of the two variables (in this scenario, the total work performed) are set equal to each other ($y_1x_1 = y_2x_2$). Using y to represent carpenters and x to represent days, the resulting equation is: $(3)(10) = (5)(x_2)$. Solving for x_2, it is determined that it should take 5 carpenters 6 days to build the frame of the house.

Solving Single- and Multistep Problems Involving Percentages

The word percent means "per hundred." When dealing with percentages, it may be helpful to think of the number as a value in hundredths. For example, 15% can be expressed as "fifteen hundredths" and written as $\frac{15}{100}$ or .15.

Converting from Decimals and Fractions to Percentages

To convert a decimal to a percent, a number is multiplied by 100. To write .25 as a percent, the equation $0.25 x 100$ yields 25%. To convert a fraction to a percent, the fraction is converted to a decimal and then multiplied by 100. To convert $\frac{3}{5}$ to a decimal, the numerator (3) is divided by the denominator (5). This results in .6, which is then multiplied by 100 to get 60%.

To convert a percent to a decimal, the number is divided by 100. For example, 150% is equal to 1.5 $\left(\frac{150}{100}\right)$. To convert a percent to a fraction, the percent sign is deleted, and the value is written as the numerator with a denominator of 100. For example, $2\% = \frac{2}{100}$. Fractions should be reduced: $\frac{2}{100} = \frac{1}{50}$.

Percent Problems

Material on percentages can include questions such as: What is 15% of 25? What percent of 45 is 3? Five is $\frac{1}{2}$% of what number? To solve these problems, the information should be rewritten as an equation where the following helpful steps are completed: (1) "what" is represented by a variable (x); (2) "is" is represented by an = sign; and (3) "of" is represented by multiplication. Any values expressed as a percent should be written as a decimal; and if the question is asking for a percent, the answer should be converted accordingly. Here are three sample problems based on the information above:

What is 15% of 25?	What percent of 45 is 3?	Five is $\frac{1}{2}$% of what number?
$x = .15 \times 25$	$x \times 45 = 3$	$5 = .005 \times x$
$x = 3.75$	$x = 0.0\bar{6}$	$x = 1,000$
$x = 6.\bar{6}\%$		

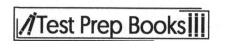

Percent Increase/Decrease

Problems dealing with percentages may involve an original value, a change in that value, and a percentage change. A problem will provide two pieces of information and ask to find the third. To do so, this formula is used:

$$\frac{change}{original\ value} \times 100 = percent\ change$$

Here's a sample problem:

> Attendance at a baseball stadium has dropped 16% from last year. Last year's average attendance was 40,000. What is this year's average attendance?

Using the formula and information, the change is unknown (x), the original value is 40,000, and the percent change is 16%. The formula can be written as:

$$\frac{x}{40,000} \times 100 = 16$$

When solving for x, it is determined the change was 6,400. The problem asked for this year's average attendance, so to calculate, the change (6,400) is subtracted from last year's attendance (40,000) to determine this year's average attendance is 33,600.

Percent More Than/Less Than

Percentage problems may give a value and what percent that given value is more than or less than an original unknown value. Here's a sample problem:

> A store advertises that all its merchandise has been reduced by 25%. The new price of a pair of shoes is $60. What was the original price?

This problem can be solved by writing a proportion. Two ratios should be written comparing the cost and the percent of the original cost. The new cost is 75% of the original cost (100% − 25%); and the original cost is 100% of the original cost. The unknown original cost can be represented by x. The proportion would be set up as: $\frac{60}{75} = \frac{x}{100}$. Solving the proportion, it is determined the original cost was $80.

Solving Single- and Multistep Problems Involving Measurement Quantities, Units, and Unit Conversion

Unit Rates

A rate is a ratio in which two terms are in different units. When rates are expressed as a quantity of one, they are considered unit rates. To determine a unit rate, the first quantity is divided by the second. Knowing a unit rate makes calculations easier than simply having a rate. Suppose someone bought a 3lb bag of onions for $1.77. To calculate the price of 5lbs of onions, a proportion could be set up as follows:

103

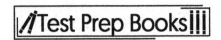
$\frac{3}{1.77} = \frac{5}{x}$. However, knowing the unit rate, multiplying the value of pounds of onions by the unit price is another way to find the solution: (The unit price would be calculated \$1.77/3lb = \$0.59/lb.)

$$5 \text{ lbs} \times \frac{\$0.59}{\text{lb}} = \$2.95$$

(The "lbs" units cancel out.)

Unit Conversion

Unit conversions apply to many real-world scenarios, including cooking, measurement, construction, and currency. Problems on this material can be solved similarly to those involving unit rates. Given the conversion rate, it can be written as a fraction (ratio) and multiplied by a quantity in one unit to convert it to the corresponding unit. For example, someone might want to know how many minutes are in 3½ hours. The conversion rate of 60 minutes to 1 hour can be written as $\frac{60 \text{ min}}{1 \text{ h}}$. Multiplying the quantity by the conversion rate results in:

$$3\frac{1}{2}\text{h} \times \frac{60 \text{ min}}{1 \text{ h}} = 210 \text{ min}$$

The "h" unit is canceled. To convert a quantity in minutes to hours, the fraction for the conversion rate would be flipped (to cancel the "min" unit). To convert 195 minutes to hours, the equation $195 \text{ min} \times \frac{1 \text{ h}}{60 \text{ min}}$ would be used. The result is $\frac{195 \text{ h}}{60}$, which reduces to $3\frac{1}{4}$ hours.

Converting units may require more than one multiplication. The key is to set up the conversion rates so that units cancel out each other and the desired unit is left. Suppose someone wants to convert 3.25 yards to inches, given that 1 yd = 3 ft and 12 in = 1 ft. To calculate, the equation $3.25 \text{ yd} \times \frac{3 \text{ ft}}{1 \text{ yd}} \times \frac{12 \text{ in}}{1 \text{ ft}}$ would be used. The "yd" and "ft" units will cancel, resulting in 117 inches.

Given a Scatterplot, Using Linear, Quadratic, or Exponential Models to Describe How Variables are Related

Scatterplots can be used to determine whether a correlation exists between two variables. The horizontal (x) axis represents the independent variable and the vertical (y) axis represents the dependent variable. If when graphed, the points model a linear, quadratic, or exponential relationship, then a correlation is said to exist. If so, a line of best-fit or curve of best-fit can be drawn through the points, with the points relatively close on either side. Writing the equation for the line or curve allows for predicting values for the variables. Suppose a scatterplot displays the value of an investment as a function of years after investing. By writing an equation for the line or curve and substituting a value for one variable into the equation, the corresponding value for the other variable can be calculated.

Linear Models

If the points of a scatterplot model a linear relationship, a line of best-fit is drawn through the points. If the line of best-fit has a positive slope (y-values increase as x-values increase), then the variables have a positive correlation. If the line of best-fit has a negative slope (y-values decrease as x-values increase),

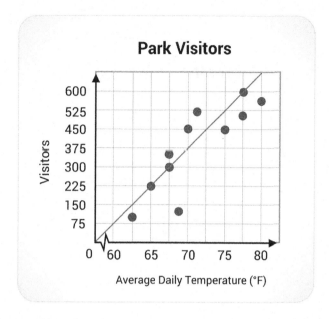
then a negative correlation exists. A positive or negative correlation can also be categorized as strong or weak, depending on how closely the points are grouped around the line of best-fit.

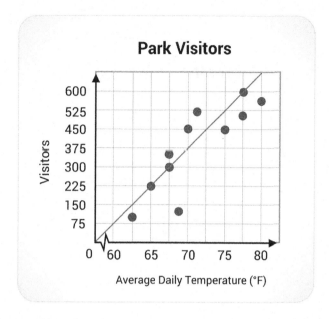

Given a line of best-fit, its equation can be written by identifying: the slope and y-intercept; a point and the slope; or two points on the line.

Quadratic Models

A quadratic function can be written in the form:

$$y = ax^2 + bx + c$$

The u-shaped graph of a quadratic function is called a parabola. The graph can either open up or open down (upside down u). The graph is symmetric about a vertical line, called the axis of symmetry. Corresponding points on the parabola are directly across from each other (same y-value) and are the same distance from the axis of symmetry (on either side). The axis of symmetry intersects the parabola at its vertex. The y-value of the vertex represents the minimum or maximum value of the function. If the graph opens up, the value of a in its equation is positive, and the vertex represents the minimum of the

function. If the graph opens down, the value of a in its equation is negative, and the vertex represents the maximum of the function.

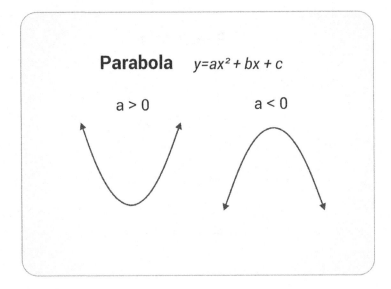

Given a curve of best-fit that models a quadratic relationship, the equation of the parabola can be written by identifying the vertex of the parabola and another point on the graph. The values for the vertex (h, k) and the point (x, y) should be substituted into the vertex form of a quadratic function, $y = a(x - h)^2 + k$, to determine the value of a. To write the equation of a quadratic function with a vertex of $(4, 7)$ and containing the point $(8, 3)$, the values for h, k, x, and y should be substituted into the vertex form of a quadratic function, resulting in:

$$3 = a(8 - 4)^2 + 7$$

Solving for a, yields $a = -\frac{1}{4}$. Therefore, the equation of the function can be written as:

$$y = -\frac{1}{4}(x - 4)^2 + 7$$

The vertex form can be manipulated in order to write the quadratic function in standard form.

Exponential Models

An exponential curve can be used as a curve of best-fit for a scatterplot. The general form for an exponential function is $y = ab^x$ where b must be a positive number and cannot equal 1. When the value of b is greater than 1, the function models exponential growth (as x increases, y increases). When the value of b is less than 1, the function models exponential decay (as x increases, y decreases). If a is positive, the graph consists of points above the x-axis; if a is negative, the graph consists of points below the x-axis. An asymptote is a line that a graph approaches.

Given a curve of best-fit modeling an exponential function, its equation can be written by identifying two points on the curve. To write the equation of an exponential function containing the ordered pairs $(2, 2)$ and $(3, 4)$, the ordered pair $(2, 2)$ should be substituted in the general form and solved for a:

$$2 = a \times b^2 \rightarrow a = \frac{2}{b^2}$$

The ordered pair $(3, 4)$ and $\frac{2}{b^2}$ should be substituted in the general form and solved for b:

$$4 = \frac{2}{b^2} \times b^3 \rightarrow b = 2$$

Then, 2 should be substituted for b in the equation for a and then solved for a:

$$a = \frac{2}{2^2} \rightarrow a = \frac{1}{2}$$

Knowing the values of a and b, the equation can be written as:

$$y = \frac{1}{2} \times 2^x$$

Exponential Curve

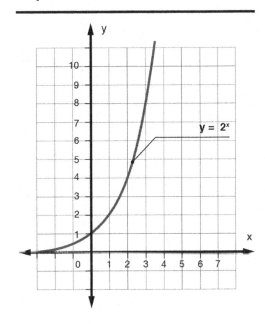

Using the Relationship Between Two Variables to Investigate Key Features of a Graph

Material on graphing relationships between two variables may include linear, quadratic, and exponential functions.

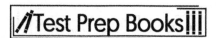
Graphing Quadratic Functions

The standard form of a quadratic function is:

$$y = ax^2 + bx + c$$

The graph of a quadratic function is a u-shaped (or upside down u) curve, called a parabola, which is symmetric about a vertical line (axis of symmetry). To graph a parabola, its vertex (high or low point for the curve) and at least two points on each side of the axis of symmetry need to be determined.

Given a quadratic function in standard form, the axis of symmetry for its graph is the line $x = -\frac{b}{2a}$. The vertex for the parabola has an x-coordinate of $-\frac{b}{2a}$. To find the y-coordinate for the vertex, the calculated x-coordinate needs to be substituted. To complete the graph, two different x-values need to be selected and substituted into the quadratic function to obtain the corresponding y-values. This will give two points on the parabola. These two points and the axis of symmetry are used to determine the two points corresponding to these. The corresponding points are the same distance from the axis of symmetry (on the other side) and contain the same y-coordinate. Plotting the vertex and four other points on the parabola allows for constructing the curve.

Quadratic Function

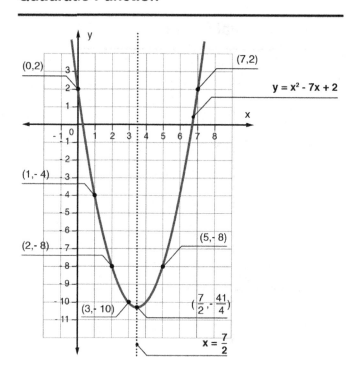

Graphing Exponential Functions

Exponential functions have a general form of $y = a \times b^x$. The graph of an exponential function is a curve that slopes upward or downward from left to right. The graph approaches a line, called an asymptote, as x or y increases or decreases. To graph the curve for an exponential function, x-values

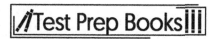

are selected and then substituted into the function to obtain the corresponding y-values. A general rule of thumb is to select three negative values, zero, and three positive values. Plotting the seven points on the graph for an exponential function should allow for constructing a smooth curve through them.

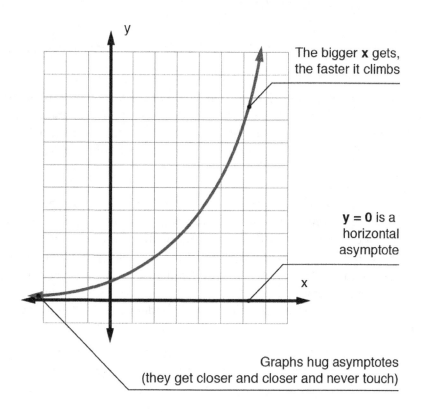

Comparing Linear Growth with Exponential Growth

Both linear and exponential equations can model a relationship of growth or decay between two variables. If the dependent variable (y) increases as the independent variable (x) increases, the relationship is referred to as growth. If y decreases as x increases, the relationship is referred to as decay.

Linear Growth and Decay

A linear function can be written in the form $y = mx + b$, where x represents the inputs, y represents the outputs, b represents the y-intercept for the graph, and m represents the slope of the line. The y-intercept is the value of y when $x = 0$ and can be thought of as the "starting point." The slope is the rate of change between the variables x and y. A positive slope represents growth, and a negative slope represents decay. Given a table of values for inputs (x) and outputs (y), a linear function would model the relationship if: x and y change at a constant rate per unit interval—for every two inputs a given

109

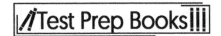

distance apart, the distance between their corresponding outputs is constant. Here are some sample ordered pairs:

x	0	1	2	3
y	-7	-4	-1	2

For every 1 unit increase in x, y increases by 3 units. Therefore, the change is constant and thus represents linear growth.

Given a scenario involving growth or decay, determining if there is a constant rate of change between inputs (x) and outputs (y) will identify if a linear model is appropriate. A scenario involving distance and time might state that someone is traveling at a rate of 45 miles per hour. For every hour traveled (input), the distance traveled (output) increases by 45 miles. This is a constant rate of change.

Exponential Growth and Decay

An exponential function can be written in the form $y = a \times b^x$, where x represents the inputs, y represents the outputs, a represents the y-intercept for the graph, and b represents the growth rate. The y-intercept is the value of y when $x = 0$ and can be thought of as the "starting point." If b is greater than 1, the function describes exponential growth; and if b is less than 1, the function describes exponential decay. Given a table of values for inputs (x) and outputs (y), an exponential function would model the relationship if the variables change by a common ratio over given intervals—for every two inputs a given distance apart, the quotients of their corresponding outputs is constant. Here are some sample ordered pairs:

x	0	1	2	3
y	3	6	12	24

For every 1 unit increase in x, the quotient of the corresponding y-values equals 2 (e.g., $\frac{6}{3}, \frac{12}{6}, \frac{24}{12}$). Therefore, the table represents exponential growth.

Given a scenario describing an exponential function, the growth or decay is expressed using multiplication. Words such as "doubling" and "halving" will often be used. A problem might indicate that the value of an investment triples every year or that every decade the population of an insect is halved. These indicate exponential growth and decay.

Using Two-Way Tables to Summarize Categorical Data and Relative Frequencies, and Calculate Conditional Probability

Categorical data consists of numerical values found by dividing the entire set into subsets based on variables that represent categories. An example would be the survey results of high school seniors, specifying gender and asking whether they consume alcohol. The data can be arranged in a two-way frequency table (also called a contingency table).

Two-Way Frequency/Contingency Tables

A contingency table presents the frequency tables of both variables simultaneously, as shown below. The levels of one variable constitute the rows of the table, and the levels of the other constitute the columns. The margins consist of the sum of cell frequencies for each row and each column (marginal

110

frequencies). The lower right corner value is the sum of marginal frequencies for the rows or the sum of the marginal frequencies for the columns. Both are equal to the total sample size.

	Drink Alcohol	Do Not Drink Alcohol	Total
Male	63	51	114
Female	37	68	105
Total	100	119	219

Conditional Frequencies

To calculate a conditional relative frequency, the cell frequency is divided by the marginal frequency for the desired outcome given the conditional category. For instance, using the table to determine the relative frequency that a female drinks, the number of females who drink (desired outcome) is divided by the total number of females (conditional category). The conditional relative frequency would equal $\frac{37}{105}$, which equals .35. If a problem asks for a conditional probability, the answer would be expressed as a fraction in simplest form. If asked for a percent, multiply the decimal by 100.

Association of Variables

An association between the variables exists if the conditional relative frequencies are different depending on condition. If the conditional relative frequencies are close to equal, then the variables are independent. For our example, 55% of senior males and 35% of senior females drink alcohol. The difference between frequencies across conditions (male or female) is enough to conclude that an association exists between the variables.

Making Inferences about Population Parameters Based on Sample Data

Statistical inference, based in probability theory, makes calculated assumptions about an entire population based on data from a sample set from that population.

Population Parameters

A population is the entire set of people or things of interest. Suppose a study is intended to determine the number of hours of sleep per night for college females in the US. The population would consist of EVERY college female in the country. A sample is a subset of the population that may be used for the study. It would not be practical to survey every female college student, so a sample might consist of 100 students per school from 20 different colleges in the country. From the results of the survey, a sample statistic can be calculated. A sample statistic is a numerical characteristic of the sample data, including mean and variance. A sample statistic can be used to estimate a corresponding population parameter. A population parameter is a numerical characteristic of the entire population. Suppose the sample data had a mean (average) of 5.5. This sample statistic can be used as an estimate of the population parameter (average hours of sleep for every college female in the US).

Confidence Intervals

A population parameter is usually unknown and therefore is estimated using a sample statistic. This estimate may be highly accurate or relatively inaccurate based on errors in sampling. A confidence interval indicates a range of values likely to include the true population parameter. These are constructed at a given confidence level, such as 95%. This means that if the same population is sampled repeatedly, the true population parameter would occur within the interval for 95% of the samples.

Measurement Error

The accuracy of a population parameter based on a sample statistic may also be affected by measurement error, which is the difference between a quantity's true value and its measured value. Measurement error can be divided into random error and systematic error. An example of random error for the previous scenario would be a student reporting 8 hours of sleep when she actually sleeps 7 hours per night. Systematic errors are those attributed to the measurement system. Suppose the sleep survey gave response options of 2, 4, 6, 8, or 10 hours. This would lead to systematic measurement error.

Using Statistics to Investigate Measures of Center of Data and Analyzing Shape, Center, and Spread

Descriptive statistics are used to gain an understanding of properties of a data set. This entails examining the center, spread, and shape of the sample data.

Center

The center of the sample set can be represented by its mean, median, or mode. The mean is the average of the data set, calculated by adding the data values and dividing by the sample size. The median is the value of the data point in the middle when the sample is arranged in numerical order. If the sample has an even number of data points, the mean of the two middle values is the median. The mode is the value that appears most often in a data set. It is possible to have multiple modes (if different values repeat equally as often) or no mode (if no value repeats).

Spread

Methods for determining the spread of the sample include calculating the range and standard deviation for the data. The range is calculated by subtracting the lowest value from the highest value in the set. The standard deviation of the sample can be calculated using the formula:

$$\sigma = \sqrt{\frac{\sum(x - \bar{x})^2}{n - 1}}$$

where $\bar{x}$ = sample mean and n = sample size.

Shape

The shape of the sample when displayed as a histogram or frequency distribution plot helps to determine if the sample is normally distributed (bell-shaped curve), symmetrical, or has measures of skewness (lack of symmetry) or kurtosis. Kurtosis is a measure of whether the data are heavy-tailed (high number of outliers) or light-tailed (low number of outliers).

Evaluating Reports to Make Inferences, Justify Conclusions, and Determine Appropriateness of Data Collection Methods

The presentation of statistics can be manipulated to produce a desired outcome. Here's a statement to consider: "Four out of five dentists recommend our toothpaste." Who are the five dentists? This statement is very different from the statement: "Four out of every five dentists recommend our toothpaste." Whether intentional or unintentional, statistics can be misleading. Statistical reports should be examined to verify the validity and significance of the results. The context of the numerical

values allows for deciphering the meaning, intent, and significance of the survey or study. Questions on this material will require students to use critical thinking skills to justify or reject results and conclusions.

When analyzing a report, who conducted the study and their intent should be considered. Was it performed by a neutral party or by a person or group with a vested interest? A study on health risks of smoking performed by a health insurance company would have a much different intent than one performed by a cigarette company. The sampling method and the data collection method should be considered too. Was it a true random sample of the population or was one subgroup over- or underrepresented? If all 20 schools included in the study were state colleges, the results may be biased due to a lack of private school participants. Also, the measurement system used to obtain the data should be noted. Was the system accurate and precise or was it a flawed system? If possible responses were limited for the sleep study to 2, 4, 6, 8, or 10, it could be argued that the measurement system was flawed.

Every scenario involving statistical reports will be different. The key is to examine all aspects of the study before determining whether to accept or reject the results and corresponding conclusions.

Geometry

Volume Formulas

Volume is the capacity of a three-dimensional shape. Volume is useful in determining the space within a certain three-dimensional object. Volume can be calculated for a cube, rectangular prism, cylinder, pyramid, cone, and sphere. By knowing specific dimensions of the objects, the volume of the object is computed with these figures. The units for the volumes of solids can include cubic centimeters, cubic meters, cubic inches, and cubic feet.

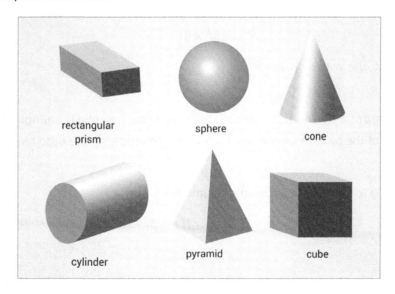

Cube
The cube is the simplest figure for which volume can be determined because all dimensions in a cube are equal. In the following example, the length, width, and height of the cube are all represented by the variable a because these measurements are equal lengths.

113

The volume of any rectangular, three-dimensional object is found by multiplying its length by its width by its height. In the case of a cube, the length, width, and height are all equal lengths, represented by the variable a. Therefore, the equation used to calculate the volume is $(a \times a \times a)$ or a^3. In a real-world example of this situation, if the length of a side of the cube is 3 centimeters, the volume is calculated by utilizing the formula:

$$(3 \times 3 \times 3) = 27 \text{ cm}^3$$

Rectangular Prism

The dimensions of a rectangular prism are not necessarily equal as those of a cube. Therefore, the formula for a rectangular prism recognizes that the dimensions vary and use different variables to represent these lengths. The length, width, and height of a rectangular prism can be represented with the variables a, b, and c.

The equation used to calculate volume is length times width times height. In a real-world application of this situation, if $a = 2$ cm, $b = 3$ cm, and $c = 4$ cm, the volume is calculated by utilizing the formula:

$$2 \times 3 \times 4 = 24 \text{ cm}^3$$

Cylinder

Discovering a cylinder's volume requires the measurement of the cylinder's base, length of the radius, and height. The height of the cylinder can be represented with variable h, and the radius can be represented with variable r.

The formula to find the volume of a cylinder is $\pi r^2 h$. Notice that πr^2 is the formula for the area of a circle. This is because the base of the cylinder is a circle. To calculate the volume of a cylinder, the slices of circles needed to build the entire height of the cylinder are added together. For example, if the radius is 5 feet and the height of the cylinder is 10 feet, the cylinder's volume is calculated by using the following equation:

$$\pi 5^2 \times 10$$

Substituting 3.14 for π, the volume is 785 ft³.

Pyramid

To calculate the volume of a pyramid, the area of the base of the pyramid is multiplied by the pyramid's height by $\frac{1}{3}$. The area of the base of the pyramid is found by multiplying the base length by the base width.

Therefore, the formula to calculate a pyramid's volume is:

$$(L \times W \times H) \div 3$$

Cone

The formula to calculate the volume of a circular cone is similar to the formula for the volume of a pyramid. The primary difference in determining the area of a cone is that a circle serves as the base of a cone. Therefore, the area of a circle is used for the cone's base.

The variable r represents the radius, and the variable h represents the height of the cone. The formula used to calculate the volume of a cone is:

$$\frac{1}{3}\pi r^2 h$$

Essentially, the area of the base of the cone is multiplied by the cone's height. In a real-life example where the radius of a cone is 2 meters and the height of a cone is 5 meters, the volume of the cone is calculated by utilizing the formula:

$$\frac{1}{3}\pi 2^2 \times 5 = 21$$

After substituting 3.14 for π, the volume is 21 m³.

Sphere

The volume of a sphere uses π due to its circular shape.

The length of the radius, r, is the only variable needed to determine the sphere's volume. The formula to calculate the volume of a sphere is $\frac{4}{3}\pi r^3$. Therefore, if the radius of a sphere is 8 centimeters, the volume of the sphere is calculated by utilizing the formula:

$$\frac{4}{3}\pi(8)^3 = 2{,}144 \text{ cm}^3$$

Right Triangles: Pythagorean Theorem and Trigonometric Ratio

The value of a missing side of a right triangle may be determined two ways. The first way is to apply the Pythagorean Theorem, and the second way is to apply Trigonometric Ratios. The Pythagorean Theorem states that for every right triangle, the square of the length of the hypotenuse is equal to the sum of the squares of the lengths of the remaining two sides. The hypotenuse is the longest side of a right triangle and is also the side opposite the right angle.

According to the diagram $a^2 + b^2 = c^2$ where c represents the hypotenuse, and a and b represent the lengths of the remaining two sides of the right triangle.

The Pythagorean Theorem may be applied a multitude of ways. For example, a person wishes to build a garden in the shape of a rectangle, having the dimensions of 5 feet by 8 feet. The garden's design

includes a diagonal board to separate various types of plants. The Pythagorean Theorem can be used to determine the length of the diagonal board.

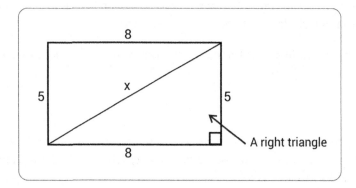

A right triangle

Given that side $a = 5$, side $b = 8$, and side c is unknown, use the following equation:

$$a^2 + b^2 = c^2$$

$$5^2 + 8^2 = c^2$$

$$25 + 64 = c^2$$

$$c = \sqrt{89}$$

$$c = 9.43$$

Degrees and Radians

Degrees are used to express the size of an angle. A complete circle is represented by 360°, and a half circle is represented by 180°. In addition, a right angle fills one quarter of a circle and is represented by 90°.

Radians are another way to denote angles in terms of π, rather than degrees. A complete circle is represented by 2π radians. The formula used to convert degrees to radians is:

$$Radians = \frac{degrees \times \pi}{180}$$

For example, to convert 270 degrees to radians:

$$Radians = \frac{270 \times \pi}{180} = 4.71$$

The *arc of a circle* is the distance between two points on the circle. The length of the arc of a circle in terms of *degrees* is easily determined if the value of the central angle is known. The length of the arc is simply the value of the central angle. In this example, the length of the arc of the circle in degrees is 75°.

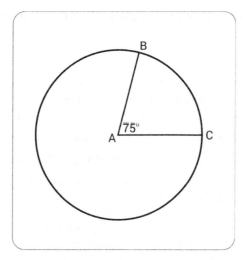

To determine the length of the arc of a circle in distance, the values for both the central angle and the radius must be known. This formula is:

$$\frac{central\ angle}{360°} = \frac{arc\ length}{2\pi r}$$

The equation is simplified by cross-multiplying to solve for the arc length.

In the following example, to solve for arc length, substitute the values of the central angle (75°) and the radius (10 inches) into the equation above.

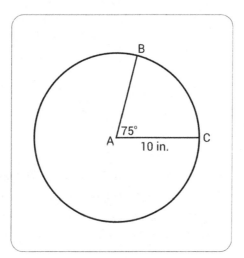

$$\frac{75°}{360°} = \frac{arc\ length}{2(3.14)(10in.)}$$

To solve the equation, first cross-multiply: $4710 = 360(arc\ length)$. Next, divide each side of the equation by 360. The result of the formula is that the arc length is 13.1 (rounded). Please note that arc length is often referred to as s.

As a special technological note for trigonometric functions, when finding the trigonometric function or an angle on the calculator, make a note using degrees or radians to get the correct value. Whether computing the sine of $\frac{\pi}{6}$ or computing the sine of 30°, the answer should come out to $\frac{1}{2}$. However, there is usually a "Mode" function on the calculator to select either radian or degree.

Circles

The equation used to find the area of a circle is $A = \pi r^2$. For example, if a circle has a radius of 5 centimeters, the area is computed by substituting 5 for the radius: $(5)^2$. Using this reasoning, to find half of the area of a circle, the formula is $A = 0.5\pi r^2$. Similarly, to find the quarter of an area of a circle, the formula is $A = 0.25\pi r^2$. To find any fractional area of a circle, a student can use the formula $A = \frac{C}{360}\pi r^2$, where C is the number of degrees of the central angle of the sector. The area of a circle can also be found by using the arc length rather than the degree of the sector. This formula is $A = rs^2$, where s is the arc length and r is the radius of the circle.

A chord is a line that connects two points on a circle's circumference. If the radius and the value of the angle subtended at the center by the chord is known, the formula to find the chord length is:

$$C = 2 \times radius \times \sin\frac{angle}{2}$$

Remember that this formula is based on half the length of the chord, so the radius is doubled to determine the full length of the chord.

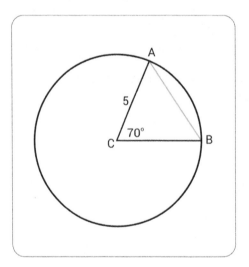

For example, the radius in the diagram above is 5 and the angle is 70 degrees. To find the chord length, plug in the values for the radius and angle to obtain the answer of 5.7.

$$5 \times \sin\frac{70}{2} = 2.87 \times 2 = 5.7$$

Chords that intersect each other at a point within a circle are related. The intersecting chord theorem states that when two chords intersect, each is cut into two portions or segments. The products of the two segments of each respective chord are equal to one another.

Other related concepts for circles include the diameter and circumference. *Circumference* is the distance around a circle. The formula for circumference is $C = 2\pi r$. The *diameter* of a circle is the distance across

118

a circle through its center point. The formula for circumference can also be thought of as $C = d\pi$ where d is the circle's diameter, since the diameter of a circle is $2r$.

Similarity, Congruence, and Triangles

Triangles are similar if they have the same shape, the same angle measurements, and their sides are proportional to one another. Triangles are congruent if the angles of the triangles are equal in measurement and the sides of the triangles are equal in measurement.

There are five ways to show that a triangle is congruent.

- SSS (Side-Side-Side Postulate): When all three corresponding sides are equal in length, then the two triangles are congruent.

- SAS (Side-Angle-Side Postulate): If a pair of corresponding sides and the angle in between those two sides are equal, then the two triangles are congruent.

- ASA (Angle-Side-Angle Postulate): If a pair of corresponding angles are equal and the side within those angles are equal, then the two triangles are equal.

- AAS (Angle-Angle-Side Postulate): When a pair of corresponding angles for two triangles and a non-included side are equal, then the two triangles are congruent.

- HL (Hypotenuse-Leg Theorem): If two right triangles have the same hypotenuse length, and one of the other sides are also the same length, then the two triangles are congruent.

If two triangles are discovered to be similar or congruent, this information can assist in determining unknown parts of triangles, such as missing angles and sides.

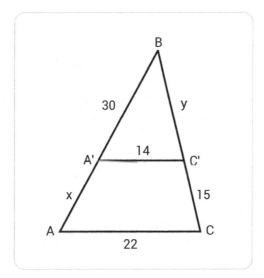

In the triangle shown above, AC and $A'C'$ are parallel lines. Therefore, BA is a transversal that intersects the two parallel lines. The corresponding angles $BA'C'$ and BAC are congruent. In a similar way, BC is also a transversal. Therefore, angle $BC'A'$ and BCA are congruent. If two triangles have two congruent angles, the triangles are similar. If the triangles are similar, their corresponding sides are proportional.

Therefore, the following equation is established:

$$\frac{30 + x}{30} = \frac{22}{14} = \frac{y + 15}{y}$$

$$\frac{30 + x}{30} = \frac{22}{14}$$

$$x = 17.1$$

$$\frac{22}{14} = \frac{y + 15}{y}$$

$$y = 26.25$$

The example below involves the question of congruent triangles. The first step is to examine whether the triangles are congruent. If the triangles are congruent, then the measure of a missing angle can be found.

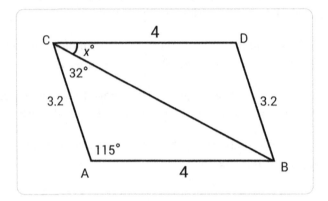

The above diagram provides values for angle measurements and side lengths in triangles CAB and CDB. Note that side CA is 3.2 and side DB is 3.2. Side CD is 4 and side AB is 4. Furthermore, line CB is congruent to itself by the reflexive property. Therefore, the two triangles are congruent by SSS (Side-Side-Side). Because the two triangles are congruent, all of the corresponding parts of the triangles are also congruent. Therefore, angle x is congruent to the inside of the angle for which a measurement is not provided in Triangle CAB. Thus:

$$115° + 32° = 147°$$

A triangle measures 180°, therefore:

$$180° - 147° = 33°$$

Angle $x = 33°$, because the two triangles are reversed.

Complementary Angle Theorem

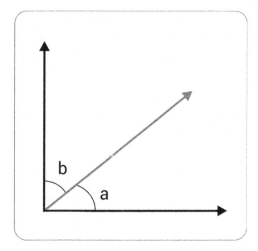

Two angles are complementary if the sum of the two angles equals 90°.

In the above diagram:

$$Angle\ a + Angle\ b = 90°$$

Therefore, the two angles are complementary. Certain trigonometric rules are also associated with complementary angles.

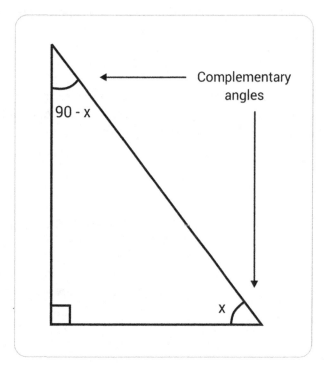

Complementary angles

121

Circles on the Coordinate Plane

If a circle is placed on the coordinate plane with the center of the circle at the origin $(0,0)$, then point (x, y) is a point on the circle. Furthermore, the line extending from the center to point (x, y) is the radius, or r. By applying the Pythagorean Theorem $(a^2 + b^2 = c^2)$ it can be stated that:

$$x^2 + y^2 = r^2$$

However, the center of the circle does not always need to be on the origin of the coordinate plane.

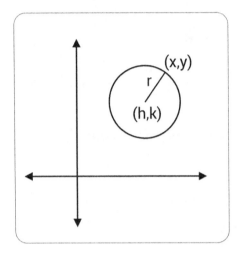

In the diagram above, the center of the circle is noted by (h, k). By applying the distance formula, the equation becomes:

$$r = \sqrt{(x - h)^2 + (y - k)^2}$$

When squaring both sides of the equation, the result is the standard form of a circle with the center (h, k) and radius r. Namely, $r^2 = (x - h)^2 + (y - k)^2$ where r equal radius and center equals (h, k). The following examples may be solved by using this information:

Example: Graph the equation:

$$-x^2 + y^2 = 25$$

To graph this equation, first note that the center of the circle is $(0, 0)$. The radius is the positive square root of 25 or 5.

Example: Find the equation for the circle below.

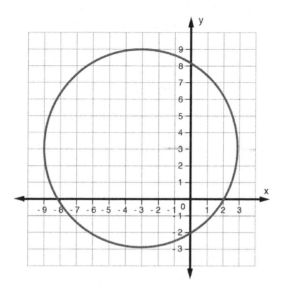

To find the equation for the circle, note that its center is not zero. Therefore, to find the circle's center, draw vertical and horizontal diameters to examine where they intersect. The center is located at point: $(-3, 3)$. Next, count the number of spaces from the center to the outside of the circle. This number is 6. Therefore, 6 is the radius. Finally, plug in the numbers that are known into the standard equation for a circle:

$$36 = \left(x - (-3)\right)^2 + (y - 3)^2$$

or

$$36 = (x + 3)^2 + (y - 3)^2$$

It is possible to determine whether a point lies on a circle or not within the coordinate plane. For example, a circle has a center of $(2, -5)$, and a radius of 6 centimeters. The first step is to apply the equation of a circle, which is $r^2 = (x - h)^2 + (y - k)^2$ where r equals radius and the center equals (h, k). Next, substitute the numbers for the center point and the number for the radius. This action simplifies the equation to:

$$36 = (x - 2)^2 + (y + 5)^2$$

Note that the radius of 6 was squared to get 36.

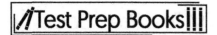

To prove that the point $(2, 1)$ lies on the circle, apply the equation of the circle that was just used and input the values of $(2, 1)$ for x and y in the equation.

$$36 = (x - 2)^2 + (y + 5)^2$$

$$36 = (2 - 2)^2 + (1 + 5)^2$$

$$36 = (0)^2 + (6)^2$$

$$36 = 36$$

Because the left side of the equation equals the right side of the equation, point $(2, 1)$ lies on the given circle.

Practice Quiz

1. Which of the following equations best represents the problem below?

> The width of a rectangle is 35 centimeters less than the length. If the perimeter of the rectangle is 112 centimeters, then what are the dimensions of the rectangle?

    a. $2l + 2(l - 35) = 122$
    b. $(l + 2) + (l + 2) + l = 124$
    c. $l \times (l - 2) = 122$
    d. $(l + 2)(l - 35) + l = 122$

2. Bernard can make $80 per day. If he needs to make $300 and only works full days, how many days will this take?

    4

3. Last year, the New York City area received approximately $27\frac{3}{4}$ inches of snow. The Denver area received approximately 3 times as much snow as New York City. How much snow fell in Denver?

    a. 60 inches

    b. $27\frac{1}{4}$ inches

    c. $9\frac{1}{4}$ inches

    d. $83\frac{1}{4}$ inches

4. A family purchases a vehicle in 2005 for $20,000. In 2010, they decide to sell it for a newer model. They are able to sell the car for $8,000. By what percentage did the value of the family's car drop?

    a. 40%
    b. 68%
    c. 60%
    d. 33%

5. A couple buys a house for $150,000. They sell it for $165,000. By what percentage did the house's value increase?

    a. 10%
    b. 13%
    c. 15%
    d. 17%

See answers on the next page.

Answer Explanations

A: The perimeter of a rectangle is $P = 2L + 2W$. We are told $P = 112$, so $2L + 2W = 112$. We are also told that the width is 35 cm less than the length: $W = L - 35$. Substituting this for W in the perimeter equation, we get $2L + 2(L - 35) = 112$, which is Choice A.

Although it's not necessary to answer the test question, we could solve the equation to find the length and width. The equation simplifies to $4L - 70 = 112$, or $4L = 182$, hence $L = 45.5$, and since $W = L - 35$, we find $W = 10.5$.

2. 4: The number of days can be found by taking the total amount Bernard needs to make and dividing it by the amount he earns per day:

$$\frac{300}{80} = \frac{30}{8} = \frac{15}{4} = 3.75$$

But Bernard is only working full days, so he will need to work 4 days since 3 days is not a sufficient amount of time.

3. D: To find Denver's total snowfall, 3 must be multiplied by $27\frac{3}{4}$. In order to easily do this, the mixed number should be converted into an improper fraction.

$$27\frac{3}{4} = \frac{27 \times 4 + 3}{4} = \frac{111}{4}$$

Therefore, Denver had approximately $\frac{3 \times 111}{4} = \frac{333}{4}$ inches of snow. The improper fraction can be converted back into a mixed number through division.

$$\frac{333}{4} = 83\frac{1}{4} \text{ inches}$$

4. C: To find the drop in value, subtract the new value from the old value. To see what percentage of the initial value this is, divide the drop in value by the initial value, then multiply by 100.

$$\frac{20,000 - 8,000}{20,000} = 0.6$$

$$(0.60) \times 100 = 60\%$$

5. A: The value went up by:

$$\$165,000 - \$150,000 = \$15,000$$

Out of \$150,000, this is $\frac{15,000}{150,000} = \frac{1}{10}$ or 0.1. To get the percentage, multiply 0.1 by 100 to get 10%.

Practice Test #1

Reading and Writing: Module 1

1. Which word, if any, is misspelled?

The director's <u>greatest acheivement</u> as the <u>leader</u> of organization may have been his <u>implementation</u> of environmental protection policies.

a. Greatest
b. Acheivement
c. Leader
d. Implementation

2. Which of the following would be the best choice for the following sentence?

<u>The Chicago City Council now are commemorating December 4th as Fred Hampton Day.</u>

a. NO CHANGE
b. Fred Hampton Day by the Chicago City Council, December 4, is now commemorated.
c. Now commemorated December 4th is Fred Hampton Day.
d. The Chicago City Council now commemorates December 4th as Fred Hampton Day.

3. Which is the best version of the underlined portion of the following sentence?

Education provides society with a vehicle for <u>raising it's children to be</u> civil, decent human beings with something valuable to contribute to the world.

a. NO CHANGE
b. raises its children to be
c. raising its' children to be
d. raising its children to be

The next question is based on the following passage:

Now when I had mastered the language of this water and had come to know every trifling feature that bordered the great river as familiarly as I knew the letters of the alphabet, I had made a valuable acquisition. But I had lost something, too. I had lost something which could never be restored to me while I lived. All the grace, the beauty, the poetry had gone out of the majestic river! I still keep in mind a certain wonderful sunset which I witnessed when steamboating was new to me. A broad expanse of the river was turned to blood; in the middle distance the red hue brightened into gold, through which a solitary log came floating, black and conspicuous; in one place a long, slanting mark lay sparkling upon the water; in another the surface was broken by boiling, tumbling rings, that were as many-tinted as an opal; where the ruddy flush was faintest, was a smooth spot that was covered with graceful circles and radiating lines, ever so delicately traced; the shore on our left was densely wooded, and the somber shadow that fell from this forest was broken in one place by a long, ruffled trail that shone like silver; and high above the forest wall a clean-stemmed dead tree waved a

127

single leafy bough that glowed like a flame in the unobstructed splendor that was flowing from the sun. There were graceful curves, reflected images, woody heights, soft distances; and over the whole scene, far and near, the dissolving lights drifted steadily, enriching it, every passing moment, with new marvels of coloring. I stood like one bewitched. I drank it in, in a speechless rapture.

Excerpt from "Two Ways of Seeing A River" by Mark Twain

4. What word best describes Twain's description of nature?
   a. Disdainful
   b. Reverential
   c. Disinterested
   d. Frightened

The next question is based on the following passage:

I went to the woods because I wished to live deliberately, to front only the essential facts of life, and see if I could not learn what it had to teach, and not, when I came to die, discover that I had not lived. I did not wish to live what was no life, living is so dear; nor did I wish to practice resignation, unless it was quite necessary. I wanted to live deep and suck out all the marrow of life, to live so sturdily and Spartan-like as to put to rout all that was not life, to cut a broad swath and shave close, to drive life into a corner, and reduce it to its lowest terms, and, if it proved to be mean, why then to get the whole and genuine meanness of it, and publish its meanness to the world; or if it were sublime, to know it by experience, and be able to give a true account of it in my next excursion.

Excerpt from Walden by Henry D. Thoreau

5. What is the author's main purpose?
   a. To reflect on his actions and how he believes life should be
   b. To criticize the reader for not simplifying their life
   c. To question how religion affects the everyday lives of men
   d. To persuade young readers to spend more time outdoors

The next question is based on the following passage:

Fellow-citizens, pardon me, allow me to ask, why am I called upon to speak here to-day? What have I, or those I represent, to do with your national independence? Are the great principles of political freedom and of natural justice, embodied in that Declaration of Independence, extended to us? And am I, therefore, called upon to bring our humble offering to the national altar, and to confess the benefits and express devout gratitude for the blessings resulting from your independence to us?

Excerpt from the speech "What to the Slave is the Fourth of July?" by Frederick Douglass, 1852

6. What is the tone of this passage?
   a. Incredulous
   b. Inclusive
   c. Contemplative
   d. Nonchalant

The next question is based on the following passage:

Four score and seven years ago our fathers brought forth on this continent, a new nation, conceived in liberty, and dedicated to the proposition that all men are created equal.

Now we are engaged in a great civil war, testing whether that nation, or any nation so conceived and so dedicated, can long endure. We are met on a great battlefield of that war. We have come to dedicate a portion of that field, as a final resting place for those who here gave their lives that that nation might live. It is altogether fitting and proper that we should do this.

Excerpt from the Gettysburg Address by Abraham Lincoln, delivered at the dedication of the cemetery at Gettysburg, 1863

7. The best description for the phrase *four score and seven years ago* is which of the following?
   a. A unit of measurement
   b. A period of time
   c. A literary movement
   d. A statement of political reform

The next question is based on the following passage:

My Good Friends,—When I first imparted to the committee of the projected Institute my particular wish that on one of the evenings of my readings here the main body of my audience should be composed of working men and their families, I was animated by two desires; first, by the wish to have the great pleasure of meeting you face to face at this Christmas time, and accompany you myself through one of my little Christmas books; and second, by the wish to have an opportunity of stating publicly in your presence, and in the presence of the committee, my earnest hope that the Institute will, from the beginning, recognize one great principle—strong in reason and justice—which I believe to be essential to the very life of such an Institution. It is, that the working man shall,

from the first unto the last, have a share in the management of an Institution which is designed for his benefit, and which calls itself by his name.

Excerpt from Charles Dickens' speech in Birmingham in 1853 on behalf of the Birmingham and Midland Institute

8. The speaker addresses his audience as "My Good Friends." What function does this salutation serve for the speaker?
   a. The speaker is an employer addressing his employees, so the salutation is a way for the boss to bridge the gap between himself and his employees.
   b. The speaker's salutation is one from an entertainer to his audience and uses the friendly language to connect to his audience before a serious speech.
   c. The salutation gives the serious speech that follows a somber tone, as it is used ironically.
   d. The speech is one from a politician to the public, so the salutation is used to grab the audience's attention.

The next question is based on the following passage:

Three years ago, I think there were not many bird-lovers in the United States who believed it possible to prevent the total extinction of both egrets from our fauna. All the known rookeries accessible to plume-hunters had been totally destroyed. Two years ago, the secret discovery of several small, hidden colonies prompted William Dutcher, President of the National Association of Audubon Societies, and Mr. T. Gilbert Pearson, Secretary, to attempt the protection of those colonies. With a fund contributed for the purpose, wardens were hired and duly commissioned. As previously stated, one of those wardens was shot dead in cold blood by a plume hunter. The task of guarding swamp rookeries from the attacks of money-hungry desperadoes, to whom the accursed plumes were worth their weight in gold, is a very chancy proceeding. There is now one warden in Florida who says that "before they get my rookery they will first have to get me."

Excerpt from *Our Vanishing Wild Life: It's Extermination and Preservation* by William T. Hornaday

9. What purpose does the quote serve at the end of the first paragraph?
   a. The quote shows proof of a hunter threatening one of the wardens.
   b. The quote lightens the mood by illustrating the colloquial language of the region.
   c. The quote provides an example of a warden protecting one of the colonies.
   d. The quote provides much needed comic relief in the form of a joke.

The next question is based on the following passage:

Insects as a whole are preeminently creatures of the land and the air. This is shown not only by the possession of wings by a vast majority of the class, but by the mode of breathing to which reference has already been made, a system of branching air-tubes carrying atmospheric air with its combustion-supporting oxygen to all the insect's tissues. The air gains access to these tubes through a number of paired air-holes or spiracles, arranged segmentally in series.

It is of great interest to find that, nevertheless, a number of insects spend much of their time under water. This is true of not a few in the perfect winged state, as for example

130

aquatic beetles and water-bugs ('boatmen' and 'scorpions') which have some way of protecting their spiracles when submerged, and, possessing usually the power of flight, can pass on occasion from pond or stream to upper air. But it is advisable in connection with our present subject to dwell especially on some insects that remain continually under water till they are ready to undergo their final moult and attain the winged state, which they pass entirely in the air. The preparatory instars of such insects are aquatic; the adult instar is aerial. All may-flies, dragon-flies, and caddis-flies, many beetles and two-winged flies, and a few moths thus divide their life-story between the water and the air. For the present we confine attention to the Stone-flies, the May-flies, and the Dragon-flies, three well-known orders of insects respectively called by systematists the Plecoptera, the Ephemeroptera, and the Odonata.

In the case of many insects that have aquatic larvae, the latter are provided with some arrangement for enabling them to reach atmospheric air through the surface-film of the water. But the larva of a stone-fly, a dragon-fly, or a may-fly is adapted more completely than these for aquatic life; it can, by means of gills of some kind, breathe the air dissolved in water.

Excerpt from The Life-Story of Insects, by Geo H. Carpenter

10. Which statement best details the central idea in this passage?
   a. It introduces certain insects that transition from water to air.
   b. It delves into entomology, especially where gills are concerned.
   c. It defines what constitutes insects' breathing.
   d. It invites readers to have a hand in the preservation of insects.

The next question is based on the following passage:

I have to admit that when my father bought a recreational vehicle (RV), I thought he was making a huge mistake. I didn't really know anything about RVs, but I knew that my dad was as big a "city slicker" as there was. <u>In fact, I even thought he might have gone a little bit crazy.</u> On trips to the beach, he preferred to swim at the pool, and whenever he went hiking, he avoided touching any plants for fear that they might be poison ivy. Why would this man, with an almost irrational fear of the outdoors, want a 40-foot camping behemoth?

11. Which of the following would be the best choice for the underlined sentence?
   a. Leave it where it is now.
   b. Move the sentence so that it comes before the preceding sentence.
   c. Move the sentence to the end of the first paragraph.
   d. Omit the sentence.

12. Which is the best version of the underlined portion of the following sentence?

If teachers set high expectations for <u>there students</u>, the students will rise to that high level.

   a. NO CHANGE
   b. they're students
   c. their students
   d. thare students

131

The next question is based on the following passage:

One of George Washington Carver's most notable contributions to the newly emerging class of Black farmers was to teach them the negative effects of agricultural monoculture, such as <u>growing the same crops in the same fields year after year, depleting the soil of much needed nutrients and results in a lesser yielding crop.</u>

13. Which of the following would be the best choice for the underlined sentence?
   a. NO CHANGE
   b. growing the same crops in the same fields year after year, depleting the soil of much needed nutrients and resulting in a lesser yielding crop.
   c. growing the same crops in the same fields year after year, depletes the soil of much needed nutrients and results in a lesser yielding crop.
   d. grows the same crops in the same fields year after year, depletes the soil of much needed nutrients and results in a lesser yielding crop.

The next question is based on the following passage:

This American government—what is it but a tradition, though a recent one, endeavoring to transmit itself unimpaired to posterity, but each instant losing some of its integrity? It has not the vitality and force of a single living man; for a single man can bend it to his will. It is a sort of wooden gun to the people themselves.

Excerpt from *Civil Disobedience* by Henry David Thoreau

14. Which choice best summarizes the passage?
   a. The government may be instituted to ensure the protections of freedoms, but this is weakened by the fact that it is easily manipulated by individuals.
   b. Unlike an individual, government is uncaring.
   c. Unlike an individual, government has no will, making it more prone to be used as a weapon against the people.
   d. American government is modeled after other traditions but actually has greater potential to be used to control people.

The next question is based on the following passage:

Assault is an unlawful and intentional act that causes reasonable apprehension in another individual, either by an imminent threat or by initiating offensive contact. Assaults can vary, encompassing physical strikes, threatening body language, and even provocative language. In the case of the latter, even if a hand has not been laid, it is still considered an assault because of its threatening nature.

Let's look at an example: A homeowner is angered because his neighbor blows fallen leaves into his freshly mowed lawn. Irate, the homeowner gestures a fist to his neighbor and threatens to bash his head in for littering on his lawn. The homeowner's physical motions and verbal threats herald a physical threat against the other neighbor. These factors classify the homeowner's reaction as an assault. If the angry neighbor hits the threatening homeowner in retaliation, that would constitute an assault as well because he physically hit the homeowner.

132

Assault also centers on the involvement of weapons in a conflict. If someone fired a gun at another person, it could be interpreted as an assault unless the shooter acted in self-defense. If an individual drew a gun or a knife on someone with the intent to harm them, that would be considered assault. However, it's also considered an assault if someone simply aims a weapon, loaded or not, at another person in a threatening manner.

15. What is the purpose of the passage?
   a. To inform the reader about what assault is and how it is committed
   b. To inform the reader about how assault is a minor example of lethal force
   c. To convince the reader to agree with their point of view
   d. To recount an incident in which the author was assaulted

16. Which of the following would be the best choice for the sentence below?

   <u>For example, Bloodhounds</u> have broad snouts and droopy ears that fall to the ground when they smell.

   a. NO CHANGE
   b. For example, Bloodhounds,
   c. For example Bloodhounds
   d. For example, bloodhounds

The next question is based on the following passage:

   I'm not alone when I say that it's hard to pay attention sometimes. I can't count how many times I've sat in a classroom, lecture, speech, or workshop and been bored to tears. <u>Usually I turn to doodling in order to keep awake.</u> This never really helps; I'm not much of an artist. Therefore, after giving up on drawing a masterpiece, I would just concentrate on keeping my eyes open and trying to be attentive. This didn't always work because I wasn't engaged in what was going on.

17. Which of the following would be the best choice for the underlined sentence?
   a. NO CHANGE
   b. Usually, I turn to doodling in order to keep awake.
   c. Usually, I turn to doodling, in order, to keep awake.
   d. Usually, I turned to doodling in order to keep awakened.

18. Which of the following would be the best choice for the sentence below?

   Discussions that make people think about educational content and <u>how it applies to there lives world and future are key.</u>

   a. NO CHANGE
   b. how it applies to their lives, world, and future are key.
   c. how it applied to there lives world and future are key.
   d. how it applies to their lives, world, and future, are key.

133

The next question is based on the following graph:

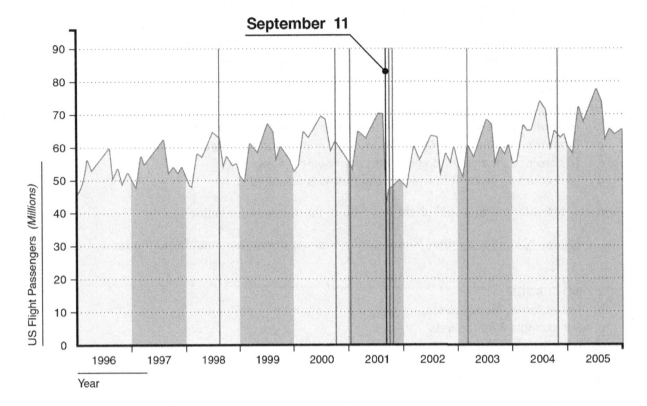

19. What statement is best supported by the graph above?
    a. As canceled flights were rescheduled, air travel became backed up and chaotic for quite some time.
    b. Over five hundred flights had to turn back or be redirected to other countries.
    c. Canada alone received 226 flights and thousands of stranded passengers.
    d. In the first few months following the attacks, there was a significant decrease in passengers boarding flights.

20. Which of the following would be the best choice for the underlined sentence below?

    Looking deeper into the myth of Prometheus sheds light not only on the character of Frankenstein but also poses a psychological dilemma to the audience. Prometheus is the titan who gave fire to mankind. <u>However, more than just fire he gave people knowledge and power.</u>

    a. NO CHANGE
    b. However, more than just fire he gave people, knowledge, and power.
    c. However, more than just fire, he gave people knowledge and power.
    d. In addition to fire, Prometheus gave people knowledge and power.

21. Which choice most effectively combines these two sentences?

> The dishwasher was invented by a woman named Josephine Cochrane in 1886. She is credited with greatly improving kitchen efficiency for homes, restaurants, and hotels.

    a. The dishwasher was invented in 1886 by a woman named Josephine Cochrane, who is credited with greatly improving kitchen efficiency for homes, restaurants, and hotels.
    b. The dishwasher was invented in 1886 by a woman named Josephine Cochrane, which led to her receiving the credit for greatly improving kitchen efficiency for homes, restaurants, and hotels.
    c. Hotels, restaurants, and homes all saw great improvements to their kitchens' efficiency in 1886 due to the invention of the dishwasher by a woman named Josephine Cochrane.
    d. Josephine Cochrane was a woman who is credited with inventing the dishwasher in 1886 and improving the kitchen efficiency in homes, restaurants, and hotels.

The next question is based on the following passage:

> Railroads revolutionized the transportation of goods and people in the 19th century. The 19th century was the time of change known as the Industrial Revolution. As a part of the Industrial Revolution, the railroad paved the way for new opportunities with the connection of the two coasts of the United States. It also changed the economy to an extreme degree.

22. Which revision improves the conciseness of the text?
    a. NO CHANGE
    b. The Industrial Revolution, which took place in the 19th century, connected the two sides of the United States through the invention of the railroad. This brought new opportunities such as the long-range transportation of goods and people. It also changed the economy greatly.
    c. The Industrial Revolution of the 19th century connected the United States from coast to coast and provided the nation with new opportunities. It revolutionized the transportation of goods and people as well as caused major change within the economy.
    d. The 19th-century Industrial Revolution was a time of great change in the country. It brought about the widespread use of the railroad. Railroads spanned from both coasts of the nation and created new opportunities for everyone with the transportation of goods and people. This heavily affected the economy as well.

The next question is based on the following passages:

> Text 1: The hikers on the expedition were told to observe the northern lights. Bright green light undulated across the sky and captivated the audience. The Native American tour guide told the story of how the northern lights were torches being carried by spirits. These spirits were lighting the way for souls that had recently passed on and needed guidance to the next life. Surviving relatives would appreciate the lights and speak to their loved ones as they traveled across the sky.

> Text 2: The Sámi, the indigenous Finno-Ugric people of northern Scandinavia, watched as the green, red, and purple northern lights flickered across the night sky. Immediately, they hurried

135

back to their tents without saying a word. The lights were a sign of the dead, and if the lights saw you, they would either steal you away or behead you!

23. Based on the texts, what can be assumed about these two cultures?
   a. The Native Americans and Sámi both look forward to the Northern Lights as an opportunity to connect with their loved ones.
   b. The Native Americans and Sámi people both believe in some form of afterlife and spirits.
   c. The two cultures have different views of the lights because they are different colors depending on the location.
   d. No assumptions can be made based on the information presented in these texts.

The next question is based on the following passage:

It is imperative that scholars of the prestigious university meticulously <u>stick to</u> the grammatical conventions of the English language.

24. Which choice best maintains the tone of the text?
   a. NO CHANGE
   b. obey
   c. agree with
   d. adhere to

The next question is based on the following passage:

Hank is a professional writer. He submits regular columns at two blogs and self-publishes romance novels. Hank recently signed with an agent based in New York. To date, Hank has never made any money off his writing.

25. The strength of the argument depends on which of the following?
   a. Hank's agent works at the biggest firm in New York.
   b. Being a professional writer requires representation by an agent.
   c. Hank's self-published novels and blogs have received generally positive reviews.
   d. Being a professional writer does not require earning money.

The next question is based on the following passage:

We were sure that ours was a nation of the ballot, not the bullet, until the murders of John Kennedy and Robert Kennedy and Martin Luther King, Jr. We were taught that our armies were always invincible and our causes were always just, only to suffer the agony of Vietnam. We respected the Presidency as a place of honor until the shock of Watergate.

We remember when the phrase "sound as a dollar" was an expression of absolute dependability, until ten years of inflation began to shrink our dollar and our savings. We believed that our Nation's resources were limitless until 1973, when we had to face a growing dependence on foreign oil.

Excerpt from "The Crisis of Confidence" by Jimmy Carter

26. What is the purpose of the paragraphs above?
    a. To point out that previous presidents have made mistakes
    b. To provide examples of why people are losing respect for government and other institutions
    c. To prove that our past is full of tragedy and our future is full of hope
    d. To suggest Americans' expectations are too high

27. Which of the following would be the best choice for the sentence below?

    Education should never discriminate on any basis, and it should create individuals who are self-sufficient, patriotic, and tolerant of <u>others' ideas</u>.

    a. NO CHANGE
    b. other's ideas
    c. others ideas
    d. others's ideas

Reading and Writing: Module 2

1. Which of the following would be the best version of the underlined portion of the sentence below?

    <u>As the leader of the BPP, Hampton organized rallies, taught political education classes, and established a free medical clinic.</u>

    a. NO CHANGE
    b. As the leader of the BPP, Hampton: organized rallies, taught political education classes, and established a free medical clinic.
    c. As the leader of the BPP, Hampton; organized rallies, taught political education classes, and established a free medical clinic.
    d. As the leader of the BPP, Hampton—organized rallies, taught political education classes, and established a medical free clinic.

The next question is based on the following passage:

> I have thought that an example of the intelligence (instinct?) of a class of fish which has come under my observation during my excursions into the Adirondack region of New York State might possibly be of interest to your readers, especially as I am not aware that anyone except myself has noticed it, or, at least, has given it publicity.
>
> The female sun-fish (called, I believe, in England, the roach or bream) makes a "hatchery" for her eggs in this wise. Selecting a spot near the banks of the numerous lakes in which this region abounds, and where the water is about 4 inches deep, and still, she builds, with her tail and snout, a circular embankment 3 inches in height and 2 thick. The circle, which is as perfect a one as could be formed with mathematical instruments, is usually a foot and a half in diameter; and at one side of this circular wall an opening is left by the fish of just sufficient width to admit her body.
>
> The mother sun-fish, having now built or provided her "hatchery," deposits her spawn within the circular enclosure, and mounts guard at the entrance until the fry are hatched out and are sufficiently large to take charge of themselves. As the embankment, moreover, is built up to the surface of the water, no enemy can very

137

easily obtain an entrance within the enclosure from the top; while there being only one entrance, the fish is able, with comparative ease, to keep out all intruders.

I have, as I say, noticed this beautiful instinct of the sun-fish for the perpetuity of her species more particularly in the lakes of this region; but doubtless the same habit is common to these fish in other waters.

Excerpt from The 'Hatchery' of the Sun-Fish by William L. Stone, Scientific American, #711

2. What is the purpose of this passage?
    a. To show the effects of fish hatcheries on the Adirondack region
    b. To persuade the audience to study ichthyology (fish science)
    c. To depict the sequence of mating among sun-fish
    d. To enlighten the audience on the habits of sun-fish and their hatcheries

3. The following sentence is an example of what literary device?

    At sunset, a broad expanse of the river was turned to blood; in the middle distance the red hue brightened into gold.

    a. Simile
    b. Allusion
    c. Oxymoron
    d. Metaphor

The next question is based on the following passage:

    Traveling in a recreational vehicle together as a family allowed us to share adventures while traveling across America, which we could not have experienced in cars and hotels. Memories like enjoying a campfire on a chilly summer evening with the mountains of Glacier National Park in the background or waking up early in the morning to see the sun rising over the distant spires of Arches National Park will always stay with us. Those are also memories that my siblings and me have now shared with our own children.

4. Which is the best version of the underlined portion of this sentence?

    Those are also memories that my siblings and me have now shared with our own children.

    a. NO CHANGE
    b. Those are also memories that me and my siblings
    c. Those are also memories that my siblings and I
    d. Those are also memories that I and my siblings

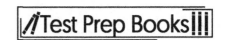

5. Which of the following words is misspelled?

> Some may <u>consider</u> compassion to be what makes us human and what <u>distinguishes us as</u> <u>civelized creatures</u>.

- a. Consider
- b. Distinguishes
- c. Civelized
- d. Creatures

6. Which is the best version of the underlined portion of the following sentence?

> Everyone has to <u>read between the lines, identify bias, and determine</u> who they can trust in the milieu of ads, data, and texts presented to them.

- a. NO CHANGE
- b. read between the lines, identify bias, and determining
- c. read between the lines, identifying bias, and determining
- d. reads between the lines, identifies bias, and determines

The next question is based on the following passage:

> As long ago as 1860 it was the proper thing to be born at home. At present, so I am told, the high gods of medicine have decreed that the first cries of the young shall be uttered upon the anesthetic air of a hospital, preferably a fashionable one. So young Mr. and Mrs. Roger Button were fifty years ahead of style when they decided, one day in the summer of 1860, that their first baby should be born in a hospital. Whether this anachronism had any bearing upon the astonishing history I am about to set down will never be known.
>
> ...
>
> On the September morning consecrated to the enormous event he arose nervously at six o'clock, dressed himself, adjusted an impeccable stock, and hurried forth through the streets of Baltimore to the hospital, to determine whether the darkness of the night had borne in new life upon its bosom.

> Excerpt from *The Curious Case of Benjamin Button* by F.S. Fitzgerald, 1922

7. According to the passage, what major event is about to happen in this story?
- a. Mr. Button is about to go to a funeral.
- b. Mr. Button's wife is about to have a baby.
- c. Mr. Button is getting ready to go to the doctor's office.
- d. Mr. Button is about to go shopping for new clothes.

The next question is based on the following passage:

> Knowing that Mrs. Mallard was afflicted with heart trouble, great care was taken to break to her as gently as possible the news of her husband's death.

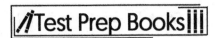

It was her sister Josephine who told her, in broken sentences; veiled hints that revealed in half concealing. Her husband's friend Richards was there, too, near her. It was he who had been in the newspaper office when intelligence of the railroad disaster was received, with Brently Mallard's name leading the list of "killed." He had only taken the time to assure himself of its truth by a second telegram, and had hastened to forestall any less careful, less tender friend in bearing the sad message.

She did not hear the story as many women have heard the same, with a paralyzed inability to accept its significance. She wept at once, with sudden, wild abandonment, in her sister's arms. When the storm of grief had spent itself she went away to her room alone. She would have no one follow her.

Excerpt from "The Story of an Hour" by Kate Chopin

8. What point of view is the above passage told in?
   a. First person
   b. Second person
   c. Third person omniscient
   d. Third person limited

9. What is the best meaning of the underlined word below?

   Upon hearing the horrible news, he wailed and fell heavily into a chair; his chest rose and fell <u>tumultuously</u>.

   a. Orderly
   b. Unashamedly
   c. Violently
   d. Calmly

The next question is based on the following passage:

I heartily accept the motto, "That government is best which governs least"; and I should like to see it acted up to more rapidly and systematically. Carried out, it finally amounts to this, which also I believe—"That government is best which governs not at all"; and when men are prepared for it, that will be the kind of government which they will have. Government is at best but an <u>expedient</u>; but most governments are usually, and all governments are sometimes, inexpedient. The objections which have been brought against a standing army, and they are many and weighty, and deserve to prevail, may also at last be brought against a standing government. The standing army is only an arm of the standing government. The government itself, which is only the mode which the people have chosen to execute their will, is equally liable to be abused and perverted before the people can act through it. Witness the present Mexican war, the work of comparatively a few individuals using the standing government as their tool; for, in the outset, the people would not have consented to this measure.

Excerpt from *Civil Disobedience* by Henry David Thoreau

10. Which phrase best encapsulates Thoreau's use of the term *expedient* in passage?
    a. A dead end
    b. A state of order
    c. A means to an end
    d. Rushed construction

The next question is based on the following passage:

Lethal force, or deadly force, is defined as the physical means to cause death or serious harm to another individual. The law holds that lethal force is only acceptable when you or another person are in immediate and unavoidable danger of death or severe bodily harm. For example, a person could be beating someone in such a way that the victim is suffering severe trauma that could result in death or serious harm. This would be an instance where lethal force would be acceptable and possibly the only way to save the victim from irrevocable damage.

Another example of when to use lethal force would be when someone enters your home with a deadly weapon. The intruder's presence and possession of the weapon indicate malicious intent and the ability to inflict death or severe injury to you and your loved ones. Again, lethal force can be used in this situation. Lethal force can also be applied to prevent the harm of another individual. If a woman is being brutally assaulted and is unable to fend off an attacker, lethal force can be used to defend her as a last-ditch effort. If she is in immediate jeopardy of rape, harm, and/or death, lethal force could be the only response that could effectively deter the assailant.

The key to understanding the concept of lethal force is the term *last resort*. Deadly force cannot be taken back; it should be used only to prevent severe harm or death. The law does distinguish whether the means of one's self-defense is fully warranted, or if the individual goes out of control in the process. If you continually attack the assailant after they are rendered incapacitated, this would be causing unnecessary harm, and the law can bring charges against you. Likewise, if you kill an attacker unnecessarily after defending yourself, you can be charged with murder. This would move lethal force beyond necessary defense, making it no longer a last resort but rather a use of excessive force.

11. Which of the following, if true, would most seriously undermine the explanation proposed by the author in the third paragraph?
    a. An instance of lethal force in self-defense is not absolutely absolved from blame. The law considers the necessary use of force at the time it is committed.
    b. An individual who uses lethal force under necessary defense is in direct compliance of the law under most circumstances.
    c. Lethal force in self-defense should be forgiven in all cases for the peace of mind of the primary victim.
    d. The use of lethal force is only evaluated on the severity of the primary attack that warranted self-defense and not based on intent at all.

The next question is based on the following passage:

When researchers and engineers undertake a large-scale scientific project, they may end up making discoveries and developing technologies that have far wider uses than originally intended. This is especially true in NASA, one of the most influential and innovative scientific organizations in America. NASA *spinoff technology* refers to innovations originally developed for NASA space projects that are now used in a wide range of different commercial fields. Many consumers are unaware that products they are buying are based on NASA research! Spinoff technology proves that it is worthwhile to invest in science research because it could enrich people's lives in unexpected ways.

The first spinoff technology worth mentioning is baby food. In space, where astronauts have limited access to fresh food and fewer options about their daily meals, malnutrition is a serious concern. Consequently, NASA researchers were looking for ways to enhance the nutritional value of astronauts' food. Scientists found that a certain type of algae could be added to food, improving the food's neurological benefits. When experts in the commercial food industry learned of this algae's potential to boost brain health, they were quick to begin their own research. The nutritional substance from algae then was developed into a product called life's DHA, which can be found in over 90% of infant food sold in America.

12. What is the organizational structure of this article?
    a. A general definition followed by more specific examples
    b. A general opinion followed by supporting evidence
    c. An important moment in history followed by chronological details
    d. A popular misconception followed by counterevidence

The next question is based on the following passage:

Mineralogy is the science of minerals, which are the naturally occurring elements and compounds that make up the solid parts of the universe. Mineralogy is usually considered in terms of materials in the Earth, but meteorites provide samples of minerals from outside the Earth.

A mineral may be defined as a naturally occurring, homogeneous solid, inorganically formed, with a definite chemical composition and an ordered atomic arrangement. The qualification *naturally occurring* is essential because it is possible to reproduce most minerals in the laboratory. For example, evaporating a solution of sodium chloride produces crystal indistinguishable from those of the mineral halite, but such laboratory-produced crystals are not minerals.

Excerpt from "Mineralogy" in Encyclopedia International by Grolier

13. According to the text, an object or substance must meet all of the following criteria to be considered a mineral EXCEPT:
    a. It must be naturally occurring.
    b. It must be a homogeneous solid.
    c. It must be organically formed.
    d. It must have a definite chemical composition.

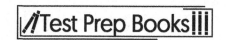

14. Which of the following would be the best choice for the sentence below?

While all dogs <u>descend through gray wolves</u>, it's easy to notice that dog breeds come in a variety of shapes and sizes.

   a. NO CHANGE
   b. descend by gray wolves
   c. descend from gray wolves
   d. descended through gray wolves

The next question is based on the following passage:

Vacationers looking for a perfect experience should opt out of Disney parks and try a trip on Disney Cruise Lines. While a park offers rides, characters, and show experiences, it also includes long lines, often very hot weather, and enormous crowds. A Disney Cruise, on the other hand, is a relaxing, luxurious vacation that includes many of the same experiences as the parks, minus the crowds and lines. The cruise has top-notch food, maid service, water slides, multiple pools, Broadway-quality shows, and daily character experiences for kids. There are also many activities, such as bingo, trivia contests, and dance parties that can entertain guests of all ages. The cruise even stops at Disney's private island for a beach barbecue with characters, waterslides, and water sports. Those looking for the Disney experience without the hassle should book a Disney cruise.

15. The main purpose of this passage is to do which of the following?
   a. Explain how to book a Disney cruise.
   b. Show what Disney parks have to offer.
   c. Show why Disney parks are expensive.
   d. Compare Disney parks to a Disney cruise.

16. Which of the following would be the best choice for the sentence below?

<u>Selective breeding which is also called artificial selection is the processes</u> in which animals with desired traits are bred in order to produce offspring that share the same traits.

   a. NO CHANGE
   b. Selective breeding, which is also called artificial selection is the process
   c. Selective breeding which is also called, artificial selection, is the process
   d. Selective breeding, which is also called artificial selection, is the process

17. Which of the following would be the best choice for the sentence below?

What I want to talk about today is that profound moment when curiosity is sparked <u>in another person drawing them to pay attention to what is before them</u> and expand their knowledge.

   a. NO CHANGE
   b. in another person, drawing them to pay attention
   c. in another person; drawing them to pay attention to what is before them
   d. in another person, drawing them to pay attention to what is before them.

143

18. Which of the following would be the best choice for the sentence below?

> Since the first discovery of dinosaur bones, <u>scientists has made strides in technological development and methodologies used to investigate </u>these extinct animals.

   a. NO CHANGE
   b. scientists has made strides in technological development, and methodologies, used to investigate
   c. scientists have made strides in technological development and methodologies used to investigate
   d. scientists, have made strides in technological development and methodologies used, to investigate

19. Which of the following would be the best choice for the sentence below?

> Some scientists believe <u>the sail serves to regulate the Spinosaurus' body temperature and yet others believe its used to attract mates.</u>

   a. NO CHANGE
   b. the sail serves to regulate the Spinosaurus' body temperature, yet others believe it's used to attract mates.
   c. the sail serves to regulate the Spinosaurus' body temperature and yet others believe it's used to attract mates.
   d. the sail serves to regulate the Spinosaurus' body temperature however others believe it's used to attract mates.

The next question is based on the following passage:

> Everyone has heard the idea of the end justifying the means; that would be Weston's philosophy. Weston is willing to cross any line, commit any act no matter how heinous, to achieve success in his goal. Ransom is repulsed by this fact, seeing total evil in Weston's plan. To do an evil act in order to gain a result that's supposedly good would ultimately warp the final act. This opposing viewpoints immediately distinguishes Ransom as the hero. In the conflict with Un-man, Ransom remains true to his moral principles, someone who refuses to be compromised by power. Instead, Ransom makes it clear that by allowing such processes as murder and lying dictate how one attains a positive outcome, <u>the righteous goal becomes corrupted.</u> The good end would not be truly good, but a twisted end that conceals corrupt deeds.

Based on an excerpt from Perelandra by C.S. Lewis

20. Which of the following would be the best choice for the sentence reproduced below?

> Instead, Ransom makes it clear that by allowing such processes as murder and lying dictate how one attains a positive outcome, <u>the righteous goal becomes corrupted.</u>

   a. NO CHANGE
   b. the goal becomes corrupted and no longer righteous.
   c. the righteous goal becomes, corrupted.
   d. the goal becomes corrupted, when once it was righteous.

144

The next question is based on the following chart:

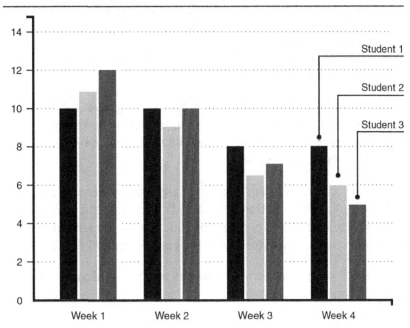

1-Mile Running Times for Three Students

21. Three students are taking a running course at their local high school. The primary goal is to improve on their mile time. This chart shows the students' mile time in minutes as it progresses over the course of four weeks. Based on the chart above, which of the following statements is true?

    a.   Student 1 did not progress as much as the other two students.

    b.   Student 2 ended up with the fastest mile time.

    c.   Student 3 had equal progress to Student 2.

    d.   No student got their mile time below 6 minutes.

The following exchange occurred after the baseball coach's team suffered a heartbreaking loss in the final inning.

    Reporter: The team clearly did not rise to the challenge. I'm sure that getting zero hits in twenty at-bats with runners in scoring position hurt the team's chances at winning the game. What are your thoughts on this devastating loss?

    Baseball Coach: Hitting with runners in scoring position was not the reason we lost this game. We made numerous errors in the field, and our pitchers gave out too many free passes. Also, we did not even need a hit with runners in scoring position. Many of those at-bats could have driven in the run by simply making contact. Our team did not deserve to win the game.

22. Which of the following best describes the main point of dispute between the reporter and baseball coach?
    a. The loss was heartbreaking.
    b. Getting zero hits in twenty at-bats with runners in scoring position caused the loss.
    c. Numerous errors in the field and pitchers giving too many free passes caused the loss.
    d. The team deserved to win the game.

The next question is based on the following passages:

Text 1: Thomas Hobbes was a philosopher who thought negatively of human nature. He believed that people naturally wish to dominate one another and are naturally at war with one another. Therefore, humans must give up their rights to their government, which has the task of protecting people from their worst desires.

Text 2: Philosopher John Locke is well known for arguing that humans are rational creatures that can act logically despite their emotions. He coined the term "natural law," which means that morals come from the human ability to reason. Due to this, the government should not be able to take away human rights. His philosophy is the basis for the US constitution.

23. Based on the texts, what are the two common themes that both philosophers focus on?
    a. Human nature and war
    b. Human nature and government
    c. Government and intelligence
    d. The United States and natural law

The next question is based on the following passage:

Turtle shells are composed of two parts. The carapace, which is the top portion of the shell, provides structural support and protection for the turtle's body. The plastron, the bottom of the shell, helps protect the turtle's organs. Both portions of the shell are made of keratin. <u>This is the same material that human nails are made out of.</u>

24. The author is considering deleting the underlined portion of text. Should this sentence be kept or deleted?
    a. Kept, because discussion of human nails is the natural continuation of the text
    b. Kept, because humans are responsible for the declining turtle population
    c. Deleted, because human nails are not relevant to the overall topic
    d. Deleted, because the information is inaccurate

The next question is based on the following passage:

While scientists aren't entirely certain why tornadoes form, they have some clues into the process. Tornadoes are dangerous funnel clouds that occur during a large thunderstorm. When warm, humid air near the ground meets cold, dry air from above, a column of the warm air can be drawn up into the clouds. Winds at different altitudes blowing at different speeds make the column of air rotate. As the spinning column of air picks up speed, a funnel cloud is formed. This funnel cloud moves rapidly and haphazardly. Rain and hail inside the cloud cause it to touch down, creating a tornado. Tornadoes move in a rapid and unpredictable pattern, making them extremely

destructive and dangerous. Scientists continue to study tornadoes to improve radar detection and warning times.

25. The main purpose of this passage is to do which of the following?
   a. Show why tornadoes are dangerous.
   b. Explain how a tornado forms.
   c. Compare thunderstorms to tornadoes.
   d. Explain what to do in the event of a tornado.

The next question is based on the following passage:

Ergonomics is a field that focuses on designing products and spaces in a way that prioritizes efficiency and comfort. This means designing things to optimize performance and decrease the opportunity for injury. For example, office chairs are designed ergonomically so that a person can sit for long periods of time without pain or the development of poor posture. Businesses must focus on ergonomics not only for the well-being of their employees but also to maximize the performance of the business as a whole.

26. Which choice best states the main idea of the text?
   a. Businesses must implement ergonomics, as it is a part of humane working conditions and workers' rights.
   b. Ergonomics is critical to the well-being and comfort of individuals, which in turn increases their performance efficiency.
   c. Ergonomics may make life easier for individuals, but it is not a necessity for the majority of people.
   d. More products should be developed with ergonomics in mind since the market is lacking in that area.

27. Which of the following would be the best choice for the sentence below?

   Usually, all news <u>outlets have some sort of bias, it's just a question of how much</u> bias clouds the reporting.

   a. NO CHANGE
   b. outlets have some sort of bias; it's just a question of how much
   c. outlets have some sort of bias it can just be a question of how much
   d. outlets have some sort of bias, its just a question of how much

Math: Module 1

1. If Danny takes 48 minutes to walk 3 miles, how long should it take him to walk 5 miles maintaining the same speed?
   a. 32 min
   b. 64 min
   c. 80 min
   d. 96 min

147

2. Evaluate the expression. Give the result in decimal form.

$$\frac{3}{5} \times \frac{7}{10} \div \frac{1}{2}$$

    a. 0.042
    b. 84%
    c. 0.84
    d. 0.42

3. Five of six numbers have a sum of 25. The average of all six numbers is 6. What is the sixth number?
    a. 8
    b. 10
    c. 11
    d. 12

4. Solve for x: $\frac{2x}{5} - 1 = 59$.
    a. 60
    b. 145
    c. 150
    d. 115

5. In Jim's school, there are a total of 650 boys and girls as students. There are 3 girls for every 2 boys. How many students are girls?

6. A train traveling 50 miles per hour takes a trip lasting 3 hours. If a map has a scale of 1 inch per 10 miles, how many inches apart are the train's starting point and ending point on the map?

7. Which of the following inequalities is equivalent to $3 - \frac{1}{2}x \geq 2$?
    a. $x \geq 2$
    b. $x \leq 2$
    c. $x \geq 1$
    d. $x \leq 1$

8. If $g(x) = x^3 - 3x^2 - 2x + 6$ and $f(x) = 2$, then what is $g(f(x))$?
    a. -26
    b. 6
    c. $2x^3 - 6x^2 - 4x + 12$
    d. -2

9. The graph of which function has an x-intercept of -2?
    a. $y = 2x - 3$
    b. $y = 4x + 2$
    c. $y = x^2 + 5x + 6$
    d. $y = 2x^2 + 3x - 1$

10. What is the solution to the following system of equations?

$$x^2 - 2x + y = 8$$

$$x - y = -2$$

    a. $(-2, 3)$
    b. There is no solution.
    c. $(-2, 0)$ and $(1, 3)$
    d. $(-2, 0)$ and $(3, 5)$

11. What is an equation for the line passing through the origin and the point $(2,1)$?
    a. $y = 2x$
    b. $y = \frac{1}{2}x$
    c. $y = x + 2$
    d. $y = x - 2$

12. What type of function is modeled by the values in the following table?

x	$f(x)$
1	2
2	4
3	8
4	16
5	32

    a. Linear
    b. Exponential
    c. Quadratic
    d. Cubic

13. The area of a given rectangle is 24 square centimeters. If the measure of each side is multiplied by 3, what is the area of the new figure?
    a. 48 cm^2
    b. 72 cm^2
    c. 216 cm^2
    d. $13,824 \text{ cm}^2$

14. Give a numerical expression for the following: "Six less than three times the sum of twice a number and one."
    a. $2x + 1 - 6$
    b. $3x + 1 - 6$
    c. $3(x + 1) - 6$
    d. $3(2x + 1) - 6$

15. $(2x - 4y)^2 =$
    a. $4x^2 - 16xy + 16y^2$
    b. $4x^2 - 8xy + 16y^2$
    c. $4x^2 - 16xy - 16y^2$
    d. $2x^2 - 8xy + 8y^2$

16. Simplify $(7n + 3n^3 + 3) + (8n + 5n^3 + 2n^4)$.
    a. $9n^4 + 15n - 2$
    b. $2n^4 + 5n^3 + 15n - 2$
    c. $9n^4 + 8n^3 + 15n$
    d. $2n^4 + 8n^3 + 15n + 3$

17. What is the product of the following expression?

$$(4x - 8)(5x^2 + x + 6)$$

    a. $20x^3 - 36x^2 + 16x - 48$
    b. $6x^3 - 41x^2 + 12x + 15$
    c. $20x^3 + 11x^2 - 37x - 12$
    d. $2x^3 - 11x^2 - 32x + 20$

18. What is the solution for the following equation?

$$\frac{x^2 + x - 30}{x - 5} = 11$$

    a. $x = -6$
    b. There is no solution.
    c. $x = 16$
    d. $x = 5$

19. The ratio of angles of a triangle is equal to 2:4:3. What is the measure of the largest angle?
    a. 20°
    b. 40°
    c. 80°
    d. 120°

20. A triangle has side lengths of 11 cm, 25 cm, and 33 cm. Which of the following types of triangles is it?
    a. Acute
    b. Right
    c. Obtuse
    d. None of the above

21. Find the volume of the following three-dimensional shape:

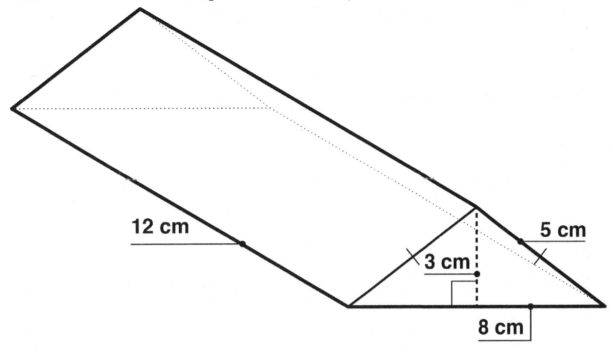

12 cm   3 cm   5 cm   8 cm

a. 240 cm^3
b. 480 cm^3
c. 144 cm^3
d. 288 cm^3

22. What is the overall median of Dwayne's current test scores: 78, 92, 83, 97?

Math: Module 2

1. What is the solution to the radical equation $\sqrt[3]{2x + 11} + 9 = 12$?
   a. −8
   b. 8
   c. 0
   d. 12

2. At the store, Jan spends $90 on apples and oranges. Apples cost $1 each and oranges cost $2 each. If Jan buys the same number of apples as oranges, how many oranges did she buy?
   a. 20
   b. 25
   c. 30
   d. 35

3. If $3x = 6y = -2z = 24$, then what does $4xy + z$ equal?
   a. 116
   b. 130
   c. 84
   d. 108

4. If $4x - 3 = 5$, what is the value of x?
   a. 1
   b. 2
   c. 3
   d. 4

5. What is $4 \times 7 + (25 - 21)^2 \div 2$?

6. Evaluate:

$$\left(\sqrt{36} \times \sqrt{16}\right) - 3^2$$

7. If $x \neq 0$, then $\dfrac{3}{x} + \dfrac{5u}{2x} - \dfrac{u}{4} =$

   a. $\dfrac{12 + 10u - ux}{4x}$

   b. $\dfrac{3 + 5u - ux}{x}$

   c. $\dfrac{12x + 10u + ux}{4x}$

   d. $\dfrac{12 + 10u - u}{4x}$

8. What are the zeros of the function $f(x) = x^3 + 4x^2 + 4x$?
   a. -2
   b. $0, -2$
   c. 2
   d. $0, 2$

9. Katie works at a clothing company and sold 192 shirts over the weekend. One third of the shirts that were sold were patterned and the rest were solid. Which mathematical expression would calculate the number of solid shirts Katie sold over the weekend?
   a. $192 \times \dfrac{1}{3}$
   b. $192 \div \dfrac{1}{3}$
   c. $192 \times \left(1 - \dfrac{1}{3}\right)$
   d. $192 \div 3$

10. Alan currently weighs 200 pounds, but he wants to lose weight to get down to 175 pounds. What is this difference in kilograms? (1 pound is approximately equal to 0.45 kilograms.)
   a. 9 kg
   b. 11.25 kg
   c. 78.75 kg
   d. 90 kg

11. What is the y-intercept for $y = x^2 + 3x - 4$?
    a. $y = -3$
    b. $y = -4$
    c. $y = 3$
    d. $y = 4$

12. Karen gets paid a weekly salary and a commission for every sale that she makes. The table below shows the number of sales and her pay for different weeks. The amount she makes can be represented by a linear equation. The table below shows the number of sales and her pay for different weeks.

Sales	?	7	4	8
Pay	$380	$580	$460	$620

Which of the following equations represents Karen's weekly pay?
    a. $y = 90x + 200$
    b. $y = 90x - 200$
    c. $y = 40x + 300$
    d. $y = 40x - 300$

13. How could the following equation be factored to find the zeros?

$$y = x^3 - 3x^2 - 4x$$

    a. $0 = x^2(x - 4)$
    b. $0 = 3x(x + 1)(x + 4)$
    c. $0 = x(x + 1)(x + 6)$
    d. $0 = x(x + 1)(x - 4)$

14. Which of the ordered pairs below is a solution to the following system of inequalities?

$$\begin{cases} y > 2x - 3 \\ y < -4x + 8 \end{cases}$$

    a. $(4, 5)$
    b. $(-3, -2)$
    c. $(3, -1)$
    d. $(5, 2)$

15. Which equation best represents the scatter plot below?

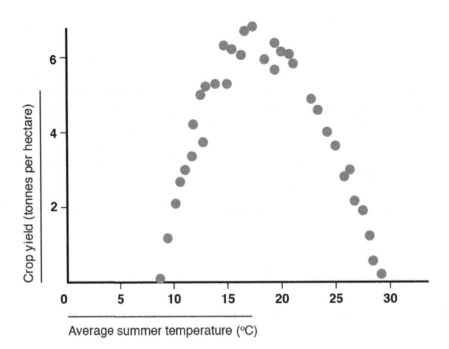

a. $y = 3x - 4$

b. $y = 2x^2 + 7x - 9$

c. $y = (3)(4^x)$

d. $y = -\frac{1}{14}x^2 + 2x - 8$

16. The table below displays the number of three-year-olds at Kids First Daycare who are potty-trained and those who still wear diapers.

	Potty-trained total	Wear diapers total	Total
Boys	26	22	48
Girls	34	18	52
Total	60	40	

If a three-year-old girl is randomly selected from this school, what is the probability that she is potty-trained?

a. 52%

b. 65%

c. 67.5%

d. 70%

17. Mom's car drove 72 miles in 90 minutes. How fast did she drive in feet per second? Round your answer to the nearest tenth. 1 mile is equal to 5,280 feet.

18. What is the slope of this line?

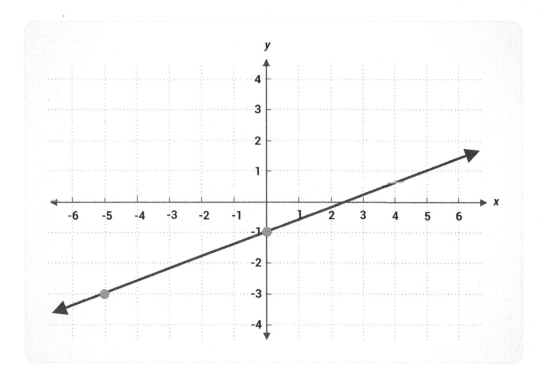

a. $\frac{-5}{-3}$

b. $\frac{4}{2}$

c. $\frac{2}{5}$

d. $\frac{1}{2}$

19. What is the value of $x^2 - 2xy + 2y^2$ when $x = 2$ and $y = 3$?

20. In cubic inches, what is the volume of a cube with the side equal to 3 inches?
    a. 6 in^3
    b. 27 in^3
    c. 9 in^3
    d. 81 in^3

21. The square and circle have the same center. The circle has a radius of r. What is the area of the shaded region?

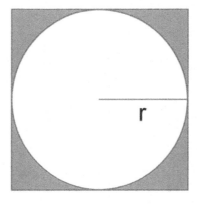

a. $r^2 - \pi r^2$
b. $4r^2 - 2\pi r$
c. $(4 - \pi)r^2$
d. $(\pi - 1)r^2$

22. In the image below, what is demonstrated by the two triangles?

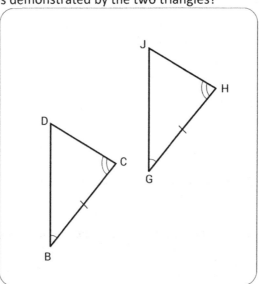

a. According to Side-Side-Side, the triangles are congruent.
b. According to Angle-Angle-Angle, the triangles are congruent.
c. According to Angle-Side-Angle, the triangles are congruent.
d. There is not enough information to prove the two triangles are congruent.

156

Answer Explanations #1

Reading and Writing: Module 1

1. B: The word *achievement* is misspelled as *acheivement*. Remember the rule *i* before *e* except after *c*. Choices *A, C,* and *D* are all spelled correctly.

2. D: The correct answer is Choice *D* because this statement provides the most clarity. Choice *A* is incorrect because the noun *Chicago City Council* acts as one, so the verb *are* should be singular, not plural. Choice *B* is incorrect because it is perhaps the most confusingly worded out of all the answer choices; the phrase *December 4* is a misplaced modifier. It is meant to modify *Fred Hampton Day* not *Chicago City Council*. Choice *C* is incorrect because it is too vague and leaves out who does the commemorating.

3. D: The possessive form of the word *it* is *its*. The contraction *it's* denotes *it is*. Thus, Choice *A* is incorrect. The word *raises* in Choice *B* makes the sentence grammatically incorrect. Choice *C* adds an apostrophe at the end of *its*. While most nouns indicate possession with an apostrophe, adding *'s* to the word "it" indicates a contraction.

4. B: Twain describes nature positively and with respect. He describes it with words such as: *graceful*, *beauty*, and *majestic*. These are all words that convey respect. He even uses the word *rapture* to describe how he feels when looking at the world. Choices *A, C,* and *D* are all incorrect because they are negatively charged words when Twain clearly speaks positively of nature.

5. A: In the paragraph, the author is describing why they went to live in the woods. This aligns with the description in Choice *A*. Choice *B* is incorrect because the author never criticizes the reader directly. Choice *C* is incorrect because the author does not connect religion with the passage. Choice *D* is incorrect because the author is not writing specifically about spending time outdoors but rather about living a simple life.

6. A: The tone of this passage is incredulous. While *contemplative* is an option because of the inquisitive nature of the text, Choice *A* is correct because the speaker is frustrated that he is expected to celebrate American independence when the principles of independence and freedom aren't extended to him or other African Americans. The speaker is not *nonchalant*, nor accepting of the circumstances which he describes.

7. B: It is apparent that Lincoln is referring to a period of time within the context of the passage because the sentence contains the words *years* and *ago*. Choices *A, C,* and *D* do not fit the language or context of the sentence and are therefore incorrect.

8. B: The speaker states that he is there to "accompany [the audience] ... through one of my little Christmas books," making him an author there to entertain the crowd with his own writing. The speech preceding the reading is the passage itself, and, as the tone indicates, it is a serious speech addressing the "working man." The speaker himself is not an employer of the audience, so Choice *A* is incorrect. Choice *C* is also incorrect, as the salutation is not used ironically, but sincerely, as the speech addresses the wellbeing of the crowd. Choice *D* is incorrect because the speech is not given by a politician, but by a writer.

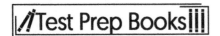

9. C: The quote gives the warden's direct statement regarding his dedication to the rookery. Choice *A* is incorrect because the speaker of the quote is a warden, not a hunter. Choice *B* is incorrect because the quote does not lighten the mood, but shows the danger of the situation between the wardens and the hunters. Choice *D* is incorrect because there is no humor found in the quote.

10. A: The passage revolves around the introduction of certain insects that transition from water to air. Choice *B* is incorrect because although the passage talks about gills, it is not the central idea of the passage. Choices *C* and *D* are incorrect because the passage does not "define" or "invite," but only serves as an introduction to stoneflies, dragonflies, and mayflies, and their transition from water to air.

11. B: For this question, place the underlined sentence in each prospective choice's position. Leaving the sentence in place is incorrect because the father "going crazy" doesn't logically follow the fact that he was a "city slicker." Choice *C* is incorrect because the sentence in question is not a concluding sentence and does not transition smoothly into another paragraph. Choice *D* is incorrect because the sentence doesn't necessarily need to be omitted since it logically follows the very first sentence in the passage.

12. C: Choice *C* is the correct choice because the word *their* indicates possession, and the text is talking about "their students," or the students of someone. Choice *A, there*, describes where something is located. Choice *B, they're*, is a contraction and means *they are*. Choice *D* is not a word.

13. B: Choice *B* is the correct answer because it puts all the verbs into the proper format. Choice *A* is incorrect because "growing the same crops, depleting the soil, and results" doesn't make sense. Choice *C* incorrectly changes *depleting* to *depletes*. Choice *D* changes all the verbs from gerunds with an *-ing* ending, to present tense verbs, which do not make sense in context

14. A: Choice *A* is the most accurate summary of the main point of Thoreau's statement. Choice *B* is totally irrelevant. Choice *C* is also incorrect; Thoreau never personifies government. Also, this doesn't coincide with his wooden gun analogy. Choice *D* is compelling because of its language but doesn't define the point of the statement.

15. A: The purpose is to inform the reader about what assault is and how it is committed. Choice *B* is incorrect because the passage does not state that assault is a lesser form of lethal force, only that an assault can use lethal force, or alternatively, lethal force can be utilized to counter a dangerous assault. Choice *C* is incorrect because the passage is informative and does not have a set agenda. Finally, Choice *D* is incorrect because although the author uses an example in order to explain assault, it is not indicated that this is the author's personal account.

16. D: Choice *D* is correct, since only proper names should be capitalized. Because the name of a dog breed is not a proper name, Choice *A* is incorrect. In terms of punctuation, only one comma after *example* is needed, so Choices *B* and *C* are incorrect.

17. B: Since the sentence can stand on its own without *Usually*, separating it from the rest of the sentence with a comma is correct. Choice *A* needs the comma after *Usually*, while Choice *C* uses commas incorrectly. Choice *D* is tempting, but changing *turn* and *awake* to *turned* and *awakened* does not fit.

18. B: Choice *C* incorrectly changes *applies* to *applied*, fails to change *there* to *their*, and fails to add the necessary punctuation. Choice *D* incorrectly adds a comma between the subject (Discussions that make people think about the content and how it applies to their lives, world, and future) and the predicate (are key).

19. D: The graph shows the number of people (in millions) boarding United States' flights between 1996-2005. The first few months following the September 11, 2001 attacks, the passengers boarding US flights dropped to around 50 million when before the attacks there were around 70 million passengers boarding flights. Therefore, the correct answer is Choice D. The graph does not show where the flights were redirected, the number of passengers that other countries received as a result of the redirected air travel, or the resulting flight schedule implications, Choice A.

20. D: Choice D is correct, adding finer details to help the reader understand exactly what Prometheus did and his impact: fire came with knowledge and power. Choice A lacks a comma after *fire*. Choice B inserts unnecessary commas since *people* is not part of the list *knowledge and power*. Choice C is a strong revision but could be confusing, hinting that the fire was knowledge and power itself, as opposed to being symbolized by the fire.

21. A: Choice A is the correct answer because it effectively combines the two sentences in a way that flows seamlessly. It retains all of the relevant facts that are presented in the original sentences. It combines them effectively with a comma and conjunction. Choice B is incorrect because although it adds a comma and conjunction, it also adds an excessive amount of wording to do the same job as Choice A. Choice C is incorrect because it changes the order of information provided so that the new sentence does not resemble the previous two. Choice D is incorrect because it also changes the order of information and makes the inventor the main subject of the text rather than the invention.

22. C: Choice C is the correct answer because it improves the concision of the text. It provides all of the relevant information while getting rid of excessive wordiness by combining sentences. Choice A is incorrect because there is an appropriate choice that is more concise than the original. Choice B is incorrect because it does not combine any sentences to become more concise. Choice D is incorrect because it is just as long as the original text and does not improve concision.

23. B: Choice B is correct because both cultures associate the northern lights with some form of spirit and with the dead carrying on after life. For the Native Americans, the lights are spirits that guide the recently deceased to the next life. For the Sámi, they are a sign of the dead and a dangerous force. Choice A is incorrect because the Sámi would not look forward to the lights since they mean danger. Choice C is incorrect because there is no indication that the color of the lights is connected to the cultural beliefs presented. Choice D is incorrect because some assumptions can be made about the cultural beliefs regarding spirits and the afterlife.

24. D: Choice D is the correct answer because it is the most appropriate word choice for this text. The language in this text is elevated and uses complex vocabulary. In this instance, the phrase *stick to* is not formal enough, which makes Choice A incorrect. *Adhere to* uses more formal vocabulary that fits the context of the text. Choice B is incorrect because the students are following rules, not laws. *Obey* has a connotation that there is an authority figure involved, which does not fit the context. Choice C is incorrect because the students are not agreeing or disagreeing with the conventions in this context. They are merely rules for the English language that will improve their academic success.

25. D: Choice A is not relevant. The argument's conclusion is that Hank is a professional writer. The argument does not depend on whether Hank's agent is the best or worst in the business. Choice B seems fairly strong at first glance. It feels reasonable to say that being a professional writer requires representation. However, the argument would still be strong if being a professional writer did not require an agent. Hank would still be a professional writer. Choice C is irrelevant. Whether Hank is a professional writer does not depend on his reviews. Choice D is strong. Negate it to determine if the

159

argument falls apart. If being a professional writer requires earning money, then Hank would not be a professional writer. The argument falls apart. Therefore, Choice *D* is the correct answer.

26. B: According to Carter, these examples are the shocks and tragedies that have gradually caused Americans to lose their faith and confidence in government and other institutions such as schools and media. While there are references to previous presidents, it is not Carter's intention to grade their time in office, making Choice *A* incorrect. The future is not mentioned in paragraphs six and seven, rendering Choice *C* incorrect. President Carter believes Americans have very reasonable expectations, even when they're not being met. For that reason, Choice *D* is incorrect.

27. A: Choice *A* is correct because the phrase "others' ideas" is both plural and indicates possession. Choice *B* is incorrect because *other's* indicates only one "other" that's in possession of "ideas," which is incorrect. Choice *C* is incorrect because no possession is indicated. Choice *D* is incorrect because the word *other* does not end in *s*. *Others's* is not a correct form of the plural possessive word.

Reading and Writing: Module 2

1. A: The sentence is correct as is, therefore Choice *A* is correct. The list of events accomplished by Hampton is short enough that each item in the list can be separated by a comma. Choice *B* is incorrect. The subject *Hampton* should not be separated from the verb *organized* by a colon. Semicolons are used to separate at least three items in a series that have an internal comma. Semicolons can also be used to separate clauses in a sentence that contain internal commas intended for clarification purposes. Neither of the two latter uses of semicolons is required in the example sentence. Therefore, Choice *C* is incorrect. Choice *D* is incorrect because a dash is not a conventional choice for punctuating items in a series.

2. D: Choice *A* is incorrect because although the Adirondack region is mentioned in the text, there is no cause or effect relationships between the region and fish hatcheries depicted here. Choice *B* is incorrect because the text does not have an agenda, but rather is meant to inform the audience. Finally, Choice *C* is incorrect because the text says nothing of how sun-fish mate.

3. D: The sentence in this question is describing the color of the river. It is the color of blood and gold because of the sun setting. This is a metaphor, which is used to compare two things. Choice *A* is incorrect because a simile uses a comparison word such as *like* or *as*. This sentence does not. Choice *B* is incorrect because an allusion is an indirect reference to something without mentioning what is being referenced. Choice *C* is incorrect because an oxymoron is when two contradictory terms are used together.

4. C: The rule for *me* and *I* is that one should use *I* when it is the subject pronoun of a sentence, and *me* when it is the object pronoun of the sentence. Break the sentence up to see if *I* or *me* should be used. To say "Those are memories that I have now shared" is correct, rather than "Those are memories that me have now shared." Choice *D* is incorrect because *my siblings* should come before *I*.

5. C: The word *civelized* should be spelled *civilized*. The words *consider*, *distinguishes*, and *creatures* are all spelled correctly.

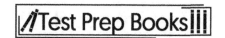

6. A: Choice *A* has consistent parallel structure with the verbs *read*, *identify*, and *determine*. Choices *B* and *C* have faulty parallel structure with the words *determining* and *identifying*. Choice *D* has incorrect subject/verb agreement. The sentence should read, "Students have to read … identify … and determine."

7. B: The passage begins by giving the reader information about traditional birthing situations. Then, we are told that Mr. and Mrs. Button decide to go against tradition to have their baby in a hospital. The next paragraph is dedicated to letting the reader know how Mr. Button dresses and goes to the hospital to welcome his new baby. There is no doctor in this excerpt, as Choice *C* indicates, and clothes are discussed, as choice *D* indicates. However, Mr. Button is not going to the doctor's office, nor is he about to go shopping for new clothes.

8. C: The passage is narrated in third person omniscient point of view. We know this because the story starts out with us knowing something that the character does not know: that her husband has died. Mrs. Mallard eventually comes to know this, but we as readers know this information before it is broken to her. In third person limited, Choice *D*, we would only see and know what Mrs. Mallard herself knew, and we would find out the news of her husband's death when she found out the news, not before.

9. C: The word *tumultuously* most nearly means *violently*. Even if you don't know the word *tumultuously*, look at the surrounding context to figure it out. We see a fearful and almost violent reaction to the emotion that he's having. Thus, his chest would rise and fall tumultuously, or violently.

10. C: This question can be solved through careful context analysis and vocabulary knowledge. One can infer that the use of *expedient*, while not necessarily very positive, isn't inherently bad in this context either. Note how in the next line, he says, "but most governments are usually, and all governments are sometimes, inexpedient." This use of *inexpedient* indicates that a government becomes a hindrance rather than a solution; it slows progress rather than helps facilitate progress. Thus, Choice *A* and Choice *D* can be ruled out because they are hindrances or problems and would work better with inexpedient rather than expedient. Choice *B* makes no logical sense. Therefore, Choice *C* is the best description of *expedient*. Essentially, Thoreau is saying that government is constructed as a way of developing order and people's rights, but the rigidness of government soon inhibits justice and human rights.

11. D: The statement in Choice *D* would most undermine the last part of the passage because it directly contradicts how the law evaluates the use of lethal force. Choices *A* and *B* are stated in the paragraph, so they do not undermine the explanation from the author. Choice *C* does not necessarily undermine the passage, but it does not support the passage either. It is more of an opinion that does not offer strength or weakness to the explanation.

12. B: This organization question asks readers to analyze the structure of the essay. The topic of the essay is about spinoff technology, and the thesis statement at the end of the first paragraph offers the opinion, "Spinoff technology proves that it is worthwhile to invest in science research because it could enrich people's lives in unexpected ways." The next paragraph provides evidence to support this opinion. Choice *A* is the second-best option because the first paragraph gives a general definition of spinoff technology, while the following paragraph offers more detailed examples to help illustrate this idea. However, it is not the best answer because the main idea of the essay is that spinoff technology enriches people's lives in unexpected ways. Choice *C* is incorrect because the essay does not provide details of any specific moment in history. Choice *D* is incorrect because the essay does not discuss a popular misconception.

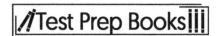

13. C: The text mentions all of the listed properties of minerals except the instance of minerals being organically formed. It specifically states they must be inorganic, which means not organic. Objects or substances must be naturally occurring, must be a homogeneous solid, and must have a definite chemical composition in order to be considered a mineral.

14. C: Choice *C* correctly uses *from* to describe the fact that dogs are related to wolves. The word *through* is incorrectly used in the original sentence, so Choice *A* is incorrect. Choice *B* does not make sense. Choice *D* unnecessarily changes the verb tense in addition to incorrectly using *through*.

15. D: The passage compares Disney cruises with Disney parks. It does not discuss how to book a cruise, so Choice *A* is incorrect. Choice *B* is incorrect because though the passage does mention some of the park attractions, it is not the main point. The passage does not mention the cost of either option, so Choice *C* is incorrect.

16. D: Choice *D* is correct because the commas serve to distinguish that *artificial selection* is just another term for *selective breeding* before the sentence continues. The structure is preserved, and the sentence can flow with more clarity. Choice *A* is incorrect because the sentence needs commas to avoid being a run-on. Choice *B* is close but still lacks the required comma after *selection*, so this is incorrect. Choice *C* is incorrect because the comma to set off the aside should be placed after *breeding* instead of *called*.

17. B: Choice *B* correctly adds a comma after the word *person*. Choice *C* inserts a semicolon where a comma is needed. Choice *D* adds a period to the middle of the sentence.

18. C: Choice *C* is correct because it fixes the core issue with this sentence: the singular has does not agree with the plural *scientists*. Choices *B* and *D* add unnecessary commas.

19. B: Choice *B* not only fixes the homophone issue from *its*, which is possessive, to *it's*, which is a contraction of *it is*, but also streamlines the sentence by adding a comma and eliminating *and*. Choice *A* is incorrect because of these errors. Choices *C* and *D* only fix the homophone issue.

20. A: Choice *A* is direct and clear, without any punctuation errors. Choice *B* is well written but too wordy. Choice *C* adds an unnecessary comma. Choice *D* is also well written but much less concise than Choice *A*.

21. A: Choice *A* is the correct answer because Student 1 did not progress from Week 1 to Week 2; they also did not progress from Week 3 to Week 4. Both of the other students progressed steadily from week to week. Choice *B* is incorrect because Student 3 ended up with the fastest mile time. Choice *C* is incorrect because Student 3 had more progress than Student 2, showing a bigger difference between Week 1 and Week 4. Choice *D* is incorrect because Student 3 had a mile time under 6 minutes in the last week.

22. B: Choice *A* is not the main point of disagreement. The reporter calls the loss devastating, and there's no reason to believe that the coach would disagree with this assessment. Choice *C* is mentioned by the coach, but not by the reporter. It is unclear whether the reporter would agree with this assessment. Choice *D* is mentioned by the coach but not by the reporter. It is not stated whether the reporter believes that the team deserved to win. Choice *B* is strong since both passages mention the at-bats with runners in scoring position. The reporter asserts that the team lost due to the team failing to get such a hit. In contrast, the coach identifies several other reasons for the loss, including fielding and pitching errors. Additionally, the coach disagrees that the team even needed a hit in those situations. Therefore, Choice *B* is the correct answer.

This material is provided for exam preparation purposes only and does not indicate an endorsement of any specific scientific, political, or religious point of view. © TPB Publishing. You have been licensed one copy of this document for personal use only. Any other reproduction or redistribution is strictly prohibited. All rights reserved.

23. B: Choice *B* is correct because both philosophers focus on the topics of human nature and how it relates to government. Choice *A* is incorrect because only the Hobbes text mentions war. Choice *C* is incorrect because intelligence is not mentioned by either philosopher. Choice *D* is incorrect because only the Locke text mentions the United States and natural law.

24. C: Choice *C* is the correct answer because it is true that human nails are not relevant to the overall discussion. Turtle shells are the main topic of the text. Therefore, it is unnecessary to bring up a comparison to human nails, and that sentence can be deleted. Choice *A* is incorrect because the two topics are not related enough for human nails to be a natural progression in discussion. Choice *B* is incorrect because human responsibility is not a topic of discussion in this text. Choice *D* is incorrect because the information is accurate; it just is not relevant to the overall text.

25. B: The main point of this passage is to show how tornadoes form. Choice *A* is wrong because while the passage does mention that tornadoes are dangerous, it is not the main focus of the passage. While thunderstorms are mentioned, they are not compared to tornadoes, so Choice *C* is incorrect. Choice *D* is incorrect because the passage does not discuss what to do in the event of a tornado.

26. B: Choice *B* is the correct answer because the text explains how important ergonomics is to making products and spaces more comfortable for humans, which in turn leads to greater efficiency and work performance. Choice *A* is incorrect because the text does not state that ergonomic products are a part of workers' rights. Choice *C* is incorrect because the text does not claim ergonomics is unnecessary for most people. Choice *D* is incorrect because the text explains the importance of ergonomics but does not mention a lack of ergonomic products on the market.

27. A: Choice *B* is correct because *all news outlets have some sort of bias* and *it's just a question of how much bias* are both independent clauses, so they need to either be joined by a semicolon or a comma and a conjunction. Choice *A* creates a run-on sentence, because it uses a comma without a conjunction to join two independent clauses. Choice *C* also creates a run-on sentence, and Choice *D* incorrectly changes *it's* to *its*.

Math: Module 1

1. C: To solve the problem, we can write a proportion consisting of ratios comparing distance and time. One way to set up the proportion is:

$$\frac{3}{48} = \frac{5}{x}$$

x represents the unknown value of time. To solve this proportion, we can cross-multiply: $(3)(x) = (5)(48)$, or $3x = 240$. To isolate the variable, we divide by 3 on both sides, getting $x = 80$.

2. C: The first step in solving this problem is expressing the result in fraction form. Multiplication and division are typically performed in order from left to right, but they can be performed in any order. For this problem, let's start with the division operation between the last two fractions. When dividing one fraction by another, invert or flip the second fraction and then multiply the numerators and denominators.

$$\frac{7}{10} \times \frac{2}{1} = \frac{14}{10}$$

163

Next, multiply the first fraction by this value:

$$\frac{3}{5} \times \frac{14}{10} = \frac{42}{50}$$

In this instance, to find the decimal form, we can multiply the numerator and denominator by 2 to get 100 in the denominator.

$$\frac{42}{50} \times \frac{2}{2} = \frac{84}{100}$$

In decimal form, this would be expressed as 0.84.

3. C: The average is calculated by adding all six numbers, then dividing by 6. The first five numbers have a sum of 25. This means $\frac{(25+n)}{6} = 6$, where n is the unknown number. Multiplying both sides by 6, we get $25 + n = 36$, which means $n = 11$.

4. C: Set up the initial equation.

$$\frac{2x}{5} - 1 = 59$$

Add 1 to both sides.

$$\frac{2x}{5} - 1 + 1 = 59 + 1$$

$$\frac{2x}{5} = 60$$

Multiply both sides by $\frac{5}{2}$.

$$\frac{2x}{5} \times \frac{5}{2} = 60 \times \frac{5}{2}$$

$$x = 150$$

5. 390: Three girls for every two boys can be expressed as a ratio: 3 : 2. This can be visualized as splitting the school into 5 groups: 3 girl groups and 2 boy groups. The number of students that are in each group can be found by dividing the total number of students by 5:

$$\frac{650 \text{ students}}{5 \text{ groups}} = \frac{130 \text{ students}}{\text{group}}$$

To find the total number of girls, multiply the number of students per group (130) by the number of girl groups in the school (3). This equals 390.

6. 15: First, the train's journey in the real world is:

$$3 \text{ h} \times 50\frac{\text{mi}}{\text{h}} = 150 \text{ mi}$$

On the map, 1 inch corresponds to 10 miles, so that is equivalent to:

$$150 \text{ mi} \times \frac{1 \text{ in}}{10 \text{ mi}} = 15 \text{ in}$$

Therefore, the start and end points are 15 inches apart on the map.

7. B: To simplify this inequality, subtract 3 from both sides to get $-\frac{1}{2}x \geq -1$. Then, multiply both sides by −2 (remembering this flips the direction of the inequality) to get $x \leq 2$.

8. D: This problem involves a composition function, where one function is plugged into the other function. In this case, the $f(x)$ function is plugged into the $g(x)$ function for each x value.

Since $f(x) = 2$, the composition equation becomes:

$$g\big(f(x)\big) = (2)^3 - 3(2)^2 - 2(2) + 6$$

Simplifying the equation gives the answer:

$$g\big(f(x)\big) = 8 - 3(4) - 2(2) + 6$$

$$g(f(x)) = 8 - 12 - 4 + 6$$

$$g\big(f(x)\big) = -2$$

9. C: An x-intercept is a point where the graph crosses the x-axis. At this point, the value of y is 0. To determine if an equation has an x-intercept of −2, substitute −2 for x, and calculate the value of y. If the value of −2 for x corresponds with a y-value of 0, then the equation has an x-intercept of −2. The only answer choice that produces this result is Choice *C*.

$$0 = (-2)^2 + 5(-2) + 6$$

10. D: This system of equations involves one quadratic equation and one linear equation. One way to solve this is through substitution.

Solving for y in the second equation yields:

$$y = x + 2$$

Plugging this equation in for the y of the quadratic equation yields:

$$x^2 - 2x + x + 2 = 8$$

Simplify the equation:

$$x^2 - x + 2 = 8$$

Set this equal to zero and factor:

$$x^2 - x - 6 = 0 = (x - 3)(x + 2)$$

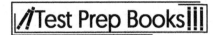
Solving these two factors for x gives the zeros:

$$x = 3, -2$$

To find the y-value for the point, plug in each number to either original equation. Solving each one for y yields the points (3,5) and (-2,0).

11. B: The slope will be given by:

$$m = \frac{y_2 - y_1}{x_2 - x_1}$$

$$m = \frac{1 - 0}{2 - 0} = \frac{1}{2}$$

The y-intercept will be 0 since it passes through the origin. Using slope-intercept form, the equation for this line is:

$$y = \frac{1}{2}x$$

12. B: The table shows values that are increasing exponentially. The differences between the inputs are the same, while the differences in the outputs are changing by a factor of 2. The values in the table can be modeled by the equation $f(x) = 2^x$.

13. C: Because area is a two-dimensional measurement, the dimensions are multiplied by a scale factor that is squared to determine the scale factor of the corresponding areas. The dimensions of the rectangle are multiplied by a scale factor of 3. Therefore, the area is multiplied by a scale factor of 3^2 (which is equal to 9):

$$24 \text{ cm}^2 \times 9 = 216 \text{ cm}^2$$

14. D: "Sum" means the result of adding, so "the sum of twice a number and one" can be written as $2x + 1$. Next, "three times the sum of twice a number and one" would be $3(2x + 1)$. Finally, "six less than three times the sum of twice a number and one" would be $3(2x + 1) - 6$.

15. B: To expand a squared binomial, it's necessary to use the First, Outer, Inner, Last (FOIL) method.

$$(2x - 4y)^2$$

$$(2x)(2x) + (2x)(-4y) + (-4y)(2x) + (-4y)(-4y)$$

$$4x^2 - 8xy - 8xy + 16y^2$$

$$4x^2 - 16xy + 16y^2$$

16. D: The expression is simplified by collecting like terms. Terms with the same variable and exponent are like terms, and their coefficients can be added. It is also important to remember to order the terms by decreasing degree.

$$2n^4 + (3n^3 + 5n^3) + (7n + 8n) + 3$$

$$2n^4 + 8n^3 + 15n + 3$$

17. A: Finding the product means distributing one polynomial to the other so that each term in the first is multiplied by each term in the second. Then, like terms can be collected. Multiplying the factors yields the expression:

$$20x^3 + 4x^2 + 24x - 40x^2 - 8x - 48$$

Collecting like terms means adding the x^2 terms and adding the x terms. The final answer after simplifying the expression is:

$$20x^3 - 36x^2 + 16x - 48$$

18. B: The equation can be solved by factoring the numerator into $(x + 6)(x - 5)$. Since $(x - 5)$ is on the top and bottom, that factor cancels out. This leaves the equation $x + 6 = 11$. Solving the equation gives the answer $x = 5$. When this value is plugged into the equation, it yields a zero in the denominator of the fraction. Since this is undefined, there is no solution.

19. C: The sum of three angles in a triangle is 180°. Using the ratio, the largest angle is $\frac{4}{9}$ of 180°. Multiplying $\frac{4}{9}(180°)$ results in 80°.

20. C: The sum of the squares of the two side lengths is $11^2 + 25^2 = 746$. The square of the other side length is $33^2 = 1089$. Because the sum of the squares is smaller than the square of the longest side, this angle is obtuse.

21. C: This is a triangular prism, and its volume is equal to the area of the triangle times the length. The triangle has an area of $\frac{1}{2} \times base \times height = \frac{1}{2}(8)(3) = 12$ cm². The length of the prism is 12 cm. Therefore, the volume of the shape is $12 \times 12 = 144$ cm³.

22. 87.5: For an even number of total values, the median is calculated by finding the mean, or average, of the two middle values once all values have been arranged in ascending order from least to greatest. In this case, $(92 + 83) \div 2$ would equal the median 87.5.

Math: Module 2

1. B: First, subtract 9 from both sides to isolate the radical. Then, cube each side of the equation.

$$\sqrt[3]{(2x + 11)} + 9 = 12$$

$$\sqrt[3]{(2x + 11)} = 3$$

$$2x + 11 = 27$$

Subtract 11 from both sides, and then divide by 2.

$$2x = 16$$

$$x = 8$$

2. C: The best way to solve this problem is by using a system of equations. We know that Jan bought $90 worth of apples ($a$) and oranges ($o$) at $1 and $2 respectively. That means our first equation is:

$$1a + 2o = 90$$

We also know that she bought an equal number of apples and oranges, which gives us our second equation $a = o$. We can then replace a with o in the first equation to give:

$$1o + 2o = 90$$

$$3o = 90$$

Which yields:

$$o = 30$$

Thus, Jan bought 30 oranges (and 30 apples).

3. A: First solve for x, y, and z. So, $3x = 24$ is $x = 8$, $6y = 24$ is $y = 4$, and $-2z = 24$ is $z = -12$. This means the expression $4xy + z$ would be $4(8)(4) + (-12)$, which equals 116.

4. B: Add 3 to both sides to get $4x = 8$. Then divide both sides by 4 to get $x = 2$.

5. 36: To solve this correctly, keep in mind the order of operations with the mnemonic PEMDAS (Please Excuse My Dear Aunt Sally). This stands for Parentheses, Exponents, Multiplication & Division, Addition & Subtraction. Taking it step by step, start with the parentheses:

$$4 \times 7 + (4)^2 \div 2$$

Then, apply the exponent:

$$4 \times 7 + 16 \div 2$$

Multiplication and division are both performed next:

$$28 + 8$$

Addition and subtraction are done last.

$$28 + 8 = 36$$

The solution is 36.

6. 15: Follow the order of operations in order to solve this problem. Evaluate inside the parentheses first, being sure to follow the order of operations inside the parentheses as well. First, simplify the square roots:

$$(6 \times 4) - 3^2$$

168

Then, multiply inside the parentheses:

$$24 - 3^2$$

Next, simplify the exponent:

$$24 - 9$$

Finally, subtract to get 15.

7. A: The common denominator here will be $4x$. Rewrite these fractions as:

$$\frac{3}{x} + \frac{5u}{2x} - \frac{u}{4}$$

$$\frac{12}{4x} + \frac{10u}{4x} - \frac{ux}{4x}$$

$$\frac{12 + 10u - ux}{4x}$$

8. B: There are two zeros for the given function. They are $x = 0$ and -2. The zeros can be found a number of ways, but this particular equation can be factored into:

$$f(x) = x(x^2 + 4x + 4) = x(x + 2)(x + 2)$$

By setting each factor equal to zero and solving for x, there are two solutions: $x = 0$ and $x = -2$. On a graph, these zeros can be seen where the line crosses the x-axis.

9. C: $\frac{1}{3}$ of the shirts sold were patterned. Therefore, $1 - \frac{1}{3}$ (that is, $\frac{2}{3}$) of the shirts sold were solid. A fraction of something is calculated with multiplication, so $192 \times \left(1 - \frac{1}{3}\right)$ solid shirts were sold. (We could calculate that this equals 128, but that's not necessary for this question.)

10. B: Using the conversion rate, the projected weight loss of 25 pounds is multiplied by 0.45 kg/lb to get the amount in kilograms (11.25 kg).

11. B: The y-intercept of an equation is found where the x-value is zero. Plugging in zero for x in the equation, we get $0^2 + 3(0) - 4 = -4$.

12. C: In this scenario, the variables are the number of sales and Karen's weekly pay. The weekly pay depends on the number of sales. Therefore, weekly pay is the dependent variable (y), and the number of sales is the independent variable (x). All four answer choices are in slope-intercept form, $y = mx + b$, so we just need to find m (the slope) and b (the y-intercept). We can calculate both by picking any two points, for example, (2, 380) and (4, 460).

The slope is given by $m = \frac{(y_2 - y_1)}{(x_2 - x_1)}$, so $m = \frac{460 - 380}{4 - 2} = 40$.

This gives us the equation $y = 40x + b$. Now we can plug in the x and y values from our first point to find b.

Since $380 = 40(2) + b$, we find $b = 300$. This means the equation is $y = 40x + 300$.

169

13. D: Finding the zeros for a function by factoring is done by setting the equation equal to zero, then completely factoring. Since there is a common x for each term in the provided equation, that should be factored out first to get $x(x^2 - 3x - 4)$. Then the quadratic that is left can be factored into two binomials, which are $(x + 1)(x - 4)$. This gives the factored equation $0 = x(x + 1)(x - 4)$.

14. B: For an ordered pair to be a solution to a system of inequalities, it must make a true statement for both inequalities when substituting its values for x and y. Substituting $(-3, -2)$ into the inequalities produces $(-2) > 2(-3) - 3$, which becomes $-2 > -9$, and $(-2) < -4(-3) + 8$, which becomes $-2 < 20$. Both are true statements.

15. D: The shape of the scatter plot is a parabola (U-shaped). This eliminates Choices A (a linear equation that produces a straight line) and C (an exponential equation that produces a smooth curve upward or downward). The value of a for a quadratic function in standard form ($y = ax^2 + bx + c$) indicates whether the parabola opens up (U-shaped) or opens down (upside-down U). A negative value for a produces a parabola that opens down; therefore, Choice B can also be eliminated.

16. B: There are 34 girls who are potty-trained out of a total of 52 girls:

$$34 \div 52 \approx 0.65 = 65\%$$

17. 70.4: This problem can be solved by using unit conversion. The initial units are miles per minute. The final units need to be feet per second. Converting miles to feet uses the equivalence statement $1 \text{ mi} = 5{,}280 \text{ ft}$. Converting minutes to seconds uses the equivalence statement $1 \text{ min} = 60 \text{ s}$. Setting up the ratios to convert the units is shown in the following equation:

$$\frac{72 \text{ mi}}{90 \text{ min}} \times \frac{1 \text{ min}}{60 \text{ s}} \times \frac{5{,}280 \text{ ft}}{1 \text{ mi}} = 70.4 \frac{\text{ft}}{\text{s}}$$

The initial units cancel out, and the new units are left.

18. C: The slope is given by the change in y divided by the change in x. Specifically, it's:

$$\text{slope} = \frac{y_2 - y_1}{x_2 - x_1}$$

The first point is $(-5, -3)$, and the second point is $(0, -1)$. Work from left to right when identifying coordinates. Thus, the point on the left is point 1 $(-5, -3)$ and the point on the right is point 2 $(0, -1)$.

Now we just need to plug those numbers into the equation:

$$\text{slope} = \frac{-1 - (-3)}{0 - (-5)}$$

It can be simplified to:

$$\text{slope} = \frac{-1 + 3}{0 + 5}$$

$$\text{slope} = \frac{2}{5}$$

170

19. 10: Start with the original equation: $x^2 - 2xy + 2y$, then replace each instance of x with a 2, and each instance of y with a 3 to get:

$$2^2 - 2 \times 2 \times 3 + 2 \times 3^2 = 4 - 12 + 18 = 10$$

20. B: The volume of a cube is the length of the side cubed, and 3 inches cubed is 27 in^3. Choice *A* is not the correct answer because that is 2×3 inches. Choice *C* is not the correct answer because that is 3×3 inches, and Choice *D* is not the correct answer because it represents $(3 \times 3) \times 3$.

21. C: The area of the shaded region is the area of the square minus the area of the circle. The area of the circle is πr^2. The side of the square will be $2r$, so the area of the square will be $4r^2$. Therefore, the difference is:

$$4r^2 - \pi r^2 = (4 - \pi)r^2$$

22. C: The picture demonstrates Angle-Side-Angle congruence. Choices *A* and *B* are incorrect because the picture does not show Side-Side-Side congruence and angles alone cannot prove congruence. Choice *D* is not the correct answer because there is already enough information to prove congruence.

Practice Test #2

Reading and Writing: Module 1

The next question is based on the following passage:

> The homes and buildings designed by renowned architect Frank Lloyd Wright, an icon in the realm of architecture, dot the landscape of the Chicagoland area. He pioneered a design _____ known as the Prairie School in the early 20th century, which went on to influence urban planning well into the current day.

1. Which choice completes the text with the most logical and precise word or phrase?
    a. philosophy
    b. life
    c. gift
    d. temperance

The next question is based on the following passage:

> Presidents' Day is a federal holiday that is celebrated in the United States on the third Monday of February. Previously, George Washington's and Abraham Lincoln's birthdays were celebrated separately. However, legislators sought to consolidate the two holidays into one. A _____ of both George Washington's and Abraham Lincoln's birthdays, Presidents' Day was officially designated as a federal holiday beginning in 1968.

2. Which choice completes the text with the most logical and precise word or phrase?
    a. opposition
    b. combination
    c. composition
    d. juxtaposition

The next question is based on the following passage:

> The Battle of Hastings was fought between the Normans and Anglo-Saxons in 1066 over control of the English domain. Anglo-Saxon king Harold Godwinson was defeated by Duke William, who would eventually become known as William the Conqueror. After the battle, the Anglo-Saxon English elite would be replaced by a French-speaking noble class that heavily _____ the modern English language.

3. Which choice completes the text with the most logical and precise word or phrase?
    a. discouraged
    b. destroyed
    c. influenced
    d. created

The next question is based on the following passage:

> The Federal Reserve, sometimes shortened to the Fed, is the central bank of the United States and was founded in 1913. The Fed sets interest rates, determines _____

policy, and controls the circulation of the US Dollar. Its primary stated goal is to curb inflation and control maximum interest percentages in order to prevent financial meltdowns and bank runs.

4. Which choice completes the text with the most logical and precise word or phrase?
   a. fiscal
   b. foreign
   c. military
   d. social

The next question is based on the following passage:

After winning eight consecutive Mr. Olympia bodybuilding competitions from 1998 to 2005, Ronnie Coleman is widely considered to be one of the greatest bodybuilders of all time. He is best known for his _____ physical stature, extremely heavy and fast workouts, and his signature catchphrase, "light weight, baby!" Coleman is credited with pioneering the "Mass Era" in bodybuilding, which emphasizes sheer size over definition and is still the dominant aesthetic in the sport today.

5. Which choice completes the text with the most logical and precise word or phrase?
   a. unremarkable
   b. unprecedented
   c. conventional
   d. average

The next question is based on the following passage:

When designing a weightlifting routine, it is important to schedule at least one rest day in which the lifter _____. This important gap in training allows the body to maximize the muscle stimulus presented to it by the training.

6. Which choice completes the text with the most logical and precise word or phrase?
   a. avoids physical activity
   b. makes up for any training that was missed
   c. works any weak spots in their physique
   d. applies heat to any sore muscles

The following passages are based on "Worth His While" by Amy Ella Blanchard:

Text 1: Benny turned to go back with a light step. It was late in the afternoon, and already growing shadowy in the deep pine grove through which he had to pass. He was not afraid, however, for he had sense enough to know that there were neither bears nor wildcats thereabouts, and he did not even consider whether he would encounter a snake. He caught sight of a gray squirrel scampering up a tree, and saw a clumsy land turtle traveling slowly along.

Text 2: He kept on steadily till he was about in the middle of the woods, when presently there came from the thicket close by a sound between a growl and a moan, and the boy stood still to listen. The sound was repeated, and this time it sounded nearer. Benny was no coward, but it must be confessed that his heart misgave him, and for a moment

173

he stood uncertain whether to run or whether to investigate the matter. "I'll see what it is, I won't be silly," he told himself. "Maybe somebody is hurt in there." And he dauntlessly followed the sound as a cry of distress reached his ears. Then he seized a stick and rushed forward.

7. What does the juxtaposition between these two passages reveal about Benny's character?
   a. Benny is an easily startled person.
   b. Benny is headstrong and tries to ignore his feelings of fear for the greater good.
   c. Benny's hubris gets him into trouble.
   d. Benny is an adventurous soul with a desire to help others.

The following passages are based on "The Medieval Stage" by E.K. Chambers:

Text 1: The great capitals of the later Greece—Alexandria, Antioch, and Pergamum—rivaled Athens itself in their devotion to the stage. Another development of drama, independent of Athens, in Sicily and Magna Graecia, may be distinguished as farcical rather than comic. After receiving literary treatment at the hands of Epicharmus and Sophron in the fifth century, it continued its existence under the name of *mime* (μῖμος), upon a more popular level.

Text 2: The vast popular audiences of the period under consideration cared but little for the literary drama. In the theater of Pompey, thronged with slaves and foreigners of every tongue, the finer histrionic effects must necessarily have been lost. Something more spectacular and sensuous, something appealing to a cruder sense of humor, almost inevitably took their place. There is evidence indeed that, while the theaters stood, tragedy and comedy never wholly disappeared from their boards. But it was probably only the ancient masterpieces that got a hearing.

8. What was the main difference between works of the stage in ancient Greece and ancient Rome?
   a. The Greek stage was rife with comedy, whereas the Roman stage was far more serious and deliberate about their choice of plays.
   b. The Greek tradition featured a need to innovate past their origins, whereas the Romans respected the classics that the Greeks rejected.
   c. The Greek stage had a refined sense of humor and was presented in a literary style, whereas Roman plays were meant to entertain plebeian audiences with limited access to literature.
   d. The Greek plays were silent and featured mimes, whereas the Roman stage was often loud and bombastic.

The next question is based on the following passage:

While many people are familiar with the typical tan-colored sand found at beaches, there are actually beaches around the world that feature sand in a variety of colors. For instance, in Hawaii, there are beaches with jet-black sand, which is the result of eroded volcanic rock from nearby volcanoes like Mauna Loa. In Greece, there is a beach with pink sand, colored by foraminifera, tiny coral organisms, as well as pink-hued shells. These are just a couple of examples; there are also beaches with purple sand and even green sand.

9. What is the main purpose of this passage?
    a.   To explain the process of how sand is made
    b.   To warn readers about organisms within sand
    c.   To highlight the diversity of sand colors
    d.   To encourage people to visit a variety of beaches

The next question is based on the following passage:

> He was in an amazing plight. His coat was dusty and dirty, and smeared with green
> down the sleeves; his hair disordered, and as it seemed to me greyer—either with dust
> and dirt or because its colour had actually faded. His face was ghastly pale; his chin had
> a brown cut on it—a cut half-healed; his expression was haggard and drawn, as by
> intense suffering. For a moment he hesitated in the doorway, as if he had been dazzled
> by the light. Then he came into the room. He walked with just such a limp as I have seen
> in footsore tramps. We stared at him in silence, expecting him to speak.

10. What is the best summary of the man in this passage?
    a.   He is disheveled and shocking in appearance.
    b.   He is filthy but healthy.
    c.   He is silent and brooding.
    d.   He is alert and looking for conflict with others.

The next question is based on the following passage:

Planet	Number of Rings
Mars	0
Jupiter	4
Saturn	8+
Uranus	2
Neptune	6

> Planetary rings are formed in several ways. The most common way is through the
> impact of moons. Moons may orbit too close to their parent planet. In a process called
> tidal disruption, the planet's tidal forces will then tear the moon apart and create a ring
> of debris. Planets that are farther from the sun generally have more moons.

11. Based on the information in both the table and text, which of the following can we assume?
    a.   Jupiter two fewer moons than Uranus because it is closer to the sun.
    b.   Saturn has more rings than the other planets because it has more moons.
    c.   Neptune has more moons than Jupiter and Uranus combined.
    d.   Even though Jupiter has fewer rings than Saturn, it must have more moons because it is bigger
         in size.

The next question is based on the following passage:

> On the seventh of January between seven and eight hundred tradesmen had assembled
> in Paris to discuss a new tax which was to be levied on house property. They deputed
> ten of their number to wait upon the Duke of Orleans, who, according to his custom,
> affected popularity. The duke received them and they informed him that they were

175

resolved not to pay this tax, even if they were obliged to defend themselves against its collectors by force of arms. They were listened to with great politeness by the duke, who held out hopes of easier measures, promised to speak in their behalf to the queen, and dismissed them with the ordinary expression of royalty, "We will see what we can do."

12. Which of the following choices best explains the tradesmen's response to the tax increase?
    a. They spoke to the queen and expressed their concerns.
    b. They sought aid from the Duke of Orleans, who is very wealthy.
    c. They paid the tax without complaint.
    d. They protested in Paris by threatening to resist forcible collection.

The next question is based on the following passage:

Mount Roraima, one of the most famous tepuis (flat-topped mountain formations), is home to several endemic species of plants and animals, including the Roraima bush toad and the Roraima black frog. The mountain, which is part of the Guiana Shield, has a unique microclimate that has encouraged an impressive level of biodiversity. It is believed that Mount Roraima served as the inspiration for *The Lost World* by Sir Arthur Conan Doyle, where explorers discover a unique world that is beyond imagination.

13. Which choice best states the main purpose of the text?
    a. To advocate for preserving Mount Roraima
    b. To show the importance of biodiversity
    c. To introduce *The Lost World* to readers
    d. To highlight the unique features of Mount Roraima

The next question is based on the following passage from Twelfth Night *by William Shakespeare:*

SIR TOBY: What a plague means my niece to take the death of her brother thus? I am sure care's an enemy to life.

MARIA: By my troth, Sir Toby, you must come in earlier o' nights; your cousin, my lady, takes great exceptions to your ill hours.

SIR TOBY: Why, let her except, before excepted.

MARIA: Ay, but you must confine yourself within the modest limits of order.

SIR TOBY: Confine? I'll confine myself no finer than I am. These clothes are good enough to drink in, and so be these boots too; and they be not, let them hang themselves in their own straps.

MARIA: That quaffing and drinking will undo you: I heard my lady talk of it yesterday; and of a foolish knight that you brought in one night here to be her wooer.

14. What is Maria attempting to explain to Sir Toby in this passage?
    a. That Sir Toby's niece is incredibly ill at the moment
    b. That Sir Toby is not respected by his friends or family
    c. That his late-night antics and drinking are concerning for his niece
    d. That Sir Toby needs to find better clothes and boots

The next question is based on the following passage:

Most men appear never to have considered what a house is, and are actually though needlessly poor all their lives because they think that they must have such a one as their neighbors have. As if one were to wear any sort of coat which the tailor might cut out for him, or, gradually leaving off palmleaf hat or cap of woodchuck skin, complain of hard times because he could not afford to buy him a crown! It is possible to invent a house still more convenient and luxurious than we have, which yet all would admit that man could not afford to pay for. Shall we always study to obtain more of these things, and not sometimes to be content with less? Shall the respectable citizen thus gravely teach, by precept and example, the necessity of the young man's providing a certain number of superfluous glow-shoes, and umbrellas, and empty guest chambers for empty guests, before he dies?

15. What is the main purpose of this passage?
    a. To criticize society for pressuring man to conform to owning a home
    b. To condemn the government for not providing housing
    c. To argue that housing is a basic human right
    d. To argue that minimalism is difficult to achieve

The next question is based on the following passage:

The new development of so-called _____ is just the next step in our journey of building more useful machines. Programs that can construct sentences are scary—and impressive—but their internal workings are hollow. They regurgitate sentences without actually thinking about a sentence's content.

16. Which choice completes the text so that it conforms to the conventions of Standard English?
    a. artificial intelligence
    b. "artificial intelligence"
    c. 'artificial intelligence'
    d. "artificial" intelligence

The next question is based on the following passage:

It had originally meant that the captain, Mr. Arrow, Hunter, Joyce, the doctor, and the squire were to occupy these six berths. Now Redruth and I were to get two of them, and Mr. Arrow and the captain were to sleep on deck in the companion, which had been enlarged on each side till you might almost have called it a round-house. Very low it was still, of course, but there was room to swing two hammocks, and even the mate seemed pleased with the _____ perhaps, had been doubtful as to the crew, but that is only a guess, for as you shall hear, we had not long the benefit of his opinion.

177

17. Which choice completes the text so that it conforms to the conventions of Standard English?
    a. arrangement, even he,
    b. arrangement. They,
    c. arrangement. Even she,
    d. arrangement. Even he,

The next question is based on the following passage:

> When is it OK to _____ agree that, in general, stealing is wrong. Yet, at the same time, there seem to be particular circumstances in which this crime is permissible. We condone the starving woman who steals bread to survive—but if she steals something valuable with which to purchase bread, we condemn her. Do we condone certain kinds of theft, or do we just forgive them?

18. Which choice completes the text so that it conforms to the conventions of Standard English?
    a. steal? We all
    b. steal? You
    c. steal. We
    d. steal? Everyone

The next question is based on the following passage:

> The principal site is Palenque, the ruins of which were among the earliest of all to attract attention. The style of the architecture with gigantic vaults and comb-shaped gables _____ from Copan and Quirigua, which it surpasses also in the magnificence of its sculptures.

19. Which choice completes the text so that it conforms to the conventions of Standard English?
    a. to distinguish Palenque
    b. distinguishes Palenque
    c. distinguished Palenque
    d. had distinguished Palenque

The next question is based on the following passage:

> Iggy snarled from where she lay curled up beneath the old pine tree. Her hackles stuck up like a hedgehog's spikes, as though she thought my hand was a viper. "Come _____ girl," I whispered.

20. Which choice completes the text so that it conforms to the conventions of Standard English?
    a. hear, poor
    b. here, poor
    c. to here, poor
    d. to hear, poor

The next question is based on the following passage:

> Seventeen steps led down into the old, cobwebby basement of Grandpa's house. Gregory shifted his feet. Just seventeen steps. "The _____ the bottom," he thought. "Top shelf, just to the right."

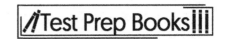

21. Which choice completes the text so that it conforms to the conventions of Standard English?
    a. flashlight's at
    b. flashlight at
    c. flash-light's at
    d. flash lights

The next question is based on the following passage:

> The best birds for culinary purposes, however, are the curlews. Some are as large as
> _____ Unfortunately, we were not provided with shot, and balls fell harmlessly
> among them.

22. Which choice completes the text so that it conforms to the conventions of Standard English?
    a. small fouls.
    b. small foils.
    c. small fowls.
    d. small fools.

The next question is based on the following passage:

> After the First World War, the United States enjoyed an unprecedented time of
> economic prosperity. The development of new technologies, _____ burgeoning
> middle class, increased the standard of living dramatically for the average person.

23. Which choice completes the text with the most logical transition?
    a. despite a
    b. alongside a
    c. in contrast with a
    d. largely dissuaded by a

The next question is based on the following passage:

> In the 1920s, the stock market entered a boom period, resulting in a large amount of
> capital being pumped into the American economy. Speculative traders made large
> amounts of money gambling on risky stocks, _____ increasing the prosperity
> experienced by many people at the time.

24. Which choice completes the text with the most logical transition?
    a. always
    b. subsequently
    c. sometimes
    d. despite

While researching a topic, a student has taken the following notes:

- Ivan the Terrible was the first Russian tsar, who reigned as a part of the Rurikid Dynasty from 1547 to 1584.

- Ivan's conquest of the remaining khanates, which held large swathes of Russia, united the lands under the Grand Duchy of Moscow.

179

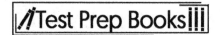

- Ivan modernized Russia by enacting legal reforms, establishing a police force, pursuing positive foreign relations with other European states, and colonizing Siberia.

- Ivan is best known for being a paranoid man who treated his family and nation with unmatched brutality, once killing his own son in a fit of rage.

- Ivan's close relationship with the Orthodox Church and his emphasis on his divine right to rule has influenced the Church's relations with the Russian head of state into the modern day.

25. The student wants to describe the changes that Ivan the Terrible brought to Russia. Which choice most effectively uses relevant information from the notes to accomplish this goal?
   a. Ivan the Terrible was a paranoid man that presided over many wars and conflicts, leading to a crisis in Russia. He even killed his own son in a fit of rage which caused a succession crisis after his death.
   b. Ivan the Terrible was an ambitious ruler that united Russia for the first time, colonized Siberia, created a police force to impose his will on the people, and established foreign relations with other European nations in pursuit of trade.
   c. The Orthodox Church, which ordained Ivan the Terrible's divine right to rule and treat his subjects poorly, is still an active force in Russian politics today despite their suspicious connection to his son's untimely death.
   d. After conquering all remaining khanate rump states and establishing a police force that terrorized the newly formed Russian Empire, Ivan the Terrible set his sights on colonizing all of Northern Asia and Eastern Europe.

The next question is based on the following passage:

Agglomerated stone is a type of material made by combining finely crushed rocks with adhesive material. One of the most abundant uses of agglomerated stone is in kitchen countertops and stone flooring.

26. Which quote would best support the claim made in the passage?
   a. "Agglomerated stone is created by mixing polymer resin with rocks, letting the composite harden, and then cutting it to size."
   b. "Normally, a completed piece of agglomerated stone is about 90 percent rock and 10 percent adhesive material."
   c. "The type of stone used for kitchen countertops is most commonly quartz, whereas flooring utilizes marble."
   d. "Agglomerated stone is a cheaper alternative to solid pieces of rock, as sourcing large enough pieces to cut is as easy as creating them beforehand."

The next question is based on the following passage:

In the American legal system, criminal and civil trials carry various differences. _____, a criminal trial is held to determine whether a person should be penalized for committing a crime, whereas a civil trial is held to determine if a monetary judgment should be awarded for a noncriminal act.

180

27. Which choice completes the text with the most logical transition?
    a. To clarify
    b. Lastly
    c. For example
    d. Primarily

Reading and Writing: Module 2

The next question is based on the following passage:

> Julius Caesar was a Roman general and dictator who is credited with having heavily contributed to the fall of the Roman Republic and the rise of the Roman Empire. After conquering a vast swath of western Europe as a general, Caesar disobeyed the Senate's stern _____ to disband his army and marched on Rome. After defeating his main political rival, Pompey, Caesar declared himself to be dictator for life of the Roman Republic. In 44 BCE, while making plans to invade the Parthian Empire, Caesar was assassinated on the Ides of March by the Roman Senate.

1. Which choice completes the text with the most logical and precise word or phrase?
    a. suggestion
    b. request
    c. plea
    d. command

The following passage is based on Oscar Wilde's The Importance of Being Earnest:

> "I haven't the smallest intention of doing anything of the kind. To begin with, I dined there on Monday, and once a week is quite enough to _____ one's own relatives. In the second place, whenever I do dine there I am always treated as a member of the family, and sent down with either no woman at all, or two. In the third place, I know perfectly well whom she will place me next to, to-night. She will place me next to Mary Farquhar, who always flirts with her own husband across the dinner-table. That is not very pleasant."

2. Which choice completes the text with the most logical and precise word or phrase?
    a. be around
    b. dine with
    c. speak to
    d. go out with

The following passage is based on Aristophanes' The Birds:

> There is nothing more useful nor more pleasant than to have wings. To begin with, just let us suppose a _____ to be dying with hunger and to be weary of the choruses of the tragic poets; if he were winged, he would fly off, go home to dine and come back with his stomach filled. Some Patroclides in urgent need would not have to soil his cloak, but could fly off, satisfy his requirements, and, having recovered his breath, return.

3. Which choice completes the text with the most logical and precise word or phrase?
    a. actor
    b. writer
    c. spectator
    d. poet

The next question is based on the following passage:

> Sometimes, passionate discussions may become heated and, through no fault of either party, begin to stir up anger and distract the participants. Oftentimes, excusing oneself from the discussion to regain composure is a valid technique to keep any discussion or debate _____.

4. Which choice completes the text with the most logical and precise word or phrase?
    a. hostile and productive
    b. relaxed and on-topic
    c. inflamed and energetic
    d. respectful and meandering

The next question is based on the following passage:

> When commuting by public transit, it is often a _____ to keep to oneself. It is acceptable to carry on a quiet conversation, but loud or uninvited conversations can often be perceived as disrespectful by other riders.

5. Which choice completes the text with the most logical and precise word or phrase?
    a. bad idea
    b. lawful requirement
    c. personal preference
    d. wise practice

The next question is based on the following passage:

> Although many financial gurus recommend cutting up one's credit cards, they are not all bad. Although credit cards do feature exorbitantly high interest rates on unpaid bills, paying one's bill in full and never overspending can provide fiscal flexibility during emergencies and improve one's credit score.

6. What should a person do with their first credit card based on the advice in the passage above?
    a. Take advantage of limited-time 0% interest offers
    b. Keep a balance to avoid hurting their credit score
    c. Always pay the balance in full and never overspend
    d. Close their account immediately

The next question is based on the following passage:

> With the advent of smartphones, time to "unplug" has become quite difficult to come by. Most experts recommend getting at least thirty uninterrupted minutes of _____ on a daily basis. This can be accomplished through meditation, quality time with family and friends, or even taking a nap.

7. Which choice completes the text with the most logical and precise word or phrase?
   a. decompressing
   b. unplugging
   c. talking
   d. driving

The next question is based on the following passages:

Text 1: Although the American public once had a fascination for the latest and greatest in architectural achievement, increasing new home prices combined with a nostalgia for a bygone era have led many new homeowners to opt to restore historic houses. Instead of tearing down old houses, many restoration specialists will use materials from dilapidated homes to create a new one for their clients.

Text 2: As of 2024, the average home price in the United States is considered to be "unaffordable" for America's mean income bracket due to high interest rates and the lack of a supply of available homes. This is leading to an increasing number of Americans who rent, live with family, or refuse to move out of their current house due to economic anxiety.

8. What advice from Text 1 can an American take who finds themselves in a situation as described by Text 2 but still wants to purchase a house?
   a. Move back in with their parents
   b. Arrange a rent-to-own agreement with their current landlord
   c. Purchase a historic house and have it restored
   d. Improve their credit score so they qualify for a mortgage on a new home

The next question is based on the following passage:

Jane Eyre by Charlotte Brontë is a prose fiction work from 1847. It follows the title character as she navigates childhood, education, her career as a governess, love, and more. She often asserts her autonomy and goes against the social expectations of the time. The themes of independence and freedom are apparent throughout the text.

9. Which quotation would be the most effective evidence for the claims about *Jane Eyre*'s themes?
   a. "To women who please me only by their faces, I am the very devil when I find out they have neither souls nor hearts—when they open to me a perspective of flatness, triviality, and perhaps imbecility, coarseness, and ill-temper: but to the clear eye and eloquent tongue, to the soul made of fire, and the character that bends but does not break—at once supple and stable, tractable and consistent—I am ever tender and true."
   b. "I remembered his fine voice; I knew he liked to sing—good singers generally do. I was no vocalist myself, and, in his fastidious judgment, no musician, either; but I delighted in listening when the performance was good."
   c. "I am no bird; and no net ensnares me: I am a free human being with an independent will, which I now exert to leave you."
   d. "I did not indeed dream of sorrow, but as little did I dream of joy; for I never slept at all. With little Adèle in my arms, I watched the slumber of childhood—so tranquil, so passionless, so innocent—and waited for the coming day: all my life was awake and astir in my frame: and as soon as the sun rose I rose too."

183

The next question is based on the following passage:

> "Bartleby the Scrivener: A Tale of Wall Street" is a short story by Herman Melville that shows life in the business world. It displays how a demanding job can suck the life out of a person and hurt human connection.

10. Which quotation from "Bartleby the Scrivener: A Tale of Wall Street" most effectively illustrates this claim?

    a. "I am a man who, from his youth upwards, has been filled with a profound conviction that the easiest way of life is the best. Hence, though I belong to a profession proverbially energetic and nervous, even to turbulence, at times, yet nothing of that sort have I ever suffered to invade my peace. I am one of those unambitious lawyers who never addresses a jury, or in any way draws down public applause; but in the cool tranquility of a snug retreat, do a snug business among rich men's bonds and mortgages and title-deeds."

    b. "I should have stated before that ground glass folding-doors divided my premises into two parts, one of which was occupied by my scriveners, the other by myself. According to my humor I threw open these doors, or closed them. I resolved to assign Bartleby a corner by the folding-doors, but on my side of them, so as to have this quiet man within easy call, in case any trifling thing was to be done."

    c. "I speak less than truth when I say that, on his own account, he occasioned me uneasiness. If he would but have named a single relative or friend, I would instantly have written, and urged their taking the poor fellow away to some convenient retreat. But he seemed alone, absolutely alone in the universe. A bit of wreck in the mid-Atlantic. At length, necessities connected with my business tyrannized over all other considerations."

    d. "Nothing so aggravates an earnest person as a passive resistance. If the individual so resisted be of a not inhumane temper, and the resisting one perfectly harmless in his passivity; then, in the better moods of the former, he will endeavor charitably to construe to his imagination what proves impossible to be solved by his judgment."

The next question is based on the following passage:

Grade Level	5	6	7	8	9	10
First responder (firefighter, police officer, EMT, etc.)	38%	28%	25%	20%	14%	10%
Business/office professional (business owner, attorney, accountant, IT)	25%	30%	28%	35%	42%	40%
Medical field (doctor, surgeon, nurse)	30%	31%	30%	29%	24%	15%
Unsure or undecided	7%	11%	17%	16%	20%	35%

> A K–12 school surveyed its students to see what career paths they could see themselves pursuing in the future. They asked students to pick between various job fields and pick which one they believed suited them best. The evaluations varied based on grade level, for example, _____

11. Which choice most effectively uses data from the table to complete the passage?
    a. the youngest students were the least likely to want to pursue a career in the medical field.
    b. as grade levels advanced, students became less likely to pursue first responder careers and more likely to choose business- or office-related careers.
    c. with each grade level advancement, more students wanted to participate in business or office jobs while fewer students were unsure.
    d. every job choice percentage consistently changes as the grade level goes up or down.

The next question is based on the following passage:

> The Angakkuit, or Inuit spiritual leaders, are believed to communicate with the spirit world. This includes animals and humans. They may perform intricate rituals that call upon guidance from the spirit world to heal the mental, physical, and spiritual ailments of the living. Their pivotal place in the community means that they are also teachers who pass down traditions to younger generations and preserve Inuit culture.

12. Which choice best states the main purpose of the text?
    a. To describe the importance of keeping cultural practices alive through every generation
    b. To prove that the spirit world is real and communicative
    c. To educate readers about the role of the Angakkuit in Inuit culture
    d. To promote spiritual practices that connect the living with spirits

While researching a topic, a student has taken the following notes:

> There are three major shapes of galaxies: elliptical, spiral, and irregular.
> Spiral galaxies are flat, rotating disks, and elliptical galaxies are round or oval.
> Irregular galaxies can be any shape, such as ring shaped.
> They were defined by Edwin Hubble in 1936.
> Elliptical galaxies are the largest.
> More than 60 percent of nearby galaxies are spirals.
> The Milky Way is a spiral galaxy.

13. The student wants to emphasize the most common type of galaxy that humans observe. Which choice most effectively uses relevant information from the notes to accomplish this goal?
    a. Elliptical galaxies are larger than spiral galaxies and are therefore easier to observe.
    b. Our own Milky Way galaxy is a spiral galaxy, meaning that it is a flat, rotating disk.
    c. Edwin Hubble determined that elliptical galaxies are the most abundant.
    d. Spiral galaxies, such as the Milky Way, are the most common type of observable galaxy.

The next question is based on the following passage from Henry VI Part 1 *by William Shakespeare. The speaking character, Joan, has been accused of witchcraft:*

> JOAN: First, let me tell you whom you have condemn'd:
> Not me begotten of a shepherd swain,
> But issued from the progeny of kings;
> Virtuous and holy; chosen from above,
> By inspiration of celestial grace,
> To work exceeding miracles on earth.
> I never had to do with wicked spirits:

But you, that are polluted with your lusts,
Stain'd with the guiltless blood of innocents,
Corrupt and tainted with a thousand vices,
Because you want the grace that others have,
You judge it straight a thing impossible
To compass wonders but by help of devils.
No, misconceived! Joan of Arc hath been
A virgin from her tender infancy,
Chaste and immaculate in very thought;
Whose maiden blood, thus rigorously effused,
Will cry for vengeance at the gates of heaven.

14. Which choice best describes the way Joan defends herself in this monologue?
    a. She argues that she has been possessed by a wicked spirit.
    b. She states that she is virtuous and chaste, therefore innocent.
    c. She claims that only God is allowed to judge her, not her abusers.
    d. She condemns her accusers for being bloodthirsty against women.

The next question is based on the following passage, a poem titled "The Ghost" from The Flowers of Evil *by Charles Baudelaire:*

Just like an angel with evil eye,
I shall return to thee silently,
Upon thy bower I'll alight,
With falling shadows of the night.

With thee, my brownie, I'll commune,
And give thee kisses cold as the moon,
And with a serpent's moist embrace,
I'll crawl around thy resting-place.

And when the livid morning falls,
Thou'lt find alone the empty walls,
And till the evening, cold 'twill be.

As others with their tenderness,
Upon thy life and youthfulness,
I'll reign alone with dread o'er thee.

15. Which choice best states the purpose of this poem?
    a. The speaker is comparing angelic flowers with evil serpents.
    b. The speaker is describing their desire to be young again.
    c. The speaker is promising to return to a loved one after death.
    d. The speaker is hoping for winter to end, as they find it dreadful.

The next question is based on the following passage:

The computer supergiant Apple was founded by Steve Jobs, Steve Wozniak, and Ronald Wayne in 1976. The latter left the company less than two weeks later. _____ is well-known to this day as the company's charismatic figurehead. He was more than an executive guiding a company. Jobs became a culture icon through his focus not just on developing technology but also on encouraging customers to believe that technology is fashionable. This vision produced the world of tablets and smartphones we live in today. But what about Wozniak?

16. Which choice completes the text so that it conforms to the conventions of Standard English?
    a. Of course he
    b. Of course, Jobs
    c. Of course, Wayne
    d. Of course Wayne

The next question is based on the following passage:

He, the young _____ who cherished

Noble longings for the strife,

By the roadside fell and perished,

Weary with the march of life!

17. Which choice completes the text so that it conforms to the conventions of Standard English?
    a. and strong
    b. and, strong
    c. and strong,
    d. but strong,

The next question is based on the following passage:

Now, few things pass by a village and leave no talk _____ Nor did this unicorn. For the three that saw it going by in the starlight immediately told their families, and many of these ran from their houses to tell the good news to others, for all strange news was well accounted for in Erl because of the talk that it made, and talk was held to be needful when work was over to pass the evenings away. So they talked long of the unicorn.

18. Which choice completes the text so that it conforms to the conventions of Standard English?
    a. behind them;
    b. behind it.
    c. behind it—
    d. behind them.

187

The next question is based on the following passage:

> Mycroft Holmes was a much larger and stouter man than Sherlock. His body was absolutely corpulent, but his face, though massive, had preserved something of the sharpness of expression which was so remarkable in that of his brother. His eyes, which were of a _____ seemed always to retain that far-away, introspective look which I had only observed in Sherlock's when he was exerting his full powers.

19. Which choice completes the text so that it conforms to the conventions of Standard English?
    a. peculiar light, watery grey,
    b. peculiarly light, watery grey,
    c. peculiarest light, watery grey,
    d. peculiarly light watery grey,

The next question is based on the following passage:

> "Didn't I tell you _____ Flask; "Yes, you'll soon see this right whale's head hoisted up opposite that parmacetti's."
>
> In good time, Flask's saying proved true. As before, the Pequod steeply leaned over towards the sperm whale's head; now, by the counterpoise of both heads, she regained her even keel, though sorely strained, you may well believe.

20. Which choice completes the text so that it conforms to the conventions of Standard English?
    a. so?", said
    b. so?," said
    c. so," said
    d. so?" said

The next question is based on the following passage:

> That same night, Max fell fast asleep as soon as he was in bed. Never in his career had he used his muscles so much in one day. His rest was dreamless, but he awoke as the clock struck six, and lay thinking. It was a glorious morning, for his window was illumined by the sunshine, and he felt warm and comfortable. _____ the same, he shivered.

21. Which choice completes the text so that it conforms to the conventions of Standard English?
    a. For all
    b. But all
    c. To all
    d. At all

The next question is based on the following passage:

> The best editing tip I've ever heard is to cut 10% of the total words when crafting the second draft. This shouldn't trim content—don't cut scenes, characters, and so on. _____ draft ought to tighten sentences by pruning excess words.

22. Which choice completes the text so that it conforms to the conventions of Standard English?
    a. Rather, these
    b. Rather, that
    c. Rather, the
    d. Rather, this

While researching a topic, a student has taken the following notes:

> The 1920s saw an unprecedented increase in economic activity in the United States.
> Speculative asset trading created an inflationary bubble in the American economy.
> Many European countries defaulted on the loans they had been given during World War I.
> The bubble, alongside these loans going into default, caused a massive sell-off in the stock market.
> This sell-off, marking the beginning of the Great Depression, came to be known as "Black Tuesday."

23. The student wants to identify the causes of the Great Depression. Which choice most effectively uses relevant information from the notes to accomplish this goal?
    a. A massive stock sell-off known as "Black Tuesday" caused the Great Depression.
    b. The unprecedented increase in economic activity during the 1920s eventually caused a speculative asset bubble known as the Great Depression.
    c. A speculative asset bubble, alongside many European countries entering default on their wartime loans, caused the Great Depression to be kicked off by a massive sell-off known as "Black Tuesday."
    d. The Great Depression led to a speculative asset bubble that caused many European countries to default on their wartime loans, which culminated in an event known as "Black Tuesday."

The next question is based on the following passage:

> After the 1929 stock market crash, the standard of living for the average American dropped significantly almost overnight. This led to a large number of people attempting to withdraw their money from banks and the stock market before it lost more value, _____ causing a bank run that wiped out many people's life savings.

24. Which choice completes the text with the most logical transition?
    a. further
    b. after
    c. nevertheless
    d. consequently

189

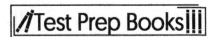

The next question is based on the following passage:

> Although experimentation with artificial fabrics has reached a fever pitch in the age of athleisure fashion, many animal products are still used in weather-resistant apparel. _____, sheep's wool and goose down are still used in thermal blankets, jackets, and winter boots.

25. Which choice completes the text with the most logical transition?
    a. For example
    b. Consequently
    c. Granted
    d. Likewise

The next question is based on the following passage:

> King George V was the King of the British Empire from 1910 until 1936. George presided over pivotal events in British history such as the Empire's territorial zenith, the establishment of the House of Windsor, and the First World War, in which George's cousins, Kaiser Wilhelm II of Germany and Tsar Nicolas II of Russia, also participated. _____ Nicolas was overthrown in a coup and taken prisoner by Bolshevik forces by the end of the war, George refused to give him and his family asylum in Britain due to their extreme unpopularity.

26. Which choice completes the text with the most logical transition?
    a. Although
    b. To demonstrate that
    c. After
    d. Since

The next question is based on the following passage:

> The Russian Revolution is a highly complicated event that spans many years and is marked by several cataclysmic turning points. The February Revolution in 1917 ended with the establishment of the Provisional Government and the overthrow of Tsar Nicolas II. _____ Nicolas's removal, the October Revolution occurred later in the year in which the Bolsheviks seized power from the Provisional Government and took Nicolas and his family prisoner.

27. Which choice completes the text with the most logical transition?
    a. Following
    b. On account of
    c. Simultaneously with
    d. Despite

Math: Module 1

1. If $6t + 4 = 16$, what is t?
   a. 1
   b. 2
   c. 3
   d. 4

2. The variable y is directly proportional to x. If $y = 3$ when $x = 5$, then what is y when $x = 20$?
   a. 10
   b. 12
   c. 14
   d. 16

3. Solve for x, if $x^2 - 2x - 8 = 0$.

   a. $2 \pm \frac{\sqrt{30}}{2}$

   b. $2 \pm 4\sqrt{2}$

   c. 1 ± 3

   d. $4 \pm \sqrt{2}$

4. A ball is drawn at random from a ball pit containing 8 red balls, 7 yellow balls, 6 green balls, and 5 purple balls. What's the probability that the ball drawn is yellow?

   a. $\frac{1}{26}$

   b. $\frac{19}{26}$

   c. $\frac{7}{26}$

   d. 1

5. In an office, there are 50 workers. A total of 60% of the workers are women. 50% of the women (and none of the other workers) are wearing skirts. How many workers are wearing skirts?
   a. 12
   b. 15
   c. 16
   d. 20

6. If Sarah reads at an average rate of 21 pages in four nights, how many nights will it take her to read 140 pages?
   a. 6 nights
   b. 26 nights
   c. 8 nights
   d. 27 nights

7. Apples cost $2 each, while oranges cost $3 each. Maria purchased 10 fruits in total and spent $22. How many apples did she buy?

8. What are the roots of the polynomial $x^2 + x - 2$?
   a. 1 and −2
   b. −1 and 2
   c. 2 and −2
   d. 9 and 13

9. The phone bill is calculated each month using the equation $c = 50g + 75$. The cost of the phone bill per month is represented by c, and g represents the gigabytes of data used that month. Identify and interpret the slope of this equation.
   a. 75 dollars per day
   b. 75 gigabytes per day
   c. 50 dollars per day
   d. 50 dollars per gigabyte

10. $x^4 - 16$ can be simplified to which of the following?
   a. $(x^2 - 4)(x^2 + 4)$
   b. $(x^2 + 4)(x^2 + 4)$
   c. $(x^2 - 4)(x^2 - 4)$
   d. $(x^2 - 2)(x^2 + 4)$

11. $(4x^2y^4)^{\frac{3}{2}}$ can be simplified to which of the following?

   a. $8x^3y^6$

   b. $4x^{\frac{5}{2}}y$

   c. $4xy$

   d. $32x^{\frac{7}{2}}y^{\frac{11}{2}}$

12. If $\sqrt{1 + x} = 4$, what is x?
   a. 10
   b. 15
   c. 20
   d. 25

13. Suppose $\frac{x+2}{x} = 2$. What is x?
   a. −1
   b. 0
   c. 2
   d. 4

192

14. A National Hockey League store in the state of Michigan advertises 50% off all items. Sales tax in Michigan is 6%. How much would a hat originally priced at $32.99 and a jersey originally priced at $64.99 cost during this sale? Round to the nearest penny.
   a. $97.98
   b. $103.86
   c. $51.93
   d. $48.99

15. A line passes through the point $(1, 2)$ and crosses the y-axis at $y = 1$. Which of the following is an equation for this line?
   a. $y = 2x$
   b. $y = x + 1$
   c. $x + y = 1$
   d. $y = \frac{x}{2} - 2$

16. A traveler takes an hour to drive to a museum, spends 3 hours and 30 minutes there, and takes half an hour to drive home. What percentage of their time was spent driving?
   a. 15%
   b. 30%
   c. 40%
   d. 60%

17. A six-sided die is rolled. What is the probability that the roll is 1 or 2? Round to two decimal places.

18. A shipping box has a length of 8 inches, a width of 14 inches, and a height of 4 inches. If all three dimensions are doubled, what is the relationship between the volume of the new box and the volume of the original box?
   a. The volume of the new box is double the volume of the original box.
   b. The volume of the new box is four times as large as the volume of the original box.
   c. The volume of the new box is six times as large as the volume of the original box.
   d. The volume of the new box is eight times as large as the volume of the original box.

19. Which measure for the center of a small sample set is most affected by outliers?
   a. Mean
   b. Median
   c. Mode
   d. None of the above

20. A right triangle has a hypotenuse of 10 inches, and one leg is 8 inches. In inches, how long is the other leg?

21. An equilateral triangle has a perimeter of 18 feet. The sides of a square have the same length as the triangle's sides. What is the area of the square?
   a. 6 square feet
   b. 36 square feet
   c. 256 square feet
   d. 1,000 square feet

193

22. Suppose an investor deposits $1,200 into a bank account that accrues 1 percent interest per month. Assuming x represents the number of months since the deposit and y represents the money in the account, which of the following exponential functions models the scenario?

    a. $y = (0.01)(1200^x)$
    b. $y = (1200)(0.01^x)$
    c. $y = (1.01)(1200^x)$
    d. $y = (1200)(1.01^x)$

Math: Module 2

1. What is the sum of $\frac{1}{3}$ and $\frac{2}{5}$?

    a. $\frac{3}{8}$

    b. $\frac{11}{15}$

    c. $\frac{11}{30}$

    d. $\frac{4}{5}$

2. Ten students take a test. Five students get a 50. Four students get a 70. If the average score is 55, what was the last student's score?

    a. 20
    b. 40
    c. 50
    d. 60

3. A map has a scale of 1 inch per 5 miles. A car can travel 60 miles per hour. If the distance from the start to the destination is 3 inches on the map, how many minutes will it take the car to make the trip?

    a. 12 minutes
    b. 15 minutes
    c. 17 minutes
    d. 20 minutes

4. 6 is 30% of what number?

    a. 18
    b. 20
    c. 24
    d. 26

5. Kristen purchases $100 worth of CDs and DVDs. The CDs cost $10 each and the DVDs cost $15. If she bought four DVDs, how many CDs did she buy?

6. A student gets an 85% on a test with 20 questions. How many questions did the student solve correctly?

7. If $f(x) = x^2 - 3x + 17$, then what is $f(x + 1)$?
   a. $x^2 - 3x + 19$
   b. $x^2 - x + 15$
   c. $x^2 + 2x + 18$
   d. $x^2 - 3x + 14$

8. For which of the following are $x = 4$ and $x = -4$ solutions?
   a. $x^2 + 16 = 0$
   b. $x^2 + 4x - 4 = 0$
   c. $x^2 - 2x - 2 = 0$
   d. $x^2 - 16 = 0$

9. Before a race of four horses, you make a random guess of which horse will get first place and which will get second place. Rounded to two decimal places, what is the probability that both your guesses will be correct?

10. Five students take a test. The scores of the first four students are 80, 85, 75, and 60. If the median score is 80, which of the following could NOT be the score of the fifth student?
   a. 60
   b. 80
   c. 85
   d. 100

11. Which graph will be a line parallel to the graph of $y = 3x - 2$?
   a. $6x - 2y = -2$
   b. $4x - y = -4$
   c. $3y = x - 2$
   d. $2x - 2y = 2$

12. A company invests $50,000 in a building where they can produce saws. If the cost of producing one saw is $40, then which function expresses the amount of money the company pays? The variable y is the money paid and x is the number of saws produced.
   a. $y = 50,000x + 40$
   b. $y + 40 = x - 50,000$
   c. $y = 40x - 50,000$
   d. $y = 40x + 50,000$

13. A line passes through the origin and through the point $(-3, 4)$. What is the slope of the line?
   a. $-\dfrac{4}{3}$

   b. $-\dfrac{3}{4}$

   c. $\dfrac{4}{3}$

   d. $\dfrac{3}{4}$

195

14. Which of the following functions represents the graph below?

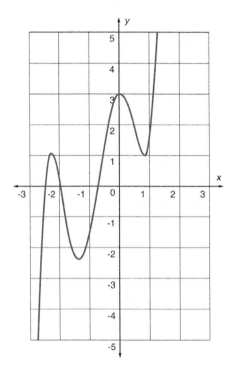

 a. $y = x^5 + 3.5x^4 - 6.5x^2 + 0.5x + 3$
 b. $y = x^5 - 3.5x^4 + 6.5x^2 - 0.5x - 3$
 c. $y = 5x^4 - 6.5x^2 + 0.5x + 3$
 d. $y = -5x^4 - 6.5x^2 + 0.5x + 3$

15. Simplify: $(5x^2 - 3x + 4) - (2x^2 - 7)$?
 a. x^5
 b. $3x^2 - 3x + 11$
 c. $3x^2 - 3x - 3$
 d. $x - 3$

16. If $-3(x + 4) \geq x + 8$, what is the value of x?
 a. $x = 4$
 b. $x \geq 2$
 c. $x \geq -5$
 d. $x \leq -5$

17. For a group of 20 men, the median weight is 180 pounds and the range is 30 pounds. If each man gains 10 pounds, which of the following would be true?
 a. The median weight will increase, and the range will remain the same.
 b. The median weight and range will both remain the same.
 c. The median weight will stay the same, and the range will increase.
 d. The median weight and range will both increase.

18. What is the volume of a cylinder, in terms of π, with a radius of 6 centimeters and a height of 2 centimeters?

    a. $36\ \pi\ \text{cm}^3$
    b. $24\ \pi\ \text{cm}^3$
    c. $72\ \pi\ \text{cm}^3$
    d. $48\ \pi\ \text{cm}^3$

19. What is the length of the hypotenuse of a right triangle with one leg equal to 3 centimeters and the other leg equal to 4 centimeters?

    a. 7 cm
    b. 5 cm
    c. 25 cm
    d. 12 cm

20. The perimeter of a 6-sided polygon is 56 cm. The lengths of three sides are 9 cm each. The lengths of two other sides are 8 cm each. What is the length of the missing side?

21. Which of the following equations best represents the problem below?

    The width of a rectangle is 2 centimeters less than the length. If the perimeter of the rectangle is 44 centimeters, then what are the dimensions of the rectangle?

    a. $2l + 2(l - 2) = 44$
    b. $(l + 2) + (l + 2) + l = 48$
    c. $l \times (l - 2) = 44$
    d. $(l + 2) + (l + 2) + l = 44$

22. How will the following algebraic expression be simplified: $(5x^2 - 3x + 4) - (2x^2 - 7)$?

    a. x^5
    b. $3x^2 - 3x + 11$
    c. $3x^2 - 3x - 3$
    d. $x - 3$

Answer Explanations #2

Reading and Writing: Module 1

1. A: In the context of the passage, the Prairie School is not necessarily a physical location, but rather a specific aesthetic that was influenced by Wright's work. In this context, *design life, design gift*, and *design temperance* do not fit into the passage.

2. B: Since both Washington's and Lincoln's birthdays are being celebrated on a combined holiday, *combination* fits best into the sentence. *Juxtaposition, opposition,* and *composition* do not accurately describe the previously mentioned consolidation of two holidays into Presidents' Day.

3. C: Since modern English could neither be discouraged nor destroyed during a time in which it did not yet exist, and *heavily created* is not grammatically correct, the word *influenced* fits best in the sentence.

4: A: Since the Federal Reserve is stated in the passage to be a central bank, *fiscal* fits best as it is the only term related to banking and finance available from among the four options.

5. B: Since Coleman has been established as one of the greatest bodybuilders of all time, the best descriptor of his stature would be *unprecedented*, as the other choices convey that Coleman's physique is unremarkable within the sport of bodybuilding.

6. A: Since the passage is discussing rest days and mentions the importance of a gap in training, exercising more would not make sense in this context. Although applying heat to a sore muscle is a valid recovery technique, avoiding physical activity fits best with the general topic at hand.

7. B: Although Benny initially talks himself out of feeling any fear, he eventually does become afraid when confronted with the reality of his perilous situation. However, heeding the situation at hand, he puts his fear aside to help whoever is hurt despite not particularly wanting to.

8. C: The Roman style, according to Text 2, dumbed down the sophisticated tones of the Greek epics designed to appeal to the masses, which were presented in a literary style that only those familiar with the theater could fully appreciate.

9. C: Choice *C* is the correct answer because it best explains the purpose of the passage. The passage describes various types of sand and where they are found. There is no further purpose than to discuss the variations. Choice *A* is incorrect because although there is mention of what colors the sand differently, the process of how sand is made is not described. Choice *B* is incorrect because there is nothing suggesting that the organisms found in sand are dangerous. Choice *D* is incorrect because although the variety of sands around the world are interesting, the information is not meant to encourage readers to visit anywhere.

10. A: Choice *A* is the correct answer because it is the best summary of the man in the passage. His appearance is dirty and haggard. The people in the room are stunned by him. Choice *B* is incorrect because although he is filthy, he does not appear to be healthy. His chin is mentioned to have a cut, and he walks with an apparent limp. Choice *C* is incorrect because although he is silent, he does not appear to be brooding or moody. He is simply haggard and in pain. Choice *D* is incorrect because he does not acknowledge anyone in the room.

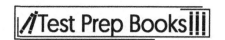

11. B: Choice *B* is the correct answer because it uses information in the chart and paragraph to make a strong assumption. Saturn has more rings than any other planet. Since the paragraph mentions that moons are one of the causes of ring creation, it is safe to assume that Saturn has many moons. Choice *A* is incorrect because Jupiter has two more moons than Uranus. Choice *C* is incorrect because Jupiter and Uranus combined have the same number of moons as Neptune. The number of moons of each planet is also never mentioned in the passage. Choice *D* is incorrect because the size of the planets is never mentioned as being significant.

12. D: Choice *D* is the correct answer because it explains the response of the tradesmen to the tax increase. They assemble in Paris and threaten to defend themselves with violence. Choice *A* is incorrect because they spoke to the Duke of Orleans, who promised to speak to the queen for them, but they did not actually speak to the queen themselves. Choice *B* is incorrect because they are not seeking aid from the Duke of Orleans, but rather are protesting against his tax. Choice *C* is incorrect because they did not pay the tax.

13. D: Choice *D* is the correct answer because it correctly identifies the purpose of the text. The text talks about the unique features of Mount Roraima, such as the endemic species and microclimate. Choice *A* is incorrect because the text does not mention that Mount Roraima is in need of preservation. Choice *B* is incorrect because although the biodiversity is important, it is not the main purpose of the text. Choice *C* is incorrect because *The Lost World* is only mentioned to show the significance of Mount Roraima.

14. C: Choice *C* is the correct answer because it identifies what Maria is telling Sir Toby. Sir Toby wishes to visit with his niece. However, Maria is telling him that he visits too late and that his niece has mentioned that his drinking needs to be controlled. Choice *A* is incorrect because Maria isn't informing Sir Toby that his niece is ill, only that she cannot visit late at night with someone drinking. Choice *B* is incorrect because Sir Toby's friends and family are not mentioned as respecting him or not, even if it may be implied with the niece. Choice *D* is incorrect because the clothing and boots comment comes from Sir Toby regarding his drinking, not from Maria.

15. A: Choice *A* is the correct answer because it identifies the purpose of the passage. Thoreau is saying that men should not be forced to buy homes if they do not want to. They should not be made to feel as if they need to own a home and material things. Choice *B* is incorrect because Thoreau doesn't mention the government or the need for housing. Choice *C* is incorrect because Thoreau is arguing that housing is not a necessity that men should obtain without good reason. Choice *D* is incorrect because although Thoreau appears to dislike material goods, he is not sharing his thoughts on minimalism directly.

16. B: Choice *B* is correct because the use of quotation marks here follows the convention of identifying a term the author wants to emphasize, often after a phrase like "so-called." These "scare quotes" can indicate sarcasm, irony, or another emotional tone that is discordant with the emphasized word's meaning. Choice *A* is incorrect because removing the quotation marks weakens the author's rhetoric. Choice *C* is incorrect because single quotation marks generally are not used in Standard English for either regular or scare quotes, except for a quotation within a quotation. Choice *D* is incorrect because, by emphasizing only *artificial,* the quotation marks imply that "artificial intelligence" is not, in fact, artificial. This doesn't agree with the author's claim that such programs' *internal workings are hollow.*

17. D: Choice *D* is correct because ending the sentence with *arrangement* and a period works well grammatically, and the pronoun corresponding to the subject—*the mate*—can be identified through the last sentence's final clause, *we had not long the benefit of his opinion.* Choice *A* is incorrect because it

creates a run-on sentence; a period, semicolon, or conjunction is necessary to join the independent clauses. Choices *B* and *C* are incorrect because they use the wrong pronoun.

18. A: Choice *A* is correct because *When is it* at the start of the first sentence indicates that it is a question, and *We all* agrees with the second sentence's verb *agree* and with the pronoun *we* used in subsequent sentences. Choice *C* is incorrect because the sentence is a question and cannot end with a period. Choice *B* is incorrect because, while *you* works with *agree,* it does not work with the use of *we* later in the passage to talk about *people in general.* Choice *D* is incorrect because *everyone* matches the passage's general meaning but doesn't work with the verb *agree.*

19. B: Choice *B* is correct because *distinguishes* is in the present tense, which matches *surpasses* later in the sentence. Choice *A* is incorrect because the infinitive *to distinguish* generally requires another verb prior to forming the infinitive. Choice *C* is incorrect because *distinguished* is in the past tense, which does not match the rest of the sentence. Choice *D* is incorrect because *had distinguished* is in the past perfect, which again does not match the tense of the sentence.

20. B: Choice *B* is correct because *here* is the correct word to use after *come* to indicate location. Choices *A* and *D* incorrectly use *hear*, a homophone of *here* and a verb synonymous with *listen*, which doesn't fit the context. Choices *C* and *D* incorrectly include the preposition *to*, which is often used with locations but not with *here* or *there*.

21. A: Choice *A* is correct because *flashlight's* forms a contraction of *flashlight* and *is* with an apostrophe, which fits the sentence grammatically. Choice *B* is incorrect because it does not provide a verb. Choice *C* is incorrect because *flashlight* is not hyphenated in Standard English. Choice *D* is incorrect because context clues about the *top shelf* indicate that this blank must be about an object, not about a flash that lights the basement.

22. C: Choice *C* is correct because *fowls* are types of birds, which fits the context of the passage. Choice *A* is incorrect because *fouls* is a homophone of *fowls* that typically refers to the breaking of rules in a sport. Choices *B* and *D* are incorrect because neither foils nor fools are relevant to the context.

23. B: Choice *B* is best because it places the development of a middle class alongside an increase in availability and sophistication of technology, thus bringing a period of economic prosperity as mentioned in the passage. The development of a middle class does not necessarily clash with the development of new technologies, but rather is spurred on by it in this instance, thus eliminating Choices *C* and *D*. Furthermore, the presence of a middle class during this time indicates economic growth and would not stifle it, thus eliminating Choice *A*.

24. B: Choice *B* is best as it provides a transition from the subject of *speculative traders* to the subject of *many people* while simultaneously connecting the two ideas together in a cause-effect relationship. Although the beginning of the passage mentions speculative traders making large amounts of money and a "boom period," this was not true for every single person in the United States at the time, eliminating Choice *A*. Although Choice *C* could technically be true for some people at the time, the sentence is attempting to explain that the boom period in the 1920s stock market increased prosperity for most people. Choice *D* is incorrect as speculative asset trading was what increased many people's prosperity rather than acting as a hindrance to it.

25. B: Choice *B* is best as it truthfully identifies the major changes that Ivan's rule brought to a newly united Russia. Choice *A*, although accurate, focuses more on Ivan's emotional demeanor and the

200

consequences of his mental instability rather than the effect it had on Russia as a whole. Choice C is mainly focused on the effect that the Orthodox Church had on Ivan's rule and Russia today rather than Ivan's overall effect on Russian history. Choice D is technically true, although it incorrectly conflates Ivan's conquests inside Russia's modern borders with a desire to conquer other countries within Europe.

26. C: Choice C is best as it continues discussing the applications of agglomerated stone by detailing the various types that are used for the purposes already mentioned in the previous sentence. Choice A is correct but somewhat redundant as the process of creating agglomerated stone is already detailed in the passage's first sentence. Choice B contains accurate information but is unfocused, as it expands on information that the passage has already moved on from. Choice D could be correct, but the focus of the passage is on the application of agglomerated stone rather than the price itself.

27. D: Choice D is best as the second sentence communicates the most basic purposes for each kind of trial being held and the stakes found therein. Choice A is incorrect as there is no concrete statement to clarify but rather only the introduction of a survey of criminal and civil trials. Choice B is incorrect as no other descriptions of criminal and civil trials preceded the sentence it introduces. Choice C is somewhat correct, but *various differences* is not a statement that is typically exemplified with such non-specific information as found in the second sentence, which makes Choice D better.

Reading and Writing: Module 2

1. D: Since the sentence mentions that Caesar *disobeyed* the Senate, it can be understood that the Senate commanded him to disband his army. The adjective *stern* is also a clue into the Senate's attitude toward Caesar. It is highly unlikely that the author would utilize the word *disobeyed* in relation to a *stern* suggestion, request, or plea.

2. B: Since the topic of the excerpt is the speaker's distaste for their weekly family dinners, *dine with* is the most correct as well as the most specific choice available to place into the excerpt.

3. C: Since *actor* is not grammatically correct due to the article *a*, a poet would not be listening to themselves, and a writer would have been writing the choruses mentioned in the sentence, the most grammatically correct and accurate choice for the excerpt is *spectator.*

4. B: The passage discusses a method to regain composure during a passionate discussion in order to prevent anger and distraction from overtaking the debate. In this instance, *relaxed* and *on-topic* are antonyms to the possible pitfalls of discussion mentioned in the passage and are thus the best choice.

5. D: Conversations on public transit are not prohibited by law. Furthermore, the second sentence in the passage elaborates on conversational etiquette on public transit, which does not amount to a *bad idea* or *personal preference*.

6. C: Although credit cards can be quite harmful to one's financial position when abused, the passage provides evidence of the benefits of using credit cards responsibly as long as the balance is paid in full and the user never overspends.

7. B: Although *decompressing* certainly works in the sentence, *unplugging* works better as it holds continuity with *unplug,* which was previously used in the passage.

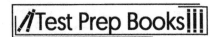

8. C: According to Text 1, new home prices outpace the price of purchasing a historic home and having it restored. Americans who find themselves unable to afford new homes could opt to buy an older house and restore it.

9. C: Choice *C* is the correct answer because it is the best quote to show the theme of independence. The quote shows someone (Jane) stating that they will not be caged like a bird. They are free of anybody's will and can do as they please. This is the meaning behind independence. Choice *A* is incorrect because it is a man discussing how women find him to be the devil before he changes their minds. This is not a show of independence. Choice *B* is incorrect because it is about a fondness for singing and enjoying a good performance. Choice *D* is incorrect because although the speaker seems to be contemplative about the state of their life and dreams, but there is no explicit mention of independence.

10. C: Choice *C* is the correct answer because it accurately picks a quote that illustrates the claims of the demanding nature of a job. The man being discussed is alone and not doing well. However, the speaker does not prioritize sympathy due to his business, even using the word *tyrannized*. Choice *A* is incorrect because the speaker is discussing their success professionally, not about the demanding nature of it. Choice *B* is incorrect because the speaker is showing a spontaneous yet careful nature. This does not show a man that has been worn out from his career. Choice *D* is incorrect because it is a discussion about passivity rather than hurt human connection.

11. B: Choice *B* is the correct answer because it fills in the blank using data from the table. Both points in Choice *B* are correct. Students strayed away from first responder careers as they got older and trended more towards business and office jobs. Choice *A* is incorrect because the younger students chose medical field jobs more often than older students. Choice *C* is incorrect because grade 7 wanted to go into office jobs less than the younger grades, so the trend was not linear. Choice *D* is incorrect due to the inconsistency of change in the business/office field and the unsure column.

12. C: Choice *C* is the correct answer because it correctly identifies the main purpose of the passage. The passage is focused on the tasks of the Angakkuit. This includes rituals and teaching. Choice *A* is incorrect because although the cultural practices being described are important to pass on, that is not why the text mentions them. It mentions them in order to describe another role of the Angakkuit. Choice *B* is incorrect because there is no evidence in the text to prove that the spiritual world is real, despite the Angakkuit's role. Choice *D* is incorrect because the text is not trying to convince the reader to partake in any of the activities mentioned.

13. D: Choice *D* is the correct answer because it uses the notes to emphasize what the student wishes to convey. The Milky Way is a galaxy that is immediately recognizable to most people, while the notes also specify that most galaxies nearby are spiral shaped. Choice *D* combines both of these points into a well-structured sentence that the student can use. Choice *A* is incorrect because it does not point out that spiral galaxies are the most common. Just because elliptical galaxies are bigger does not mean they are the most common. Choice *B* is incorrect because although it describes the Milky Way as being spiral, it does not specify that it is the most common type. Choice *C* is incorrect because the notes do not state that elliptical galaxies are most abundant.

14. B: Choice *B* is the correct answer because it is Joan's primary defense for herself when she is accused of witchcraft. This is primarily apparent in the last five lines of the monologue. She states that she is virginal, chaste, and immaculate. These are traits that would not have been applied to someone that is practicing witchcraft. They are the traits of an innocent, God-fearing person. Choice *A* is incorrect

202

because when she mentions wicked spirits, it is to say that she has nothing to do with them. Choice *C* is incorrect because although Joan insults her accusers for judging others, that is not her primary defense. Choice *D* is incorrect because Joan condemns her accusers for lusting for blood; however, she does not specifically call out bloodthirst against women.

15. C: Choice *C* is the correct answer because it is the choice that best states the purpose of the poem. The poem's speaker is writing about a loved one with whom they wish to reconnect in death. This is evidenced by lines such as "I shall return to thee silently" and "I'll crawl around thy resting-place," which refer to the death of the loved one. Choice *A* is incorrect because the flowers and serpents are not the main purpose of the poem; they are just forms of figurative language. Choice *B* is incorrect because the speaker is speaking of a passed lover, not of youth, although it is mentioned. Choice *D* is incorrect because winter is not the focus of this poem. The cold is mentioned in reference to grief.

16. B: Choice *B* is correct because it refers to the appropriate person, agreeing with *Jobs* two sentences later, and uses a comma correctly after the introductory phrase *of course*. Choice *A* is incorrect because it lacks the comma and because the pronoun *he* would refer to Ronald Wayne, not Jobs, based on the previous sentence referring to the last person named; the subject needs to be explicitly stated to clarify that this sentence is talking about Jobs. Choices *C* and *D* are incorrect because they use the wrong name, and Choice *D* is missing the comma as well.

17. C: Choice *C* is correct because this answer uses the correct conjunction and places the comma correctly at the end of the appositive phrase, *the young and strong*, describing the subject *he*. Choices *A* and *B* are incorrect because they do not use the comma correctly. Choice *D* is incorrect because the conjunction *but* is used to indicate a contrast between opposites. However, *young* and *strong* are logically similar, not opposite.

18. D: Choice *D* is correct because *them* is a plural pronoun that agrees with the subject *things*, and the capitalization of *Nor* requires the blank to end in a period, completing the sentence. Choice *A* is incorrect because a semicolon is not generally followed by a capitalized word. Choice *B* is incorrect because the singular *it* does not match the sentence's subject. Choice *C* is incorrect because the answer uses both a singular pronoun and incorrect punctuation.

19. B: Choice *B* is correct because it correctly uses the adverb *peculiarly* to modify the adjective *light* and uses a comma to separate the adjectives describing the color of Mycroft Holmes' eyes. Choice *A* is incorrect because the adverb form *peculiarly* better modifies the adjective *light*. Choice *C* is incorrect because *peculiarest* is an incorrect superlative; *most peculiar* would be the correct superlative form. Choice *D* is incorrect because commas are necessary in this list to divide up the specific attributes of Mycroft's eyes.

20. D: Choice *D* is correct because, in Standard English, a question in dialogue ends with the question mark followed by the ending quotation mark. Choices *A* and *B* are incorrect because Standard English does not add a comma after the question mark. Choice *C* is incorrect because a question mark is required to make the sentence a question.

21. B: Choice *B* is correct because the preposition *but* logically completes the sentence by providing a contrast between *warm* and *shivered*. Choice *A* is incorrect because *For* provides a sense of purpose, which does not create a contrast. Choice *C* is incorrect because *To* provides a sense of direction, which does not create a contrast. Choice *D* is incorrect because *At* provides a sense of place, which does not create a contrast.

22. D: Choice *D* is correct because *this* specifies that the speaker is discussing the same draft (the second draft) as mentioned in the first sentence. Choice *A* is incorrect because the plural *these* does not match the singular *draft*. Choice *B* is incorrect because, while *that* can point to a specific object like *this*, *this* more clearly refers to what was just discussed and aligns with *this* in the previous sentence. Choice *C* is incorrect because, while using the article *the* is not incorrect here, using *this* is more precise and thus preferable.

23. C: Choice *C* is best as it identifies the two named causes of the Great Depression as speculative asset trading and European countries defaulting on wartime loans. It properly states that these two factors led to Black Tuesday, which marks the official beginning of the Great Depression. Although Choice *A* is partially correct, Black Tuesday did not cause the Great Depression; rather, it was a direct result of the symptoms that did and could be considered the first event of the Depression. Choice *B* is incorrect as it identifies the speculative asset bubble as the Depression itself. Choice *D* is incorrect as it implies that the Great Depression began before the factors that are stated to have caused it.

24. D: Choice *D* is best as it connects the idea of a bank run to the actions that people took after the crash (withdrawing money from banks and the stock market) and illustrates their direct cause-and-effect relationship. Choice *A* is inaccurate, as the bank run was not exacerbated by the actions of people after the crash but induced by them. Choice *B* places the timing of events out of logical order, placing the bank run before the events that caused it. Choice *C* insinuates that the bank run happened in spite of people's actions after the crash rather than as a direct result of them.

25. A: Choice *A* is best as it sets up the specific usage of sheep's wool and goose down as noteworthy examples of animal products that are used in weather-resistant apparel. Choice *B* is incorrect as the specification of which animal products are being used in clothing is not a consequence of the usage of the animal products themselves. Choice *C* is incorrect as it attempts to concede a point that is being expanded upon further. Choice *D* is somewhat correct as it attempts to agree with the assertion made in the first sentence, but it is implying that the usage of sheep's wool and goose down is *like* the animal products being used in clothing rather than being the products themselves.

26. C: Choice *C* is best as it communicates that George responded to Nicolas's capture after the fact with refusal, establishing a strong chronological order of events. Choice *A* is partially correct as it contrasts the dire nature of Nicolas's situation with George's refusal to help his cousin, but Choice *C* better demonstrates the sequence of events as presented due to George's reasoning already being detailed later in the sentence. Choice *B* is incorrect as George refusing to give Nicolas asylum is not an example of Nicolas's capture. Choice *D* is incorrect as George refused to give Nicolas asylum due to his unpopularity, not because he was captured.

27. A: Choice *A* is best as it establishes the October Revolution as having occurred later in 1917 than the February Revolution and Nicolas's removal from power. Choice *B* is incorrect as the October Revolution did not occur solely as a result of Nicolas's removal since he was never reinstated as Tsar. Choice *C* is incorrect because the October Revolution occurred after the February Revolution, hence its namesake. Choice *D* is partially correct as Nicolas's removal did not stop Russia from being engulfed in further turmoil, but the specific reasons for the October Revolution are not discussed and thus still make Choice *A* best.

Math: Module 1

1. B: First, subtract 4 from each side. This yields $6t = 12$. Now, divide both sides by 6 to obtain $t = 2$.

2. B: The variable y is directly proportional to x, which means that whenever x is multiplied by a number, y is multiplied by that same number. When x changes from 5 to 20, it is multiplied by 4, so the original y value must also be multiplied by 4. That means $y = 3 \times 4 = 12$.

3. C: The quadratic formula can be used to solve this problem. Given the equation, use the values $a = 1$, $b = -2$, and $c = -8$.

$$x = \frac{-b \pm \sqrt{b^2 - 4ac}}{2a} = \frac{-(-2) \pm \sqrt{(-2)^2 - 4(1)(-8)}}{2(1)}$$

From here, simplify to solve for x.

$$x = \frac{2 \pm \sqrt{4 + 32}}{2} = \frac{2 \pm \sqrt{36}}{2} = \frac{2 \pm 6}{2} = 1 \pm 3$$

4. C: The sample space is made up of $8 + 7 + 6 + 5 = 26$ balls. The probability of pulling each individual ball is $\frac{1}{26}$. Since there are 7 yellow balls, the probability of pulling a yellow ball is $\frac{7}{26}$.

5. B: If 60% of 50 workers are women, then there are 30 women working in the office. If half of them are wearing skirts, then that means 15 women wear skirts. Since nobody else wears skirts, this means there are 15 people wearing skirts.

6. D: This problem can be solved by setting up a proportion involving the given information and the unknown value. The proportion is:

$$\frac{21 \text{ pages}}{4 \text{ nights}} = \frac{140 \text{ pages}}{x \text{ nights}}$$

We can cross-multiply to get $21x = 4 \times 140$. Solving this, we find $x \approx 26.67$. Since this is not an integer, we round up to 27 nights. 26 nights would not give Sarah enough time.

7. 8: Let a be the number of apples Maria buys and o be the number of oranges she buys. Then, the total cost is $2a + 3o = 22$, while it also known that $a + o = 10$. Using the knowledge of systems of equations, cancel the o-variables by multiplying the second equation by –3. This makes the equation $-3a - 3o = -30$. Adding this to the first equation, the o-values cancel to get $-a = -8$, which simplifies to $a = 8$. Therefore, Maria bought 8 apples.

8. A: Finding the roots means finding the values of x that make the polynomial equal zero. The quadratic formula could be used, but in this case, it is possible to factor by hand, since the numbers –1 and 2 add to 1 and multiply to –2. So, factor $x^2 + x - 2 = (x - 1)(x + 2) = 0$, then set each factor equal to zero. Solving for each value gives the values $x = 1$ and $x = -2$.

9. D: The slope from this equation is 50, and it is interpreted as the cost per gigabyte used. Since the g-value represents the number of gigabytes and the equation is set equal to the cost in dollars, the slope relates these two values. For every gigabyte used on the phone, the bill goes up 50 dollars.

205

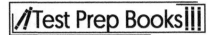

10. A: This has the form $t^2 - y^2$, where $t = x^2$ and $y = 4$. It's also known that $t^2 - y^2 = (t + y)(t - y)$, and substituting the values for t and y into the right-hand side gives $(x^2 - 4)(x^2 + 4)$.

11. A: Simplify this to:

$$(4x^2 y^4)^{\frac{3}{2}} = 4^{\frac{3}{2}}(x^2)^{\frac{3}{2}}(y^4)^{\frac{3}{2}}$$

$$4^{\frac{3}{2}} = (\sqrt{4})^3 = 2^3 = 8$$

For the variables, recall that the exponents must be multiplied, so this yields:

$$8x^{2 \cdot \frac{3}{2}} y^{4 \cdot \frac{3}{2}} = 8x^3 y^6$$

12. B: Start by squaring both sides to get $1 + x = 16$. Then subtract 1 from both sides to get $x = 15$.

13. C: Multiply both sides by x to get $x + 2 = 2x$. Then, subtract x from both sides to get $2 = x$.

14. C: List the givens.

$$\text{Tax} = 6.0\% = 0.06$$

$$\text{Sale} = 50\% = 0.5$$

$$\text{Hat} = \$32.99$$

$$\text{Jersey} = \$64.99$$

Calculate the sale prices.

$$\text{Hat Sale} = 0.5\,(32.99) = 16.495$$

$$\text{Jersey Sale} = 0.5\,(64.99) = 32.495$$

Total the sales prices.

$$\text{Hat sale} + \text{jersey sale} = 16.495 + 32.495 = 48.99$$

Calculate the tax and add it to the total sales prices.

$$\text{Total after tax} = 48.99 + (48.99 \times 0.06) = \$51.93$$

15. B: Since we are given the y-intercept (where the graph crosses the y-axis) as $y = 1$, we can substitute this value in for b in the slope-intercept form equation $y = mx + b$.

$$y = mx + 1$$

From here, the slope needs to be found. Given the two points (1,2) and (0,1) (from the y-intercept), use the slope formula.

$$m = \frac{y_2 - y_1}{x_2 - x_1} = \frac{2 - 1}{1 - 0} = \frac{1}{1} = 1$$

Therefore, the equation for the line is $y = 1x + 1$, or $y = x + 1$.

206

16. B: The total trip time is $1 + 3.5 + 0.5 = 5$ hours. The total time driving is $1 + 0.5 = 1.5$ hours. So, the fraction of time spent driving is $\frac{1.5}{5}$ or $\frac{3}{10}$. To get the percentage, convert this to a fraction out of 100. The numerator and denominator are multiplied by 10, with a result of $\frac{30}{100}$. The percentage is the numerator in a fraction out of 100, so 30%.

17. 0.33: When a die is rolled, each outcome is equally likely. Since it has six sides, each outcome has a probability of $\frac{1}{6}$. The chance of a 1 or a 2 is therefore $\frac{1}{6} + \frac{1}{6} = \frac{1}{3}$.

18. D: The formula for finding the volume of a rectangular prism is $V = l \times w \times h$, where l is the length, w is the width, and h is the height. The volume of the original box is calculated:

$$V = 8 \times 14 \times 4 = 448 \text{ in}^3$$

The volume of the new box is calculated:

$$V = 16 \times 28 \times 8 = 3{,}584 \text{ in}^3$$

The volume of the new box divided by the volume of the old box equals 8.

19. A: An outlier is a data value that is either far above or far below the majority of values in a sample set. The mean is the average of all the values in the set. In a small sample set, a very high or very low number could drastically change the average of the data points. Outliers will have no more of an effect on the median (the middle value when arranged from lowest to highest) than any other value above or below the median. If the same outlier does not repeat, outliers will have no effect on the mode (value that repeats most often).

20. 6: The Pythagorean theorem tells us that $8^2 + x^2 = 10^2$, where x is the unknown side. This simplifies to $64 + x^2 = 100$, so $x^2 = 100 - 64 = 36$, and $x = \sqrt{36} = 6$ inches.

21. B: An equilateral triangle has three sides of equal length, so if the total perimeter is 18 feet, each side must be 6 feet long. A square with sides of 6 feet will have an area of $6^2 = 36$ square feet.

22. D: Exponential functions can be written in the form: $y = a \times b^x$. The equation for an exponential function can be written given the y-intercept (a) and the growth rate (b).

The y-intercept is the output (y) when the input (x) equals zero. It can be thought of as an "original value," or starting point. The value of b is the rate at which the original value increases ($b > 1$) or decreases ($b < 1$).

In this scenario, the y-intercept, a, would be $1200, and the growth rate, b, would be 1.01 (100% of the original value combined with 1% interest, or $100\% + 1\% = 101\% = 1.01$).

Math: Module 2

1. B: Fractions must have like denominators to be added. We are trying to add a fraction with a denominator of 3 to a fraction with a denominator of 5, so we have to convert both fractions to equivalent fractions that have a common denominator. The common denominator is the least common multiple (LCM) of the two original denominators. In this case, the LCM is 15, so both fractions should be changed to equivalent fractions with a denominator of 15.

To determine the numerator of the new fraction, the old numerator is multiplied by the same number by which the old denominator is multiplied to obtain the new denominator.

For the fraction $\frac{1}{3}$, 3 multiplied by 5 will produce 15.

Therefore, the numerator is multiplied by 5 to produce the new numerator:

$$\frac{1 \times 5}{3 \times 5} = \frac{5}{15}$$

For the fraction $\frac{2}{5}$, multiplying both the numerator and denominator by 3 produces $\frac{6}{15}$. When fractions have like denominators, they are added by adding the numerators and keeping the denominator the same:

$$\frac{5}{15} + \frac{6}{15} = \frac{11}{15}$$

2. A: Let the unknown score be x. The average will be:

$$\frac{5 \times 50 + 4 \times 70 + x}{10} = \frac{530 + x}{10} = 55$$

Multiply both sides by 10 to get $530 + x = 550$, or $x = 20$.

3. B: The journey will be 5 mi/1 in × 3 in = 15 mi. A car traveling at 60 miles per hour is traveling at 1 mile per minute. The resulting equation would be:

$$\frac{15 \text{ mi}}{1 \text{ mi/min}} = 15 \text{ min}$$

Therefore, it will take 15 minutes to make the journey.

4. B: 30% is $\frac{3}{10}$, so if 6 is 30% of some number n, we can write this as $6 = \left(\frac{3}{10}\right) n$. To solve for n, multiply both sides by the reciprocal: $n = \left(\frac{10}{3}\right) \times 6 = \frac{60}{3} = 20$.

5. 4: Kristen bought four DVDs, which would cost a total of $4 \times \$15 = \$60$. She spent a total of $100, so she spent $100 - \$60 = \$40$ on CDs. Since they cost $10 each, she must have purchased $\$40 \div 10 = 4$ CDs.

6. 17: To get 85% of a number, multiply it by 0.85.

$$0.85 \times 20 = \frac{85}{100} \times \frac{20}{1}$$

This can be simplified to:

$$\frac{17}{20} \times \frac{20}{1} = 17$$

208

7. B: The function presented is being evaluated for $x + 1$; therefore, $x + 1$ must be substituted into the original function as follows:

$$f(x + 1) = (x + 1)^2 - 3(x + 1) + 17$$

The squared portion of the function becomes $x^2 + 2x + 1$, and distributing the -3 results in:

$$f(x + 1) = x^2 + 2x + 1 - 3x - 3 + 17$$

Combining like terms results in:

$$x^2 - x + 15$$

8. D: Because we know that $x = 4$ and $x = -4$ are solutions to a quadratic equation, we know that $(x - 4)$ and $(x + 4)$ are factors of the quadratic equation. To find the quadratic equation, use the FOIL method to multiply these two factors by one another.

$$(x - 4)(x + 4) = 0$$

$$x^2 + 4x - 4x - 16 = 0$$

$$x^2 - 16 = 0$$

9. 0.083: The probability of picking the winner of the race is $\frac{1}{4}$ or:

$$\left(\frac{\text{number of favorable outcomes}}{\text{number of total outcomes}} \right)$$

Assuming the winner was picked on the first selection, three horses remain from which to choose the runner-up (these are dependent events). Therefore, the probability of picking the runner-up is $\frac{1}{3}$. To determine the probability that multiple events all happen, multiply the probabilities of the events:

$$\frac{1}{4} \times \frac{1}{3} = \frac{1}{12}$$

10. A: Putting the scores in order from least to greatest, we have 60, 75, 80, and 85, as well as one unknown. The median is 80, so 80 must be the middle data point out of these five. Therefore, the unknown data point must be the fourth or fifth data point, meaning it must be greater than or equal to 80. The only answer that fails to meet this condition is 60.

11. A: Parallel lines have the same slope. The slope of the given equation is 3. The slope of Choice C can be seen to be $\frac{1}{3}$ by dividing both sides by 3. The other choices are in standard form $Ax + By = C$, for which the slope is given by $\frac{-A}{B}$. For Choice A, the equation can be written as $6x - 2y = -2$. Therefore, the slope is:

$$\frac{-A}{B} = \frac{-6}{-2} = 3$$

209

This is the same as the given equation. The slope of Choice B is:

$$\frac{-A}{B} = \frac{-4}{-1} = 4$$

The slope of Choice B is 4. The slope of Choice D is:

$$\frac{-A}{B} = \frac{-2}{-2} = 1$$

The slope of Choice D is 1. Therefore, the only equation with a parallel slope of 3 is $6x - 2y = -2$.

12. D: The total amount the company pays, y, equals the cost of the building ($50,000) plus the cost of the saws. Since the saws cost $40 each, the overall cost of the saws is $40 times x, where x is the number of saws. Putting all this together, we have $y = 50,000 + 40x$, which is equivalent to Choice D.

13. A: The slope is given by:

$$m = \frac{y_2 - y_1}{x_2 - x_1} = \frac{0 - 4}{0 - (-3)} = -\frac{4}{3}$$

14. A: The graph contains four turning points (where the curve changes from rising to falling or vice versa). This indicates that the degree of the function (highest exponent for the variable) is 5 because a function of degree n can have no more than $n - 1$ turning points, eliminating Choices C and D. The y-intercepts of the functions can be determined by substituting 0 for x and finding the value of y. The function for Choice A has a y-intercept of 3, and the function for Choice B has a y-intercept of –3. Therefore, Choice B is eliminated.

15. B: By distributing the implied one in front of the first set of parentheses and the $- 1$ in front of the second set of parentheses, the parentheses can be eliminated:

$$1(5x^2 - 3x + 4) - 1(2x^2 - 7)$$

$$5x^2 - 3x + 4 - 2x^2 + 7$$

Next, like terms (same variables with same exponents) are combined by adding the coefficients and keeping the variables and their powers the same:

$$5x^2 - 3x + 4 - 2x^2 + 7$$

$$3x^2 - 3x + 11$$

16. D: Solving a linear inequality is similar to solving a linear equation. First, start by distributing the –3 on the left side of the inequality.

$$-3x - 12 \geq x + 8$$

Then, add 12 to both sides.

$$-3x \geq x + 20$$

210

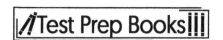

Next, subtract x from both sides.

$$-4x \geq 20$$

Finally, divide both sides of the inequality by –4. Don't forget to flip the inequality sign because you are dividing by a negative.

$$x \leq -5$$

17. A: If each man gains 10 pounds, every original data point will increase by 10 pounds. Therefore, the man with the original median will still have the median value, but that value will increase by 10. The smallest value and largest value will also increase by 10, so the difference between the two (the range) will remain the same.

18. C: The volume of a cylinder is $\pi r^2 h$, and $\pi \times 6^2 \times 2$ is $72\,\pi$ cm³. Choice A is not the correct answer because that is only $6^2 \times \pi$. Choice B is not the correct answer because that is $2^2 \times 6 \times \pi$. Choice D is not the correct answer because that is $2^3 \times 6 \times \pi$.

19. B: This answer is correct because $3^2 + 4^2$ is $9 + 16$, which is 25. Taking the square root of 25 is 5. Choice A is not the correct answer because that is $3 + 4$. Choice C is not the correct answer because that is stopping at $3^2 + 4^2$ is $9 + 16$, which is 25. Choice D is not the correct answer because that is 3×4.

20. 13: The perimeter is found by calculating the sum of all sides of the polygon:

$$9 + 9 + 9 + 8 + 8 + s = 56$$

s is the missing side length. Therefore, $43 + s = 56$. The missing side length is 13 cm.

21. A: The first step is to determine the unknown, which is in terms of the length, l.

The second step is to translate the problem into the equation using the perimeter of a rectangle:

$$P = 2l + 2w$$

The width is the length minus 2 centimeters. The resulting equation is:

$$2l + 2(l - 2) = 44$$

The equation can be solved as follows:

$2l + 2l - 4 = 44$	Apply the distributive property on the left side of the equation
$4l - 4 = 44$	Combine like terms on the left side of the equation
$4l = 48$	Add 4 to both sides of the equation
$l = 12$	Divide both sides of the equation by 4

The length of the rectangle is 12 centimeters. The width is the length minus 2 centimeters, which is 10 centimeters. Checking the answers for length and width forms the following equation:

$$44 = 2(12) + 2(10)$$

The equation can be solved using the order of operations to form a true statement: $44 = 44$.

22. B: $3x^2 - 3x + 11$. By distributing the implied one in front of the first set of parentheses and the -1 in front of the second set of parentheses, the parentheses can be eliminated:

$$1(5x^2 - 3x + 4) - 1(2x^2 - 7)$$

$$5x^2 - 3x + 4 - 2x^2 + 7$$

Next, like terms (same variables with same exponents) are combined by adding the coefficients and keeping the variables and their powers the same:

$$5x^2 - 3x + 4 - 2x^2 + 7 = 3x^2 - 3x + 11$$

PSAT 8/9 Practice Tests #3, #4, #5, & #6

To keep the size of this book manageable, save paper, and provide a digital test-taking experience, the 3rd, 4th, 5th, & 6th practice tests can be found online. Scan the QR code or go to this link to access it:

testprepbooks.com/bonus/psat89

The first time you access the tests, you will need to register as a "new user" and verify your email address.

If you have any issues, please email support@testprepbooks.com.

Dear PSAT 8/9 Test Taker,

Thank you for purchasing this study guide for your PSAT 8/9 exam. We hope that we exceeded your expectations.

Our goal in creating this study guide was to cover all of the topics that you will see on the test. We also strove to make our practice questions as similar as possible to what you will encounter on test day. With that being said, if you found something that you feel was not up to your standards, please send us an email and let us know.

We would also like to let you know about other books in our catalog that may interest you.

ACCUPLACER

amazon.com/dp/1637756356

SAT

amazon.com/dp/1637750714

TSI

amazon.com/dp/1637754434

We have study guides in a wide variety of fields. If the one you are looking for isn't listed above, then try searching for it on Amazon or send us an email.

Thanks Again and Happy Testing!
Product Development Team
info@studyguideteam.com

FREE Test Taking Tips Video/DVD Offer

To better serve you, we created videos covering test taking tips that we want to give you for FREE. **These videos cover world-class tips that will help you succeed on your test.**

We just ask that you send us feedback about this product. Please let us know what you thought about it—whether good, bad, or indifferent.

To get your **FREE videos**, you can use the QR code below or email freevideos@studyguideteam.com with "Free Videos" in the subject line and the following information in the body of the email:

   a. The title of your product

   b. Your product rating on a scale of 1-5, with 5 being the highest

   c. Your feedback about the product

If you have any questions or concerns, please don't hesitate to contact us at info@studyguideteam.com.

Thank you!

Made in the USA
Columbia, SC
05 September 2024